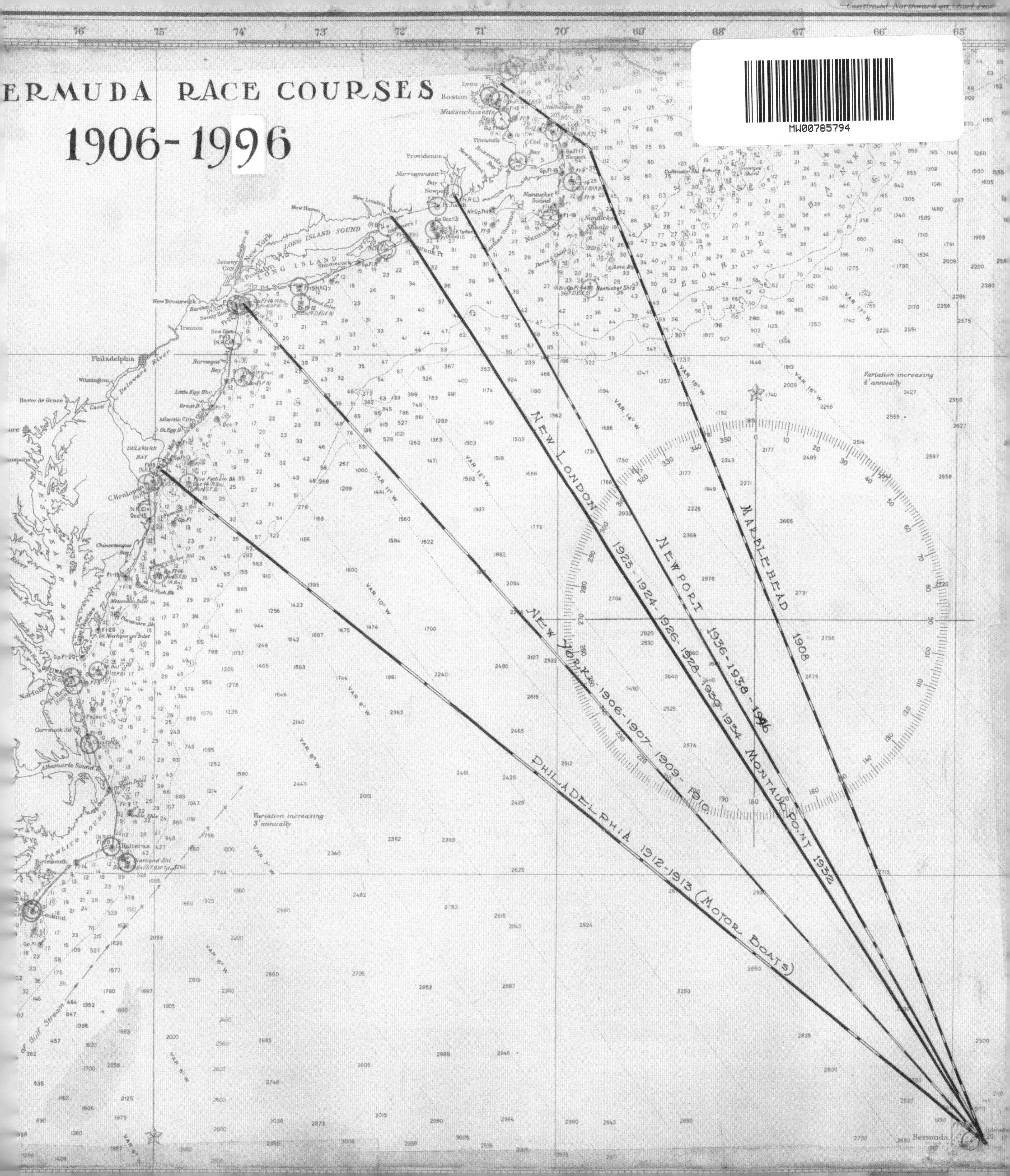

# ERMUDA RACE COURSES
## 1906-1996

MARBLEHEAD 1908

NEW LONDON 1923-1924-1926-1928-1930-1934

NEW PORT 1936-1938-1946

NEW YORK 1906-1907-1909-1910

MONTAUK POINT 1932

PHILADELPHIA 1912-1913 (MOTOR BOATS)

Variation increasing 4' annually

Variation increasing 3' annually

Gulf Stream

Bermuda

*A Berth to*
# Bermuda

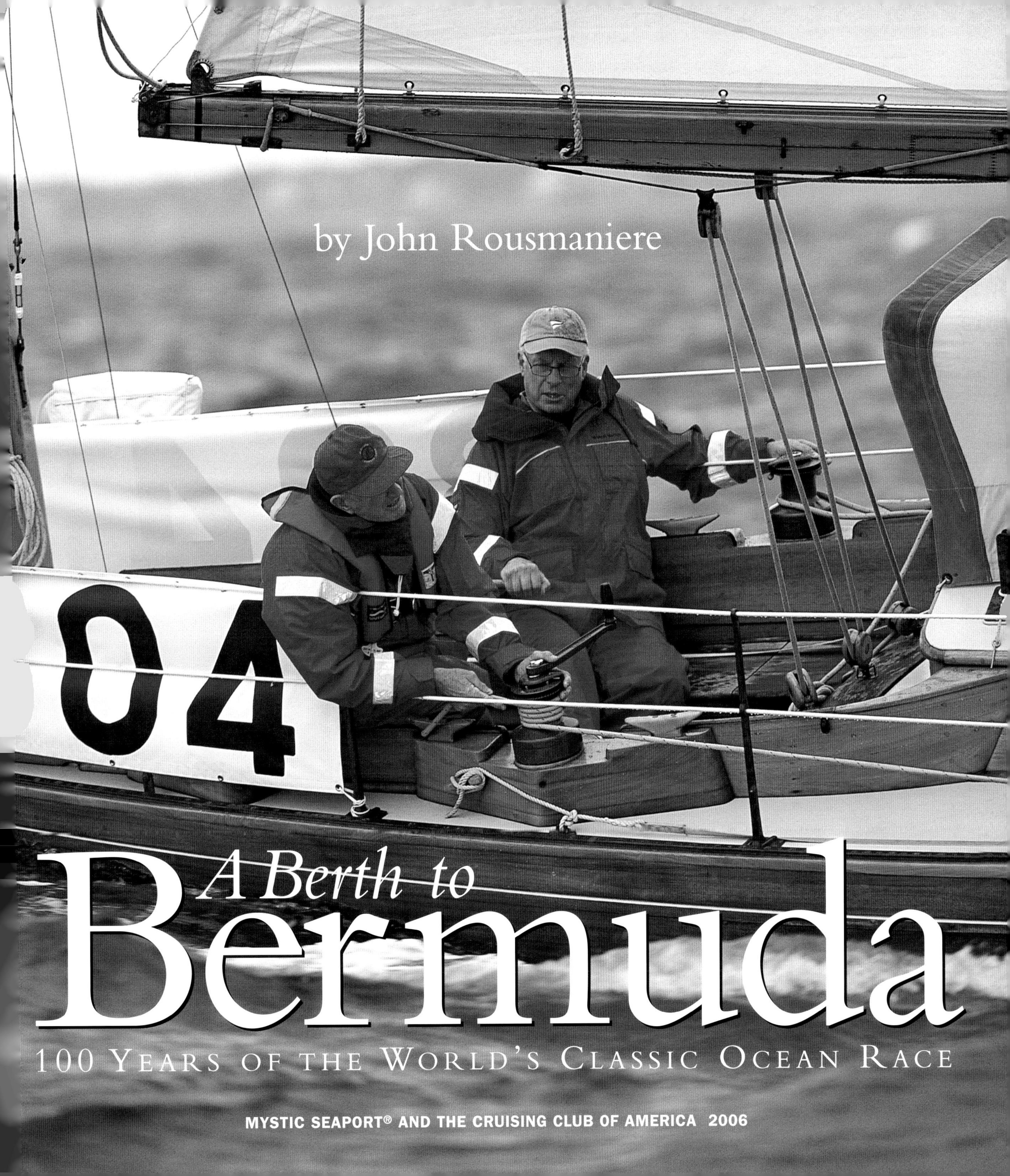

by John Rousmaniere

04

# *A Berth to* Bermuda

## 100 YEARS OF THE WORLD'S CLASSIC OCEAN RACE

MYSTIC SEAPORT® AND THE CRUISING CLUB OF AMERICA  2006

Mystic Seaport
75 Greenmanville Ave., P.O. Box 6000
Mystic, CT 06355-0990
www.mysticseaport.org

The Cruising Club of America
www.cruisingclub.org

Designed by Clare Cunningham

ISBN (cloth):0-939511-17-7
ISBN (limited edition): 0-939511-18-8

This book is printed on acid-free paper.

**Related Books by John Rousmaniere:**

*In a Class by Herself: The Yawl Bolero and the Passion for Craftsmanship* (2006)

*Sailing at Fishers* (2004)

*Sleek* (2003)

*After the Storm* (2002)

*The Annapolis Book of Seamanship* (3rd edition, 1998)

*Desirable and Undesirable Characteristics of Offshore Yachts* (edited, 1987)

*The Golden Pastime* (1986)

*Fastnet, Force 10* (1980)

(Endpaper, right)
Bermuda Race courses over the years. (Left to right)
Philadelphia-Bermuda powerboat race, 1912-1913.
Brooklyn-Bermuda, 1906-1907, 1909-1910
New London-Bermuda, 1923-1930, 1934, and Montauk-Bermuda, 1932
Newport-Bermuda,1936-present
Marblehead-Bermuda, 1908

# Table of Contents

*Dedicated to the race's scribes:*

THOMAS FLEMING DAY

HERBERT L. STONE

ALFRED F. LOOMIS

WILLIAM W. ROBINSON

(Previous photographs) The essential navigational tool throughout most of Bermuda Race history, a sextant goes to work on 1950 winner *Argyll*. The crew trims for speed in *Dame of Sark*, a 41-year-old wooden Concordia yawl, early in the 2002 race. *Finisterre*—the race's only three-time winner (and in consecutive races)—rises to a wave. Their gunmetal gray carbon fiber sails shimmering, two modern maxis, *Sagamore* and *Sayonara*, match up in 2000. (This page) It's 2002, and the rail meat assumes position for one of the toughest of all thrashes to the Onion Patch.

Thomas Fleming Day gazes out at "our great green mother." Insisting that ocean racing was inevitable, he made it so. (Opposite) The 40-footer *Lila* sails on Great Sound after winning her class in 1907. A year earlier she recovered from a dismasting but was unable to cross the Gulf Stream.

# Tom Day Invents a Sport

The Bermuda Race and modern ocean racing were born at three o'clock on the afternoon of Saturday, May 26, 1906, when Thomas Fleming Day, Thora Lund Robinson, and 13 other daredevils in three sailboats between 28 and 40 feet long crossed a starting line off Brooklyn, New York, and commenced smashing into a stiff south wind. Astern of these three modest vessels lay a tumult of wild accusations that their adventure was irresponsible if not insane. Ahead lay a difficult passage stretching east-southeast through 700 miles of blue water. The crews would cross that stormy, swirling river in the sea, the Gulf Stream, then carefully edge around a sharp-toothed coral reef, and (assuming they actually got this far) cross a finish line extending out from the eastern point of the fishhook-shaped archipelago that Shakespeare, who knew its reputation for wrecks and wild weather, had called "the still vex'd Bermoothes."

# Ocean Racing, the Past

**F**aint odors of weirdness surrounded ocean racing and small-boat voyaging. Most of the entries in the four transatlantic yacht races that had occurred were immense, professionally managed schooners owned by millionaires. Six sailors lost their lives in the first race, in 1866, and—while there were no more fatalities—the 11 boats in the 1905 race from New York to the English Channel were far too big to seem real. The winner, the 184-foot three-masted schooner *Atlantic*, was 78 feet longer than the cumulative length of the starters in 1906, and her mostly professional crew of 48 was more than three times the total number of sailors in the three boats racing to Bermuda.

Another path of ocean adventure was taken by stunt sailors in tiny craft. The floodgates were opened in 1876 by a fisherman named Alfred Johnson who celebrated the centennial of the United States by crossing the Atlantic in a 20-foot dory, followed the next year by Captain and Mrs. Crapo in a 19-foot whaleboat. Later, a piano-builder, William A. Andrews, set out on a total of seven west-to-east transatlantic cruises or races in 12- to 20-foot boats. Most of the time, either he or his competitor had to hitch rides from passing steamers.

Andrews finally disappeared at sea in 1901.

The breakthrough to normality came with Joshua Slocum's singlehanded circumnavigation in 1895-98 in a boat the length of the first Bermuda racers. Formerly a successful sea captain, Slocum had made a 5,000-mile passage with his wife and sons in a 35-foot boat after the loss of his ship. Spit out onshore by the collapse of American commercial sail in the 1890s, Slocum then was thrown out of his house by his grumpy wife. To rehabilitate himself, he first rehabilitated an ancient fishing sloop, then took it to sea. Simplicity, practicality, and joy permeate his book, *Sailing Alone around the World*, in declarations such as "The sea has been much maligned" and "To young men contemplating a voyage, I would say go." After reading it, many young men decided to do just that, and to find out how, they read the inspirational and instructional writings of Thomas Fleming Day.

**Before the Bermuda Race, ocean racing was done in immense yachts like *Atlantic* (top), and small-boat voyaging was known for stunts like the Crapos' transatlantic crossing in a whaleboat named *New Bedford*. It took Joshua Slocum and Tom Day to bring legitimacy to both sports.**

T here would be much larger Bermuda fleets with much larger boats, but otherwise the first slog to what was called the Onion Patch was typical, with the blend of gales and calms, joys and miseries, fears and ennui that would become familiar to the tens of thousands of sailors who would sail in the race over the next hundred years. Yet, never again would the voyage seem so bold and the euphoria of making landfall feel so complete. The first Bermuda Race was the first test of the revolutionary notion that the ocean is a home not just for professional sailors in large vessels engaged in commerce, war, or tycoons' competitions, but serves as a playground where amateur seamen can not only sail small boats, but actually *race them offshore*. The race's instigator and organizer, Thomas Fleming Day, was filling the pages of his magazine, *The Rudder*, with this unfamiliar notion expressed in language that still shocks. The sea, he said, is a nurturing "great green mother," and "The danger of the sea for generations has been preached by the ignorant. Small vessels are safer than large, providing they are properly designed, strongly built, thoroughly equipped, and skillfully manned." These were not comfortable thoughts in 1906. His legion of critics, with furrowed brows, quoted Mark Twain's famous warning, "Bermuda is Paradise but you have to go through Hell to get to it," and declared that these little vessels would never survive the Gulf Stream. Even if they did (warned Day's own navigation teacher) they would never find the tiny island. It was rumored that funeral wreaths were delivered to the little fleet so the sailors would be prepared to make a decent burial at sea.

Those fears took their toll. Where five crews had spoken seriously of racing, four entered and just three started. They were Richard D. Floyd's 40-foot-overall yawl *Lila*, Frank Maier's 38-foot yawl *Tamerlane* (with Tom Day as sailing master), and then the little boat that had been taking most of the heat, George Robinson's 28-foot sloop *Gauntlet*. Robinson apparently was so eager to escape the shoreside uproar that had arisen around him that he crossed the Brooklyn Yacht Club's starting line a few seconds early and was obliged to loop back through the large spectator fleet and restart in the wake of her two opponents. Of the three, *Gauntlet* attracted the most rancor.

*Gauntlet*'s problems had nothing to do with her small size. Although to our eye she seems suitable only for a weekend cruise in protected waters to, say, Oyster Bay or Nyack, a year earlier she and the other two starters, and eight other small boats, had sailed and finished a race that Day had organized from Brooklyn to Newport News, Virginia. That was the second long-distance race he had organized. In 1904, in possibly the first long race for small boats in U.S. history, he ran a race from Brooklyn around Long Island and Cape Cod to Marblehead, Massachusetts.

After the finish at Newport News in 1905, some sailors asked Day to put on what he called "a real ocean race, one that would take them well

**Today's Bermuda Race winners receive elegant replicas of the island's lighthouses. The founding race in 1906 had this fantastically ornate trophy donated by Sir Thomas Lipton and awarded to Tom Day as *Tamerlane*'s sailing master.**

off shore and into blue water." He decided the destination should be Bermuda. He arranged with the Brooklyn Yacht Club (which had started the two coastal races) to run the start and with the Royal Bermuda Yacht Club to manage the finish and award ceremony. For a prize, he approached Sir Thomas Lipton, the three-time America's Cup challenger and full-time publicity hound who was then cheerfully distributing trophies all

over North America and England. To call the Lipton Cup for the first Bermuda Race "ornate" is a profound understatement.

The question that wracked the first Bermuda Race was not little *Gauntlet*'s proportions, but the makeup of her crew. As the race committee was making the required boat inspections, they were disconcerted to be told that one of *Gauntlet*'s crew was the owner's 20-year-old wife of six weeks. Thora Lund Robinson admitted she was not much of a sailor, but she promised the committee that, having married George, she was not about to permit him to risk his life alone. The Brooklyn Yacht Club was horrified. Headquartered in a Victorian mansion on the banks of Gravesend Bay, a shoal indent off lower New York Harbor, it was one of the half-dozen oldest yacht clubs in the country and a well-established, proud sponsor of races. As the committee, Day, and the Robinsons negotiated, the journalists on hand energetically competed to produce the best euphemism for "helpless" to characterize Thora Robinson. The winner probably was the fellow who described her as "of the petite, frail type." A slightly more enlightened reporter looked at her a little more respectfully. She was, he said, "a very slender young woman, with tawny hair and level gaze."

Thora Lund Robinson's level gaze caught Tom Day between the proverbial devil and the deep blue sea. To bar her from racing would undermine his conviction that the sea was potentially safe for everyone.

In the end, as a newspaper headline put it, "Bride Thwarts Committee." As the small fleet of small boats banged out of lower New York Harbor on the end of the ebb tide, into a fresh head wind, among the spray-soaked sailors in *Gauntlet*'s cockpit was Thora Lund Robinson.

Then came a disaster that had the potential of ending the race. Ninety minutes after the start, *Lila* was opening up a big lead when her mainmast broke in two. As her five-man crew picked up the pieces, *Tamerlane*, with Tom Day, came alongside and tossed a line. They would tow *Lila* back to get a new spar. The towline snapped and a tug took over, but still *Tamerlane* escorted *Lila* back to the Brooklyn Yacht Club. While Day was praised for his seaman's big heart, it was true that he also had a big ambition for his race. If *Lila* went back alone, her discouraged sailors might scatter to the winds. *Gauntlet*, meanwhile, was doggedly pounding her way around Sandy Hook into the open sea.

## Skipper Day

"Deep sea racing was inevitable—it simply had to come," Tom Day announced in his confident way shortly before the first Bermuda Race. Like all prophets, Day identified his convictions with the Zeitgeist so closely that he would not take personal credit for his own contribution. "Invention" may be too strong a word for it; what Joseph J. Ellis has said of George Washington might also be said of Tom Day: he personally

# Rules and Boats

*G*auntlet and *Tamerlane*, the two finishers in the first Bermuda Race, were designed and built by Larry Huntington of the then yachting capital of New Rochelle, New York. A distant relative of the 1990 Bermuda Race winner, he was a former bond salesman who switched to full-time yacht design and building. It was said that his boats "were all interesting, often experimental, usually fast, but not always attractive"—although *Gauntlet* and *Tamerlane* had striking looks.

The first Bermuda Race's rules were simple enough to fit into just two and a half pages. First, the event was solely for true cruising boats between 25 and 50 feet in overall length. At a time when there was a great divide between racers and cruisers, "cruising boat" meant a long keel, water-tight cockpit, wineglass sections instead of a flat, scow bottom, a decent-sized cabin, and overhangs so short that they totaled less than 25 percent of overall length. (The popular Herreshoff New York Yacht Club 30, a racing boat, would not have qualified with its 30 percent proportion.) The rule specifically defined minimum cabin size and height. For example, a boat between 28 and 32 feet had to have no less than five feet, two inches of headroom extending over 28 square feet of cabin floor, exclusive of bunks and lockers. (Sailors then were not smaller than we are, but brought up with smaller expectations. To quote the boating writer E. F. Knight, "If one wishes to assume an erect position one can always go on deck.") Typical accommodations then consisted of little more than four benches to serve as bunks, and a small enclosed toilet. Each boat was required to carry water and food for two weeks, a small boat, navigation equipment, a life belt (life jacket) for each sailor, and ground tackle.

As for a rating rule, the big news was that the race had one. The owners of the big schooners in the transatlantic races had cared only about being first to finish, but Day wanted a fair comparison of

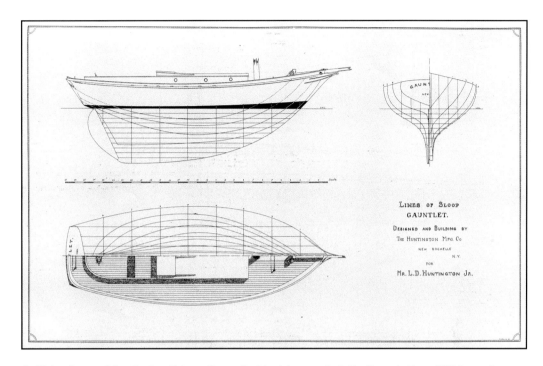

At 28 feet in overall length, *Gauntlet* was the smallest boat to compete in the Bermuda Race. With her springy sheer, wineglass sections, and large cockpit, she was a typical small cruiser of her time. She would never pass a pre-race inspection today.

performance by boats of different size. The rule was amazingly simple: measured length was length overall, rounded up or down to the nearest whole foot. The time allowance was based on a progressive scale in which, for instance, a 50-footer gave 1 hour to a 49-footer (5.5 seconds a mile over a 650-mile course), and a 40-footer gave a 39-footer 90 minutes (8.3 seconds). This rule was considered fair so long as boats had the same proportions. It was used in the first nine Bermuda Races.

Except that topsails were barred, sail area was unregulated. Day believed it was up to the sailors to judge how much sail to carry; as he put it, "A tax on sail is a tax on skill." *Gauntlet*'s working sail area of 616 square feet was just 100 feet less than the measured sail area of the ten-foot-longer *Finisterre*, winner of the 1956, 1958, and 1960 Bermuda Races.

The most startling rule was that the crews, as Day put it, had to be "real simon-pure pleasure sailors." This was a new direction at a time when many boats this size had at least one professional sailor to handle sails, cooking, and maintenance. Amateur status had to be confirmed by submitting a list of professions. Day proudly pointed out that the crew of *Tamerlane* consisted of "a telegrapher, an artist, an artisan, a gentleman-of-leisure, a school boy, and an editor." The man of leisure was the owner, Frank Maier; the artist was the navigator, Warren Sheppard, an illustrator and painter who contributed to the magazine, *The Rudder*, edited by *Tamerlane*'s first mate, Thomas Fleming Day himself.

## "The Wind-Satisfied Sail"

One night Day perched himself on the bowsprit to observe *Tamerlane* flying through a sea of phosphorescence:

*The bow waves broke away on either side a mass of fire just as if her stem was a plough being driven through a field of glowing sparks. The red and green side lights showed like the eyes of a dragon, the spray, like the breath from the monster's nostrils, coloring as it drifted across the path of the beams. Except for the sound of the bow treading down the overtaken wave, nothing was audible save a faint rustle of the canvas—the song of the wind-satisfied sail. Boys, I wish you had been with me that night. Such a night as puts into your being that life-love, that affection, nay, passion, for existence, that gives to earth an enchantment so that all things assume an aspect of immutability, when the soul in its longing to share cries out in ecstasy, "Let me live forever!"*

transformed "the improbable into the inevitable."

Born in England in 1861, Thomas Fleming Day came over as a boy, discovered sailing canoes (then the poor man's cruiser), and became a sponge for maritime knowledge. In 1890 he took over as editor of a canoeing magazine based in Watertown, New York, renamed it *The Rudder*, moved it to New York City, and made it into the first national boating magazine. His magazine and book publishing empire was founded on the needs of a growing population of men and women hungry not just for reading about adventure but for doing it. Up to the challenge of providing the necessary information and inspiration, Day also was a natural leader. One of his friends said he had "the eyes of a dynamic personality—eyes that held you, and sometimes told you more than any spoken word." Yet there were plenty of words, great gales of them, and often carrying the force of a breaking wave, for Day was not one to engage in understatement or, for that matter, blandness.

His favorite targets were the established yacht clubs, with their steam yachts and day races and their "carpet admirals." "I am sick of hearing that we are a lot of shore-skulkers, Central Park sailors; that while we can build racing machines and win with them, we have neither the craft nor the skill and pluck to sail on deep water, or even to go out of sight of land." The blue-blazer crowd—the "gray-headed, rum-soaked piazza yachtsmen"—had no idea of true sailing. "What do these miserable old hulks, who spend their days swigging booze on the front steps of a club-house, know about the danger of the deep?" When L. Francis Herreshoff, Captain Nat's son, sniffed, "Day himself was a boatsman at heart and not a yachtsman or racer," Day would have been pleased. Others respectfully nicknamed him "The Old Man," "The Skipper," or "Offshore Tommy," although there were places where mention of "The Crank" indicated only one individual.

Every now and then Day's crusty shell gave way to allow his romanticism to shine, for example, in an interview just before the Bermuda Race start when he explained why he started the race: "Sailors wanted to get a smell of the sea and forget for the time being that there is such a thing as God's green earth in the universe." Offshore sailing, in short, made people better. The reporter was not converted, suggesting the Bermuda Race proved only that the average sailor is a masochist. "In the world of sport, glory always lies on the further side of the Town of Tribulation," he wrote, adding sailing to the roster of sports whose justification is that discomfort inspires character growth. When another reporter asked Day to justify risking one's neck in a small vessel upon the ocean, he jauntily replied, "My dear boy, death is everywhere, and he is just as certain to get you on land as he is on sea. And why not, if you have to die, die doing something?"

An early historian of ocean racing, Samuel Wetherill, provided a fair evaluation of the man at the time of Day's death in 1927: "Some thought him foolish, others downright crazy. But, despite the doleful howls and lugubrious prophecies, Skipper Day persisted. He knew that small craft, if properly designed, built, and handled, were just as safe at sea as large ones. So he preached, prayed, and cajoled and cussed a lot; organized his race, and ran it to a successful conclusion, without damage or loss of a boat, or harm to an individual."

The Bermuda course could be counted to provide plenty of tribulation-triggered character growth. Taking about a week, it was long enough to test endurance and seamanship and, out of sight of land except for a few miles, it provided a challenging navigational exercise. In the prevailing south-to-southwest breeze, the south-southeast course meant either a beat or a close reach, but anything might happen to the weather. The upper part of the course lay among North America's fast-moving spring weather systems, while the lower part was on the boundary of the great mid-Atlantic High, with its calms. Whole races have been sailed upwind or downwind, whether taking solid water on deck or seeing nary a wave break.

Yet there were two constants. One was the predictably rough Gulf Stream crossing. The other constant was the population of hospitable Bermudians, whose sailing tradition reached back 300 years.

## The Race

And so the first Bermuda Race was organized and started, and then immediately came to grief when *Lila* lost her mast. It took two days to find a replacement. Meanwhile, the wind had hauled into the northwest and Tom Day was chomping at the bit to get *Tamerlane* under way. As *Lila*'s crew was rigging the spar on Tuesday morning, *Tamerlane* weighed anchor and set out after *Gauntlet*, which now had a 65-hour head start. The northerly gave way to a southwest gale in the Gulf Stream, which *Tamerlane* handled easily under jib and jigger with the mainsail secured. On the fourth day came a calm so flat that the crew launched the dinghy to row around the little yawl as she sat drying out in the warm sun.

Longtail boatswain's-birds appeared, and a concentrated patch of white clouds rose over the island. At noon on the fifth day, a pilot's whaleboat arrived, leading a fleet (as Day would write) of "tugs, yachts, steamers, skiffs, canoes by the dozen, crowded with cheering people." *Tamerlane* finished in 120 hours, averaging almost 5 1/2 knots. *Gauntlet* arrived 25 hours later on her eighth day out. In a southeast gale she had been under bare poles for two days with the helmsmen lashed in place. As she crossed the finish line, Thora Lund Robinson was at the helm and waving an American flag. Lipton sent her a prize "for her great pluck, skill, and endurance." *Gauntlet* then won a special day race and Thora Robinson became the toast of Bermuda. By then Day knew how right he was to allow her to race. As he put it, getting in one more whack at his critics, "Her having gone and having safely survived the ordeal will forever silence the piazza sailors and bar-room mariners who spent their time

denouncing the race as dangerous, and calling the backers of it murderers."

As for unlucky *Lila*, she had dropped out once again, this time for keeps in the southeast gale. "We stuck our nose into it and failed," explained one of her crew. "We tried again and failed, and we repeated the effort six times." This sign that contemporary boats of that size just weren't up to the Gulf Stream suggested that yacht design had to improve if Tom Day's vision were to be fulfilled.

When *Tamerlane* reached the Royal Bermuda Yacht Club quay under tow, 4,000 of the island's 14,000 residents were there to greet her (the club's officers apologized for the small turnout; this was, after all, a Sunday). The yacht club provided a special anchorage off White's Island for the race boats, set aside rooms for the skippers and navigators in the clubhouse (which was then on Front Street), and laid on many parties culminating with a traditional turtle dinner at the prize banquet, where His Excellency the Governor-General and Tom Day vied for the honor of giving the most colorful speech.

Then it came time to sail home. *Tamerlane*'s passage was one of those return trips that is more dreadful than the race itself. In a northeast gale blowing against the axis of the Gulf Stream, the cockpit filled, a sea broke through a skylight and filled the bilge, and when she ran off before it, the yawl threatened to pitchpole, stern over stem. Frank Maier, Tom Day, and their crew hove-to for almost 24 hours with oil bags deployed to flatten the sea. One of the sailors, Percy A. Cook, later wrote, "By 6 a.m. we were clear of the Gulf Stream, which place, I am under the impression, might be improved upon." He summarized the voyage in a way familiar to five generations of sailors: "I really enjoyed it, only I thought it would be kind of nice to be dry again for a change."

That was *Tamerlane*'s first and last Bermuda Race. She later spent several years in and around Greenwich, Connecticut, a celebrity as the first winner of a Bermuda Race. After *Gauntlet* arrived home, the Robinsons sold her and raced a catboat on Long Island Sound. The next that was heard of *Gauntlet*, she was back in Bermuda in the day-charter business. In 1930 her owner sailed her up to America with the intention of entering another Bermuda Race (or Ocean Race, as it is called in Bermuda) but was turned down as too small. Back she went to Bermuda, where she was still taking tourists out for day sails in the 1940s.

## 1907: Bermuda Sends Two Boats

Always the enthusiast, Day decided to hold another race the next year and also run a parallel motorboat race to Bermuda. (Day commanded one of the two entries, the 59-foot powerboat *Ailsa Craig*, to win handily.) Day asked Frank Maier to take charge of the sailboat race. The "man of leisure" in *Tamerlane*'s crew, Maier was in the securities business and a noted book collector. He offered a first-place trophy valued at $1,000 and formed a race committee with a member each from his own New

BATTLE AXE.

DINGHYS STARTING.

THE HARBOR.

CREW AT GIBBS HILL.

THE CROWD ON QUAY.

TAMERLANE.

DINGHYS ROUNDING.

WRECK OF THE CONTEST.

Snap Shots at Bermuda

Tom Day's Bermuda, 1906: a sloop at the yacht club wharf; fitted dinghies (one capsized) and the crowd watching their races from the yacht club; sightseeing; and *Tamerlane* under sail—her gaff rig standing out among the many Bermuda rigs. This page of snapshots ran in *The Rudder*.

Henry Morss's 85-footer *Dervish* won the large class in 1907 and in 1908 (when Morss ran the race out of Marblehead). Morsses would be winning Bermuda Race silver in the 1960s. Note the yard for the squaresail sometimes carried by schooners for offshore work.

Rochelle Yacht Club, the Brooklyn Yacht Club, and the Royal Bermuda
Yacht Club (the Bermuda representative was the surgeon on one of the
steamships making regular runs between America and the island).
Deciding after his rough ride in 1906 that *Tamerlane* was a bit small for
the Gulf Stream, Maier replaced her with a Larry Huntington-designed
schooner, *Hyperion*, that at 49 feet just under the maximum limit.

Entries were dribbling in when Henry A. Morss, commodore of the
Corinthian Yacht Club of Marblehead, Massachusetts, announced that if
the ban on professionals and the 50-foot upper limit on length were
eliminated, he would enter his 85-foot schooner, *Dervish*, and encourage
owners of other large yachts to do the same. Though this was not what
Day had in mind, he was in no position to be a purist. Of the 12 boats
on the Brooklyn Yacht Club starting line, only two were smaller than 40
feet and four were 80 feet or longer. The biggest boat was the first freshwater entry, an 86-foot Gloucester fisherman schooner named *Priscilla*
with nine paid hands and an afterguard from Rochester, New York.
Bermuda was represented by its first entry, too—in fact two entries: the
American-built cutter *Isolt* from the St. George's Yacht Club and the 37-
foot sloop *Zena*. An island product, *Zena* was the first boat built specifically for the race and the first race entry to carry the three-cornered
Bermudian rig. Her owner, D. R. W. Burrowes, was a member of the
Royal Bermuda Yacht Club and also the Hamilton Dinghy Club, which
helped organize hospitality. The Bermudian entries stimulated considerable enthusiasm on the island, including wagers, judging from a letter
home from *Zena*'s professional captain, John F. Leseur: "I shall be very
much disappointed in mind and pocket if I don't keep the credit of the
old rock up. Never fear, she is as good as you can do in Bermuda." Alas,
*Zena* had structural problems and finished last in the small class. (*Zena*
raced twice more in the 1930s with a ketch rig. In 1946 she sank while
trying to get to Newport for the start; the crew was rescued.)

Day and Morss decided that with such a disparate fleet it would be
useless to try to award overall prizes. Morss's *Dervish* won Class A and
was first to finish, reaching the island so quickly that the race committee
arrived too late to finish her. Maier's much smaller *Hyperion*, with Warren
Sheppard as navigator and a young ace named Robert N. Bavier there,
too, came in only five hours later but must have had an unhappy rating
because she ended up only second in Class B on corrected time behind
the only boat with an all-amateur crew, Richard D. Floyd's *Lila*, whose
race in 1906 had experienced so many setbacks.

Although the sailing conditions were relatively benign, the race had
its moments. One boat had a fire in the Gulf Stream, another suffered a
sprung mast and a bad leak, and the long, spoon-shaped racing bow of a
third boat pounded so badly that the furious owner bet the designer that
if he ever spent several days offshore in her, he would never again draw
those lines. Other owners would place similar bets.

Snap Shots on Tamerlane

Day's camera came out
when *Tamerlane* became
the first racer to find the
notorious "parking lot" near
Bermuda. In time the breeze
came up and boats came
out to greet her.

## 1908: A Marblehead Start

That turnout was the high point until the 1920s. With Henry A. Morss in charge, the 1908 race started at Marblehead. (The angry officers of the Brooklyn Yacht Club appealed to the Royal Bermuda Yacht Club for assistance getting the start back, but to no avail.) Eleven boats entered, only six started, and five finished. The American economy was a wreck following the Wall Street panic of 1907, and the race's reputation for heavy weather frightened amateurs away; even Frank Maier could not find a crew. This was by far the toughest race yet, with a hard beat all the way down. One boat was said to have buried her leeward rail for 48 hours straight. Conditions were so gnarly that one owner complained that the professional crew was too preoccupied with sail-handling to get around to polishing the ship's brass. On corrected time, *Dervish* won

one class and the schooner *Venona* the other. After a hundred hours of smashing into it, including losing her foretopmast, *Venona* made St. David's Head under storm canvas and circled the boat at the outer end of the line to see how she had done. When her owner, an old sea dog named E. Jared Bliss, learned that he had *Dervish* and other larger boats in his wake and was first to finish, he leaned down into the companionway and shouted to his seasick crew, "Below there, we win!"

Island of Bermuda completely Won by E.J. BLISS

First Prize Won by The Venon

Although Jared Bliss's 65-footer *Venona* did not actually win Bermuda (as an artist-crewmember suggested), she won everything else in 1908. Note the snappy sailing outfit. (Opposite) Harold Vanderbilt at the helm of one of the big, professionally crewed schooners that were so different from Tom Day's ideal.

## 1909: Charlie Barr in the Running

After its only excursion north of Cape Cod, the race start returned to Brooklyn under the mantle of the Atlantic Yacht Club, the arch-rival of the Brooklyn Yacht Club. Five boats started, four of them big schooners and the other a large cutter commanded by Warren Sheppard. The fleet had lost all pretense of being normal and amateur, and the 98-foot schooner *Crusader II* was under the command of the most successful professional racing skipper of that era, Charlie Barr, winner of three America's Cup matches and the 1905 Transatlantic Race. Barr won the start, but not the finish. The excitement came at the end with the most thrilling finish for many years. Two big schooners, *Amorita* and *Margaret*, were almost bow to bow as they came in from Kitchen Shoals and finished just two minutes apart. *Amorita* set an elapsed time record of 78 hours, 19 minutes that would stand until *Highland Light* broke it in the eleventh race in 1932. The Lawley-built 93-footer *Margaret* won on corrected time.

## 1910: A Match Race to the Onion Patch

Five boats entered the next race, but four dropped out, leaving only the 75-foot Herreshoff schooner *Vagrant*, owned and commanded by Harold S. Vanderbilt, who was three years out of Harvard. Finally the race was started on July 9 after a Midwesterner, Demarest Lloyd, arranged to have a lawsuit postponed in Chicago so he could go sailing with his wife (the second woman to race a sailboat to Bermuda after Thora Lund Robinson) in his big schooner, *Shiyessa*. In the crew was a young naval architect from Boston named John Alden.

After leading *Vagrant* for over 600 miles through a series of gales, *Shyessa* had a comfortable weather berth when the wind flip-flopped from southwest to northeast, leaving her on the outside of the shift and almost becalmed. "We had made the mistake of thinking we had won the race, especially as we had a time allowance of an hour and a half, as I remember it." John Alden would recall. "To our great surprise and disappointment, the *Vagrant* sailed around us, and while we were so close to the finish we could see the bottom plainly, we didn't have a breath of wind." Lloyd was so mad he wanted to quit the race right then and there, but Alden talked him out of it. Vanderbilt won narrowly on corrected time and is one of only two sailors to be skipper of winners of both a Bermuda Race and an America's Cup match. (The other is Ted Hood, who won the Bermuda Race in 1968 and the Cup six years later.)

The race had lost its energy. Amateur sailors in wet smaller boats did not want to race all that distance only to stand by as most of the attention and prizes were lavished on mammoth schooners sailed by tycoons and professionals. As for those tycoons, while a handful of them might be prepared to race across the Gulf Stream once, their enthusiasm for repeat-

ing the experience was limited. In the end, the amateurs opted for overnight races on Long Island Sound and Massachusetts Bay, while the wealthy owners preferred to go cruising. Interest in the race was lagging even in Bermuda, where the time had long passed when post-race arrangements were on a scale that the *Royal Gazette* described as "more or less elaborate." When the summer of 1911 rolled around, there was no racing to Bermuda in any boats. Powerboats would later come back in races from Philadelphia, but the sailing race was dead until new blood and better boats appeared.

Tom Day had moved on. In 1911 he sailed his 26-foot yawl, *Sea Bird*, from New York to Gibraltar, and a year later he commanded a 35-foot powerboat named *Detroit* on an improbable promotional voyage for American gasoline engines that began in Michigan and concluded in St. Petersburg, Russia. All that took a toll on his frail body. In 1917 he retired from *The Rudder* to manage a ship chandlery in Manhattan. He cruised the New England coast singlehanded in an outboard-powered sailing dinghy, camping on the beach and once making the 230 miles from New York to Boston in 52 hours. When the Cruising Club of America elected him an honorary member in its founding year, 1922, the yachting writer and historian W. P. Stephens said in his tribute, "To Captain Day must be given the sole credit for all that is done today in offshore cruising and ocean racing in the smaller yachts, as well as all that has been accomplished in the near past." On his deathbed, Day whispered to a friend, "I am slipping, but life is sweet still."

John Alden yachted-up the fishing schooner into the first cruiser-racer. It helped revive the Bermuda Race. This is his 47-foot *Malabar IV*, winner in 1923. (Opposite) Alden at the helm of his 58-foot *Malabar IX* before the 1928 start. The young man with his hand on the boom is Olin Stephens.

# The Schooner Era

Thirteen years passed before the next sailboat race to Bermuda. When the starting gun finally fired, said the man who revived the race, Herbert L. Stone, "an instinctive cheer, releasing pent-up enthusiasm, broke from the crew of every boat, to be echoed by the spectators." It was 1923, at the other side of a world war and at the far end of the patience of a rising generation of young sailors.

Like Tom Day, Herb Stone was a sailor-editor who was convinced that racing offshore produced better cruising boats and amateur sailors, and who was eager to promote races for his magazine. He ran the Bermuda Race until the CCA and the Royal Bermuda Yacht Club took over in 1926.

There were cheers down in Bermuda, too. The race's revival was a sign of the restoration of postwar normalcy to an island that was not only increasingly dependent on visitors, but whose national pastime was sailing. Bermuda had sent two boats — one built specifically for the race — to America to participate and then had finished races and entertained visiting crews. In 1922 Vice-Commodore Eldon Trimingham of the Royal Bermuda Yacht Club had gone up to New York to take the pulse of the Americans. Would the New York Yacht Club take on the race's complex management? After all, the commodore was none other than the winner of the last one, Harold Vanderbilt. But there was no interest there. Everybody who had been around the race knew the difficulty of managing it, what with its start in one country, its finish in another, and its collection of strong-minded participants and noisy critics. Even the indomitable Thomas Fleming Day had admitted the administrative burdens. "It should be kept up," he wrote in 1908. "But who is going to keep it going? That is the problem under my wood-ends. These races cost considerable money, and what is more valuable than money to some people — time." Day had proposed forming an international ocean racing club. In 1922 Eldon Trimingham was echoing the idea.

Trimingham surely knew that a new organization of offshore sailors was in formation in New York. Down in Greenwich Village, a few young and middle-aged yachtsmen with a hankering for blue water were gathering regularly in a speakeasy called Beefsteak John's to tell sea stories and plan their next voyages. Some of them were navy veterans who had gained offshore experience the hard way during World War I in 110-foot submarine chasers. As wet, unstable, and demanding as any racing sailboat, these little warships had crossed the Atlantic, surviving terrible weather. After the peace, six "splendid splinters" completed their passage home by racing from Bermuda to New York.

Out of the subchasers came four men who helped revive the Bermuda Race and whose names are on race trophies. William W. Nutting was the instigator of the gatherings at Beefsteak John's and the first commodore of the organization that sprang out of them, the Cruising Club of America (the CCA). Alfred F. Loomis was the winning navigator in the subchaser race, became sailing's best writer, sailed 17 races, and analyzed them meticulously in *Yachting* magazine for almost fifty years. Samuel Wetherill was an editor at *Yachting* magazine, where his regular assignments included editing the influential design section, where most new trends were announced. The fourth subchaser veteran was the CCA's second commodore, *Yachting*'s long-time editor-in-chief and publisher, Herbert L. Stone, and it was he who played the essential role in restarting the race.

They and their friends were adventurers and idealists. As we have seen, Tom Day had founded the Bermuda Race on the new idea that amateur sailors belonged far at sea and were better people for it. Here is how Nutting explained why he built a boat and sailed her to England and back: "We did it for the fun of the thing, and we believe that no further explanation is necessary." The fun of the thing lay in the risk of the thing: "Is 'Safety First' going to become our national motto? . . . In this day when life is so very easy and safe-and-sane and highly-specialized and steam-heated, we need, more than we ever needed before, sports that are big and raw and — yes, dangerous." Another founder of the CCA, Henry A. Wise Wood, who had made long-distance sailing-canoe passages with his wife, would go so far as to announce, "We popularize the use of the open sea for pleasure." Though such language would seem naïve after Bill Nutting disappeared at sea off Greenland in 1924, the spirit of risk-taking adventure continued to thrive, in large part through the Bermuda Race.

**The Essential Herb Stone**

If Day was the George Washington of ocean racing, Herb Stone was its Abraham Lincoln — the leader who brought peace among its warring sides. Like Day, Stone believed that racing helped cruisers. "There is nothing that develops all-around seamanship and resourcefulness as much as a long-distance ocean race that keeps the contestants going night and day," he told his readers in 1921, around the time he began pressing his fellow CCA founders to sponsor a race to Bermuda.

He wrote from long experience. Herbert L. Stone (1871-1955) went to sea as a teenager. He eventually came ashore, did some writing about ships and sailing, and in 1908 was rescued from a clerical job at the New York Central Railroad by the publisher of a foundering new magazine. Stone quickly made *Yachting* into a competitor of Tom Day's *The Rudder* — more handsome, better written, and, though friendlier to the establishment, covering a broader sweep.

Stone commanded a subchaser squadron during World War I and later ran a fleet of commercial schooners before returning to *Yachting*, determined to revive ocean racing, which he believed was sailing's next big thing. It took a while for that to happen. In 1921 he promoted a transatlantic race for a trophy put up by the King of Belgium, but nobody entered. A year later he was talking up a singlehanded transatlantic match race between the Duke of Leinster and Bill Nutting when the "daredevil nobleman" was exposed as a bankrupt gambler with a history of making fraudulent claims. As Herb Stone put those embarrassments behind him and plugged on, along came a cause. That cause's name was the Alden schooner, the first successful dual-purpose cruising-racing boat. It became the Bermuda Race's first secure anchor.

After Stone helped the designer John Alden deliver his 42-foot semifisherman *Malabar II* through a gale in the spring of 1922, he told his readers, "For ease of handling, she has anything I have ever been on

beaten, coming and going." Later that year, he and Sam Wetherill sailed with Alden in *Malabar II* in a 282-mile race around Long Island in which, despite plenty of upwind sailing in smooth water — conditions unfavorable to schooners — she finished third on both elapsed and corrected time, beating several larger sloops.

Stone decided that here was a good reason to sail an ocean race, and he told the Cruising Club of America that it should run that race because it would be good for cruising sailors. Many CCA members, however, saw a deep contradiction for a cruising organization to run a race. Such purism seemed a little hypocritical. "When two cruising men fall in with each other afloat, little things happen in common," Alf Loomis accurately observed. "Both trim sails more efficiently and both pay closer attention to helmsmanship." Yet, sailors of strong credentials in and out of the CCA were sure racing was inherently dangerous. The most influential writer on deep-sea voyaging, Claud Worth, the English author of the book *Yacht Cruising*, complained that a long-distance race "might very well include some owners whose keenness is greater than their experience," sailors who would not know when and if they should heave-to when running in a wild sea. Worth seems not to have considered the possibility that experience would quickly season sailors into competent seamen and that yacht designers would develop boats that could sail through a gale without having to heave-to. (Worth eventually came around in the late 1920s and complimented the Bermuda Race for having a distant offshore island as a destination, unlike the Fastnet.)

Even in his role as CCA commodore, Stone was unable to win over more than half the members to the proposition that the club should run this race, or for that matter any race.

**1923: The Race Returns**

So Stone decided to put on a Bermuda Race himself. Implicitly he was acting under the banner of *Yachting*. Subtle commercial sponsorship was not new; when Tom Day stuck his neck out in 1906, so did *The Rudder*. Day had protected himself by bringing in yacht clubs and owners to handle the details. Stone did recruit the New Rochelle Yacht Club to start the race and the Royal Bermuda Yacht Club to finish it, and prizes came in from several sources. Otherwise, the 1923 race was in the hands of Stone and his management committee of experts. Four of the six members came from the burgeoning boating industry that was thriving in the 1920s. Yacht designers John Alden and Charles D. Mower, and magazine editors Sam Wetherill and Race Chairman Stone provided considerable technical knowledge and widespread influence. The two businessmen-sailors on the committee gave that and more. One was the Royal Bermuda Yacht Club's representative, Kenneth T. Trimingham. MIT-educated, he was Eldon Trimingham's brother, regular crew, and partner in the famous Front Street department store. The other was

Alfred Darrell and his brothers knew their home waters. After they brought the 37-foot yawl *Dainty* up from Bermuda for the 1923 race, they proceeded to finish second in fleet by taking a shortcut through the reef in North Rock Channel. The tactic was barred in subsequent races.

Robert N. Bavier, a banker who competed successfully on Long Island Sound and was taking leadership roles in the sport. (His son, Robert N. Bavier Jr., played the same part and succeeded Stone as a publisher of *Yachting* magazine. *Yachting* staff members would serve on Bermuda Race committees from the 1920s into the 1970s.)

These men's demonstration of faith in their colleagues and their common enterprise was noteworthy and brave. Stone raised the stakes by declaring that the race would be a test of the modern breed of cruising boats — those semifisherman schooners that Alden was designing and he and Wetherill were praising to the skies. Had Alden's new *Malabar IV* or any of the other new schooners broken down, the reputations of these six men would have been deeply scarred, and this surely would have been the last Bermuda Race for many years. Afterwards, Sam Wetherill answered the critics with a bravado that surely was mingled with relief: "I hope that these gentlemen will kindly note that 22 boats started, and that 22 boats found the islands. And that's that." Stone and his committee drafted a set of rules that set a tight limit on professional sailors, laid down safety requirements, and established the race's broad purpose in its preamble: "In order to encourage the designing, building, and sailing of small seaworthy yachts, to make popular cruising upon deep water, and to develop in the amateur sailor a love of true seamanship, and to give opportunity to become proficient in the art of navigation." Only slightly modified, those words would remain in the race notice for decades.

Stone expected a half-dozen entries, all of them larger boats. Instead he got 32 entries, many small, and 22 starters, which was just five boats less than the total entries in the five races before the war. The range in size was about what it was in the 1980s, from 37 feet (there were three boats that size) to an 81-foot schooner. The fleet represented three countries. From Bermuda came the colorful, gifted sailing Darrell family in the 37-foot yawl *Dainty*, and Captain Alwayrd E. Dingle of the Royal Nova Scotia Yacht Squadron, the oldest yacht club in the Americas, came down with the first Canadian entry, the 51-foot schooner *Gauntlet*, with a Nova Scotia crew that included Mary S. Manning, the third woman to race in a sailboat to Bermuda.

The only boat that was not gaff-headed was *Memory*, a Herreshoff New York 40 yawl owned and sailed by Bob Bavier and flying the then-new, exotic, and extremely intimidating Marconi rig. With 19 feet of overhang on her 59-foot overall length, she easily exceeded the 25 percent rule of thumb for maximum overhangs that differentiated cruising and racing boats. When the committee accepted her entry, it was no doubt out of respect for both Bavier and Herreshoff, though

# John Alden

The race needed a central figure, and it got one with John Alden. As a sailor, he had one of the longest records of success in the race's history. He raced to Bermuda ten times between 1910 and 1954. In seven he commanded his own boat, and in six of those seven he won a prize — three overall victories in 1923, 1926, and 1932, plus a third, a first, and a second in his class in 1928, 1930, and 1950, respectively. He is the only three-time winner other than Carleton Mitchell. As with Mitchell's little yawl *Finisterre*, the success of the *Malabar*s triggered a new boom in boatbuilding that circled back to feed the Bermuda Race, which was revived thanks to these boats.

John Alden (1884-1962) was a skilled sailor, a gifted technician, a brilliant marketer, and—like many sailors—a romantic. A shipmate recalled that Alden "would practically go into a trance gazing at nice examples of the fishing schooners or coasters we met so often afloat in those days." In the 1923 Bermuda Race, Alden offered a trophy for the top boat with a traditional clipper or straight-stemmed bow.

Alden got his start drawing commercial fishing schooners in a Boston naval architecture office. As interest in small cruising boats blossomed, he considered various alternatives. What he did not want to do (he wrote in an article for Herb Stone's *Yachting* in 1913) was produce "racers in disguise," which he was sure were too tender and uncomfortable and would "bring speedy disillusionment to the trusting smooth-water sailors who attempted to take them to sea." He opted for a slightly yachted-up, smaller version of the fishing schooners he was designing. Pretty with their jaunty sheer, inexpensive (*Malabar II* reportedly cost $1,800, the equivalent of about $17,000 today), easy to sail by a small amateur crew, seakindly, and, while not close-winded, fast on a reach, they opened a large market.

Alden's first efforts were boats for himself that he named for a long-disappeared sandspit on Cape

Designer and skipper of three winners, John Alden had both an eye and a feel for a boat. Someone once said of an Alden schooner that she "looked so warm and friendly we thought of her as alive."

Cod. In all there were 13 *Malabar*s, and a great many sisters and cousins (and hundreds of other designs, too). The semifisherman concept caught on quickly and was picked up by other designers, most notably William Hand. The course seemed made for the type because in almost every race there is a long stretch of sailing on a close reach in a good breeze. In the 1930s Olin Stephens, Phil

Rhodes, and other designers, working with cutting-edge builders like Henry Nevins and Quincy Adams, turned out different types of boats that proved faster, and the era of the schooner passed. Yet John Alden's schooners are some of the most beloved yachts in history.

With her towering Marconi rig, long overhangs, and deep ballast keel, the Herreshoff New York 40 *Memory* challenged the prevailing wisdom about a suitable offshore boat. But under Bob Bavier Sr. she had a superb record and indicated yacht design's future. (Opposite) The traditional fisherman *Lloyd W. Berry* won her class in 1924 and inspired a freshwater classic.

very likely Herb Stone wanted to test the limits of the common wisdom about what constituted a good offshore boat. Some knowledgeable people took a look at *Memory* and predicted she would win everything. As the fleet assembled at New London, Connecticut, other knowledgeable people announced that once the *Memory* got into the Gulf Stream, she would open up or her rig would topple.

New London had good boatyards, was accessible by train from New York and New England, and was the site of the crew races between Harvard and Yale, where many of the sailors had gone to college (for years the Bermuda Race start was keyed to the rowing races). The trade-off was that the first 25 miles of the 662-mile racecourse could be lousy sailing. The fleet usually got away lethargically in baffling light air and fog, and then had to battle violent tidal currents before rounding Montauk Point and finally aiming toward Bermuda in deep, blue water.

In 1923, after a day and a half of light northerlies, the wind came up and clocked through east into the south-southwest, where it stayed and provided strenuous windward work in the Gulf Stream. The going was hard and it was wet. "The next time I come to Bermuda it will be in a submarine," announced the owner of *Seafarer* — and this was a 63-foot schooner under severely shortened sail. The experience intimidated the sailors. *Seafarer*'s navigator, Alfred F. Loomis, would confess that long after the wind had dropped to a mere shadow of its peak, she was still under shortened sail. Even Bob Bavier nursed *Memory* for a while on her way to finish first.

The overall winner had not been coddled. This was John Alden's 47-foot gaff-headed schooner *Malabar IV*, the first of his boats designed with racing in mind, with a cloud of sail that pushed her through the whole fleet in the light going after the start and carried her brilliantly to the finish. Where *Malabar* won the race on corrected time through sheer power, in second place was the little Bermuda yawl *Dainty*, which almost won on cunning and local knowledge when her crew of Bermudians cut miles off her distance by guiding her through the reefs at North Rock Channel. No Bermuda racer would be allowed to do that again.

### 1924: *Memory*, a Double Winner

Stone wanted to keep up the momentum but was not sure if a quick return to Bermuda was the way to do it. There was talk of racing to Halifax, but he decided to race to the Onion Patch again in 1924. The error of his ways became clear when only 14 boats appeared on the starting line, just four of them repeaters, including *Memory*. The race obviously was just too much trouble to do every year.

The start was like the previous one, with wind so flat that Eldon Trimingham launched the dinghy from the Bermuda entry *Sylvia II* and took an oar-powered tour of the fleet drifting about in the fog. Then a hard southwesterly came in, and Trimingham found himself in a bit of

trouble far beyond his experience as Bermuda's champion small-boat helmsman. As his son Eldon tells the story, "There was a problem of who was to go forward on the bowsprit to get a headsail down when running off in deteriorating weather. He volunteered, but told the helmsman on no account to let the boat broach. He got out there all right, but the boat broached and he learned it was possible to shinny up a wire headstay."

*Memory*, meanwhile, scorched down the course in four days, but with Bob Bavier in his bunk with a strained back. Aboard was the fine small-boat racing sailor Sherman Hoyt, taking his first break from what he called "normal racing." *Memory* was driven hard and crossed the finish line at St. David's Head late at night. She hove-to until daylight as her crew climbed out of their wet clothes and celebrated their safe passage. After a bit of this, Hoyt became inspired to launch the dinghy, row over to the finish-line boat, and check the results. Only after he and a shipmate burst in on a coed gathering did they become aware that they had dressed down a little far for Bermuda's warm weather, in fact were wearing almost nothing. At least they came back with the news that *Memory* not only was once again first to finish, but had won the race on corrected time, too.

The 1924 Bermuda Race was the direct inspiration of two other famous long-distance classics. A crew of sailors from Port Huron, Michigan, came east, chartered the fisherman schooner *Lloyd W. Berry*, and with Herb Stone as navigator won the special class for commercial sailing vessels (the first of many of the race's special and demonstration divisions). They then went home and founded a race up Lake Huron to

Five of the nine members of the CCA-RBYC race committee gather before the 1926 race, the first under the clubs' joint management: (left to right) Edward H. Tucker, Charles D. Mower, C. Sherman Hoyt, A. F. Masbury, and Henry A. Jackson. Absent were John Alden, Robert N. Bavier, Sam Wetherill, and Henry A. Wise Wood. Today the Bermuda Race Organizing Committee has more than 30 members—still all volunteers—from both clubs. (Opposite) Bob Bavier's *Dragoon* rapidly overhauls a schooner just before the starting gun as their crews break out their big jibs from stops.

Mackinac Island (the Chicago-Mackinac race was founded in 1898). Another visitor was an English yachting journalist, Weston Martyr, who was so excited by his race in the schooner *Northern Light* that he went back home and in a letter to a yachting magazine announced that ocean racing was "without question the very finest sport a man can possibly engage in." He explained, "to play this game at all it is necessary to possess, in the very highest degree, those hallmarks of a true sportsman: skill, courage and endurance." A year later, Martyr and other English yachtsmen organized the first Fastnet Race. When they later founded the Royal Ocean Racing Club, they specified that membership was restricted to veterans of what was already called "The Grand National of ocean racing"—with one exception, and that was Herb Stone.

## 1926: The CCA and RBYC Team Up

This was the year the Cruising Club of America and the Royal Bermuda Yacht Club agreed to be the race's co-sponsors. Ocean racing was still new and still considered by many cruising sailors to be an iffy proposition. But with Stone as mediator, and with the popularity of the semi-

fisherman schooners and the success of a converted racing boat, *Memory*, the two sides in the argument agreed that a race was good for sailing in general.

The proof was in the boats themselves. "The gaff-headed sails seemed better cut than formerly," reported Alf Loomis, no sentimentalist, "and there was every evidence that offshore racing had already lifted the standards of the sport." Of the 16 boats that raced in 1926, the average age was only three years and just three boats were older than six years. One of the youngest boats won. In another one of those famous mixed bags of sailing conditions with the breeze mostly on or near the nose, John Alden won again, and again he was in a schooner, although the 54-footer *Malabar VII* was in fact a ketch on the drawing board. (When Alden realized at almost the last minute he did not have a design ready for the Bermuda Race, he quickly redrew the ketch as a schooner, put a triple-headsail rig on her because the jib topsail was not measured under the rating rule, and got her built.) "Seven" was a lucky vessel. As she was entering New London Harbor two days before the start, her steering gear broke within sight of a number of good shipyards. Although Alden

thought she was an indifferent performer upwind, *Malabar VII* won easily, with Bob Bavier first to finish for the third race in a row, this time in *Dragoon*, a 66-foot ketch with an 85-foot mast—the first boat whose concept was shaped around the Bermuda Race measurement rule.

Alden's and Bavier's repeated successes were splendid, but the star of the first RBYC-CCA Bermuda Race was one of the oldest entries and the first British boat to come over and race. Just as Herb Stone was worrying whether his baby would ever walk, the 1925 Fastnet Race winner, the English Channel pilot cutter *Jolie Brise*, turned up unannounced. Her owner, Commander George E. Martin, explained that he had made the 48-day passage across the Atlantic as a thank-you to the Americans for creating ocean racing and inspiring the Fastnet. He recruited Stone as his navigator and they quickly found *Jolie Brise*'s weather. As she threaded her way through the fleet in the light going after the start, her immense club topsail pulling like a team of horses, a cheer arose from her competitors. She finished fifth in fleet on both corrected and elapsed times, then turned her bow east and sailed home to sail in that year's Fastnet Race (she was fifth once again). She had made a 9,000-mile round-trip voyage so that Commander Martin could race 650 miles to Bermuda. Later that year the Cruising Club of America awarded Martin its Blue Water Medal "for a most meritorious example of seamanship," the first given in part for racing. Six years later, *Jolie Brise* would return to race to Bermuda, and earn another Blue Water Medal for a very different type of seamanship.

### 1928: Families and Cruisers

The reign of the *Malabar*s was not all-conquering. In a 24-boat fleet, the largest yet, the winner was another Marconi-rigged converted Herreshoff New York 40, *Rugosa II,* which ghosted to the finish through the last 70 miles of calm. Later owned by Halsey Herreshoff, *Rugosa II* was sailed by Russell Grinnell of New Bedford, a member of one of the first of many families closely identified with the Bermuda Race. Six brothers, sons, and cousins named Grinnell filled 15 Bermuda Race berths between 1923 and 1934.

Another Grinnell, the overall winner's brother, Lawrence, won the special class for big schooners in his *Flying Cloud II*. This was the second race with a class for boats allowed to race but not in the running for prizes. Sometimes they did not fit in the envelope of minimum or maximum measurements, and sometimes they had unique designs (for instance, in 2004 boats with canting keels were allowed to enter in a demonstration division). There were two special classes in 1928, the second for small cruising boats. When the great California seaman Harry Pidgeon, the second solo sailor around the world after Joshua Slocum, arrived on the East Coast in his self-built yawl *Islander* (a cousin of Tom Day's *Sea Bird*), the race committee set up a class for him and other small

ocean cruisers under the usual minimum of 35 feet. With a crew that included CCA Commodore George P. Bonnell (the CCA's Bonnell Cove Foundation is named for him), *Islander* won the class by more than a day over a Herreshoff cutter. Farther back still was William Albert Robinson in his little Alden ketch *Svaap*, which ran into a gale off Hatteras and took 12 days to reach St. David's Head. Robinson then proceeded to sail to Panama and around the world, mostly singlehanded, while *Islander* and Pidgeon later accomplished their second circumnavigation.

Also worth noticing was the first boat from the Great Lakes, *Elizabeth*, from Chicago and sailed by Lynn Williams with his son, the future owner of many *Dora*s, in her crew. Add five Marconi-rigged boats, one of them an Alden schooner called *Teal*, with 18-year-old Rod

Though carrying a great spread of sail, the schooners had small crews. Graham Bigelow, at the helm, and his men in the Alden schooner *Teal* pose for Morris Rosenfeld's camera before the 1928 start. The fellow in the white shirt may well be the paid hand, one of whose jobs was to cook in the tomb-like galley. The fourth man from the left is young Rod Stephens, sailing his first Bermuda Race. A decade later he would set a new standard for pushing hard.

Stephens aboard. *Teal* pulled off what seems to be the first recorded exploitation of a Gulf Stream squall by a Bermuda racer. As two black clouds bore down on her, the crew were moving toward the halyards when the navigator (who had the expressive name of M. Carrington Stanford) leapt out of the companionway and ordered the helmsman to tack and everybody else to sit down. "Sail the port tack! Hold everything! We've got to pass between them clouds." The helmsman dutifully put the helm down and the overpowered boat labored her way through the eye of the needle between the two squalls, and when she tacked back to starboard *Teal* had the wind and her competitors down to leeward sat becalmed. *Teal* finished third overall, beating John Alden's new, *Malabar VIII* (with Olin Stephens in the crew).

## 1930: The First Small Boat Victory

The 1930 race was even more successful. The 42 boats made up by far the largest fleet. It was still largely a schooner race, both in numbers (30 boats as against five yawls, four ketches, and just three singlemasters) and in results. Semifisherman schooners were the top three boats in Class A and the first and third boats in Class B. After a fast reach, a calm spread like an ink blot out from the island and the small boats caught up, and for the first time the overall winner came from Class B. This was *Malay*, a semifisherman schooner owned, commanded, and navigated by Raymond W. Ferris and sailed by a crew of young sailors. At 45 feet she was the smallest winner since *Tamerlane* in 1906. She also was the first winner created outside the United States, built in Nova Scotia and

designed there by William Roué, a well-known designer of fishing schooners and the only naval architect other than Starling Burgess (designer of the 1962 winner *Niña*) to break John Alden's stranglehold on schooner-rigged Bermuda Race winners (five in all). Another *Malay* would triumph in 1954 when Ferris's son-in-law, Dan Strohmeier, won the Bermuda Race in his Concordia yawl.

Despite the schooner success, new ideas were appearing and succeed-ing. The Stephens family's *Dorade*, which was not much more than a yawl-rigged, 52-foot Six Meter with a cabin, finished second in Class B after a navigational problem. For the first time in the race's history visibil-ity was poor near the island, and among those who suffered was *Dorade*, which instead of reaching into Northeast Breaker, as her navigator, Olin Stephens, expected, had to spend several hours hard on the wind. That was a stroke of good luck in the long term, because it was then that the qualities of the new breed of narrow, heavily ballasted boats became clear for all to see. *Dorade* passed 12 larger boats approaching St. David's Head, catching a 66-foot schooner at the end to beat her by nine seconds. That beat, Stephens would write, "confirmed all I had hoped for in *Dorade* — a real sea boat that could go to windward with the out-and-out racers."

The finish results do not say it, but Tom Day's and Herb Stone's dream had become an institution. The most clear sign was the rapidly increasing number of repeat appearances. Of the 16 skippers in 1926,

only four had previously raced to Bermuda. In 1930 the return rate doubled to 50 percent; twenty of the forty skippers had raced to Bermuda at least once. The Bermuda Race, in short, was on the way to becoming a fairly popular habit. As the headline over an article in *Yachting* put it, "Bermuda Fever: A Malady that Usually Strikes Yachtsmen in the Spring of Every Other Year."

## 1932: Tragedy and Heroism

Although the eleventh Bermuda Race had a small fleet of only 27, thanks to the Great Depression, it turned out to be one of the two or three most significant runnings in the race's history. In hard weather, four entries withdrew due to damage or leaks (Bermudian Alfred Darrell's *Dainty*, which had been second overall in 1923, almost foundered 18 miles out from the finish and, under power, raced the leak to St. George's, just beating it.) There were another two dropouts, and both stemmed from a terrible accident that made this the most tragic Bermuda Race in history.

This start was at Montauk Point in order to avoid the usual miseries between there and New London, giving a course of just 628 miles. To encourage entries in a time of financial hardship, the race committee lim-ited light sails to only one of each type — spinnaker, mizzen staysail, and so on. Neither experiment was repeated.

(Opposite) The decline of the schooners began when the Stephens family's *Dorade* was launched in 1930. With her narrow beam, simple rig, deep, heavy keel, and easily driven hull, she outperformed them upwind. (Left) The tragic schooner *Adriana* at the start of the 1930 race. Only hours later she was aflame, with her 11 sailors desperately improvising life rafts.

# Jolie Brise

The Bermuda Race has been especially closely identified with a handful of boats. There was *Tamerlane*, the first winner in 1906, and later came the first *Malabars* and Bob Bavier's long-ended, Bermudian-rigged yawl *Memory*, which made the tall rig respectable. Then there was the race's hero: an anachronistic 56-foot French-built cutter with fortress-like bulwarks, ten feet of draft, a towering 32-foot topmast, and a 12-foot bowsprit at one end, and, at the other, a 12-foot tiller in the capable hands of this extraordinary vessel's six-foot, seven-inch owner and captain, George Martin.

Twice in six years *Jolie Brise* appeared at just the right moment. The first time was in 1926, the year after she won the first Fastnet Race, when her owner sailed her over from England to race to Bermuda, taking 48 days on a route that swept south to the latitude of Jamaica, and then carried her north through a gale off Cape Hatteras in which she hove-to for two days before arriving in America to bring excitement to the race. The next time *Jolie Brise* made a timely appearance, it was in 1932 and she would save ten lives.

Launched at Le Havre in 1913, she had a brief career as a French pilot boat until steam power overtook her and she went into fishing. In 1923 a Royal Navy veteran, Lieutenant Commander Evelyn George Martin, bought her

***Jolie Brise*** **played crucial roles in two Bermuda Races. (Opposite) Here she is before the 1932 start. Owner Bobby Somerset is seated near the tiller, Sherman Hoyt is second from the left, and Paul Hammond is steering.**

and went racing. Many sailors at the dawn of modern ocean racing preferred the heavy, ultra-seamanlike, gaff-rigged, heavily sparred look of traditional commercial craft. In America's case, it was semifisherman schooners. In Britain, it was fishing ketches and pilot cutters. "The essential quality in a yacht designed for deep water sailing," Martin wrote in his book *Deep Water Cruising*, "is ability and not speed." By "ability" he meant

an aptitude for surviving a hard blow. Speed was a relative term with *Jolie Brise*, with her remarkable displacement of 48 tons on a waterline length of 48 feet.

George Martin raced *Jolie Brise* for another year. She subsequently finished second in the 1928 Fastnet under another owner, and was then bought by the man who would be the Bermuda Race's greatest hero, Henry Robert Somers Fitzroy de Vere Somerset. "Bobby" Somerset, as he was called, was descended from two dukes, had been decorated for his services in the trenches on the Western Front, had lost a lung, and was described as "a man of outrageously good looks" who exuded "an element of the devil-may-care buccaneer." An early member of the Royal Ocean Racing Club (which today awards its Boat of the Year with the Somerset Memorial Trophy), he became England's missionary for the new sport. When the Stephens family in *Dorade* won the 1931 transatlantic race by two days, *Jolie Brise* and Bobby Somerset greeted them at the finish line at Plymouth. On April 1, 1932, Somerset turned *Jolie Brise*'s long bowsprit back again to the west and her second Bermuda Race. It was in that race where *Jolie Brise* won her second Blue Water medal and Bobby Somerset became an international hero.

On the first night, the fleet was banging into a squally southwester that left a sailor describing the sea as "valleys and mountains"; his 43-foot schooner was dipping her leeward kerosene running lights underwater. It was somewhat easier going in James H. Ottley's five-year-old, 78-foot schooner *Adriana*, which though too large to qualify as an official entry, had been allowed to sail in a special division with the promise of a prize if she beat the Class A boats. Though her decks were relatively dry, *Adriana*'s cabin was cold and damp, and the off-watch professional crew stoked the coal stove until it glowed red-hot. Nobody noticed that the heat migrated through an insulated bulkhead into an adjacent locker, where rope and oilskins — literally cotton clothing soaked in linseed oil — were stored. At 0240 in the morning, 79 miles southeast of Montauk, the oilskins burst into flames, and as the oily, smoky fire quickly spread, Ottley determined there was nothing to do but abandon ship and fire rockets (what we call flares).

Three miles ahead of *Adriana* were the cutter *Jolie Brise* and 35-year-old Bobby Somerset, with an afterguard that included Sherman Hoyt and Paul Hammond, owner of the radical staysail schooner *Niña*. *Jolie Brise*'s crew fired answering flares and turned back (as did a racing schooner, *Amberjack II*). Of course, the flaming schooner was sighted almost instantly, and as the English cutter reached down on her, her crew were seen struggling to launch the ship's boat and heave spinnaker poles into the water to serve as improvised floats. With Somerset at the long tiller, the engineless *Jolie Brise* reached past *Adriana*, jibed around her stern, and came along the burning schooner's leeward side and stopped, as *Adriana*'s helmsman, Clarence Kozaly, held position. The rails banged together, the upper rigging tangled, and *Jolie Brise*'s tarred deadeye lanyards were charred. *Adriana*'s sailors piled onto the cutter's deck; a witness would recall a naked Indian, the ship's cook, leaping out of the companionway, brandishing a large knife. Only the dutiful Kozaly was left. The two yachts were several feet apart when he finally let go the wheel and made his jump, only to tumble into the gap. Sherman Hoyt desperately

threw him a line, but Kozaly's heavy clothing drew him under once, then twice. "The second time we never saw him again," Ottley mournfully told the race committee.

As Somerset jibed *Jolie Brise* around again, he ordered all the *Adriana* crew to go below while his crew conducted the search, but Kozlay's body never came up. Deeply saddened by this bitter end to a feat of courageous seamanship on the part of the two helmsmen, the crew and guests sailed *Jolie Brise* back to Montauk. Along the way they passed a schooner called *Twilight* sailing in the other direction. *Twilight*'s crew believed there had been an injury, but very soon they came upon the smoking hulk of *Adriana*. "It was a ghastly sight," one of them, Edward Southworth wrote in his journal. "Her masts had fallen and the whole deck was a roaring furnace and the flames were licking out between the planks above her waterline. Just as we were abeam the fuel tanks exploded with a tremendous blast of flame and smoke."

Somerset was later awarded the Blue Water Medal by the Cruising Club and a lifesaving medal by the United States Department of State. *Jolie Brise* went on to a very long, successful, and distinguished career as a cruising and sail-training vessel, competing in the 1993 Fastnet and winning the 2000 and 2002 sail-training races.

### *Highland Light* Sets a Record

The shadow of the *Adriana* tragedy fell upon a triumph, for a new elapsed-time record was set that year. Back in 1909 the big schooner *Amorita* had covered the 673 miles from Brooklyn to St. David's Head in 72 hours, 19 minutes, averaging 8.25 knots. That standard held through six races until 1932, when the 64-foot cutter *Highland Light* averaged half a knot better speed and finished the 45-mile-shorter course in 71 hours,

25 minutes, or just under three days.

Frank Paine, the boat's designer and builder, was in command of *Highland Light* on a charter from her owner, Dudley Wolfe, who was off climbing mountains in Switzerland. Paine pushed her exceptionally hard. A true cutter, with her mast almost amidships, *Highland Light* had an immense mainsail that was never reefed for the good reason that the exceptionally stiff Number 00, 12-ounce cotton sailcloth was too stiff. Yawls then shortened sail by dousing the main and going under "jib and jigger" (small jib and mizzen), schooners lowered the foresail, and some crews were adept at setting small mainsails or storm trysails. But *Highland Light* carried that big mainsail. "Frank Paine loved this creation of his and drove her with merciless intelligence in the Bermuda Race," one of the crew, Jack Parkinson, would write in his memoir, *Yarns for Davy Jones*. With frequent headsail changes and a lot of flogging of the mainsail during squalls, *Highland Light* pressed on. Fetching Kitchen Shoals on one long starboard tack before the short beat to the finish, she never dropped below six knots.

*Malabar X,* generally considered the best boat John Alden ever designed, never shortened sail either. John Alden would have liked to, but he was in no position to take charge because he was in his bunk, desperately seasick after hours wrestling with a leaky toilet. His crew was indecisive, so they just eased sheets and spilled wind in the gusts and hoped for the best. After the finish they discovered that they could not have doused the sail even if they had tried because the Manila foresail halyard had swelled so far it would not render through the sheave. At the end of the day, *Malabar X* won the 1932 Bermuda Race — Alden's third victory — by only three minutes, 16 seconds, by far the narrowest victory to date.

Driven "with merciless intelligence" by her designer, Frank Paine, the cutter *Highland Light* sets a new elapsed-time record in 1932. The triple-headsail and double-headsail rigs soon disappeared with the development of low-stretch genoa jibs and big winches. The contraption hanging off the stern to support the permanent backstay was nicknamed "the permanent erection."

Rod Stephens's well-drilled crew ties in a reef in his New York 32 *Mustang* after the 1950 start. (Opposite) A big 'un rolls by in a typical messy Gulf Stream sea.

# Wet Fannies and Rod Stephens

Ocean racing was growing fast and becoming ever more competitive. When he published his history of the new sport in 1935, Alfred F. Loomis listed 2,000 men and women known to have raced to Bermuda or Hawaii, or around Fastnet Rock, or across the Atlantic—a million miles of sailing by 350 yachts, with a total of only ten fatalities.

More significant even than the numbers was the seriousness of this new breed of sailors. By our standards, crews were remarkably small; the notion of moveable ballast in the form of "rail meat" on the open ocean was far in the future. A 41-foot Alden schooner sailed the 1923 race with a crew of just four because that was all the bunks she had. The typical approach to racing was nicely exemplified by the anecdote about the skipper who was asked why he had tacked just before arriving at a turning mark. "Had to put the roast in the oven!" he replied. That attitude would slowly disappear.

## 1934: The First Single-Masted Victory

**W**hile the *Adriana* tragedy encouraged the race committee to lengthen the required equipment list, it did not discourage ocean racing. Twenty-nine boats, including half a dozen new ones, started the next race at New London. After drifting out to the ocean, they enjoyed what everybody prefers to think are typical Bermuda Race conditions, what Alfred F. Loomis called "another of those starboard tack sleighrides," with started sheets in a southwester that hit the high thirties and rarely dropped into the teens. As a sign that boats were improving, the fleet came through relatively unscathed. When a sailor said, "We broke a cleat, and that's about all," he was testifying to the recent advances in boatbuilding and seamanship. Perfect as these conditions may have seemed from a distance, "sleighride" was not a word that came to the minds of some sailors. The race, Loomis added, was "extremely fast going for the big fellows, and fast going and extremely wet work for the little ones." The big fellows got wet, too. "Lucky was the man who found a berth where water would not drip in his face," complained a sailor in the hard-driven 59-foot schooner *Grenadier*, owned by the brothers Sherman Morss and Henry A. Morss Jr., sons of the owner of a top boat almost 30 years earlier. Obviously, this fellow was more concerned with domestic comfort than with fast sailing, of which *Grenadier*—third on elapsed time—did more than her share.

The first 16 places on corrected time went to Class A boats, and the main award, the Bermuda Trophy, was taken by the brand-new Sparkman & Stephens 56-foot sloop *Edlu*, the first singlemaster to win the race. Though owned by Rudolph J. Schaefer, a New York brewer, she was commanded by Bob Bavier, who gained his fifth major race trophy and second overall win since 1923. Most older boats did poorly. When the Darrell brothers entered their little yawl *Dainty*, which had been second overall back in 1923, it was considered a "sporting gesture." She finished second to last. Some of the old schooners were back, too, including Raymond W. Ferris's *Malay*, the winner of the 1930 race, which this time took second in Class B, her third trophy in four races.

There were fewer schooners this year—only 55 percent of the fleet as against 77 percent in 1923—yet the traditional rig was holding on. There were three reasons. One was the abiding affection that sailors held for this shippy rig and the handy semifisherman hull under it. Second, the rig had been updated in the late 1920s when *Malay* and other boats were built with towering, more weatherly Marconi mainsails. The major holdouts for the stubby, gaff-headed mains were John Alden's own *Malabar*s, though some of their sisters carried the modern arrangement.

As for reason three, the Bermuda Race seemed made for the schooner, with all its sail spread wide. "Schooner weather," a close or beam reach, usually was on hand for at least a third of the race, sometimes over almost the entire 660 miles—as in 1934 when schooners won

*Baccarat* came east for the 1934 race, and with Prohibition over, her crew is taking aboard some brew from back home. Previously, alcohol came aboard in Bermuda, not the U.S.

three of the six corrected-time trophies. The other three cups were won by sloops, including Class B winner *Baccarat*, which had come east from Michigan with a crew that had never before raced in the ocean. "*Baccarat*'s skipper and crew proved, tradition to the contrary, that it is not the salt in the water that makes sailors," Carl Weagant wrote in *Yachting*. After collecting his silver, her owner, Russell A. Alger Jr., turned right around, went home, and won that year's Port Huron-Mackinac Race.

Taking a regular trick at the helm of the new Sparkman & Stephens yawl *Stormy Weather*—reportedly the only boat in the fleet that did not shorten sail in the Gulf Stream squalls—was Lorna Whittlesey, a 22-year-old ace one-design sailor from Long Island Sound. The first woman to race to Bermuda who was not a member of the owner's family, she was recruited at the last minute. Luckily, her father was away on a business trip and not around to say no, though her mother approved. Still, Laura wasn't allowed to go forward of the mast. Her job was to steer. Asked if she got some strange looks from other boats, she replied, "Oh, plenty." After the race she went home and won the women's sailing championship of Long Island Sound for the fifth time in eight years.

## CCA Rating Rule

The 1934 race was the first sailed under the Cruising Club of America's rating rule, which was created in part to better handicap the increasingly diverse fleet, in part to add some muscle to the race's original mission of developing better offshore cruising boats. The original, simple method of calculating time allowances based solely on overall length survived for the first eight races. It says something about the relatively low level of competitiveness in those days that not until 1926 did someone make the effort to have a boat built especially for this rule and this race. The boat was Bavier's ketch *Dragoon*, with a snubbed bow that trimmed her overall length and a powerful shape conducive to fast reaching.

In 1928 the CCA and Royal Bermuda Yacht Club adapted a variation on the rating rule of England's Royal Ocean Racing Club. The new, simple formula balanced the two major speed-making factors, length and sail area, against the major speed-limiting factor of volume or displacement:

$$\frac{\text{Length} \times \sqrt{\text{Sail Area}}}{\sqrt{(\text{Beam} \times \text{Depth})}}$$

The result was multiplied by .02 in order to bring the rating near the boat's actual length. There were allowances for different types of rigs, with the gaff schooner and ketch getting a 10 percent discount on their ratings while the more weatherly Marconi-rigged sloop or cutter got none. Bavier developed a rule that provided allowances for the resistance of a propeller. Nathanael Greene Herreshoff proposed that Length (L)

The masthead Marconi yawl *Dragoon* was the first boat designed for the Bermuda Race rating rule, with a snubbed bow and stern to minimize sailing length. The height of her 85-foot mainmast was unprecedented in an offshore boat. She was first to finish in 1928 and might have saved her time on the fleet if she had not suffered the big-boat agony of stumbling into a calm and watching the small boats come up on her.

should approximate the boat's actual effective sailing length, or the waterline length of a heeled hull, by measuring along a plane in the hull at a distance above the water equal to 4 percent of the upright waterline length.

Despite the onset of the Great Depression, new, innovative boats began to appear in such numbers that Alf Loomis joked that the CCA should be renamed "The Racing and Designing Association of America." As boats became more diverse, pressure built to introduce a new rule that would more accurately compare different types, sizes, and rigs while discouraging light displacement, huge sail areas, and other features thought to be undesirable if not plain unsafe.

The CCA formed a committee. One member, a Chicago sailor named Wells Lippincott, introduced the notion of an ideal boat—sometimes called a "normal" or "base" boat—that would embody the desirable characteristics of a fast, seakindly offshore vessel and serve as a standard for other boats. Any deviation from that boat would earn a rating credit or incur a rating penalty. An example was the measurement for maximum beam at L (sailing length). The base or ideal beam was set at 0.23 x L, plus 2 feet. If L was 40 feet, the base beam was 11.2 feet. If the actual beam was other than that, the difference was multiplied by 2 and inserted

Compared with *Malabar X* (opposite), *Kirawan* and the other new boats were remarkably simple with their all-inboard Marconi rigs. Their lighter construction, with plenty of metal rein-forcement, allowed for more weight in the keel and greater stability.

The mid 1930s were a transition period, with Marconi yawls and gaff-headed schooners often in the same water, plus the unique three-masted main trysail ketch *Vamarie* (center, in the distance) adding spice.

in the rating formula either as a plus factor (if narrower) or a minus factor (if wider). One early casualty was *Dorade*, with her unusually narrow beam of just 10.25 feet on deck. Though she was the smallest boat in Class A in 1934, her new rating required her to give time to eight boats in the class. The price for this added precision was complexity, but the CCA Rule was effective until it was replaced by the International Offshore Rule in 1969. Still today, there are people who say that the high point of the cruiser-racer came under the CCA Rule.

Under the pressure of loophole-seeking owners and designers, the rule was constantly tweaked by the measurement committee and its advisory group of technical advisors. To encourage good stability while barring extreme light construction and exceptionally heavy keels, in 1936 the rule established a maximum ballast-to-displacement ratio of 46 percent (in the 1950s that ratio gave way to an inclining test to measure actual stability). Owners tried to get around the limit on ballast by filling the bilges with water tanks so large that even a crew of Ancient Mariners had nothing to fear from thirst, and then cramming the niches between the tanks with canned goods, anchors, and chain. The rule was altered to require that ground tackle carried aft of the mainmast be counted as ballast, and measurers were instructed that "abnormal supplies" must not be carried in order to bolster stability unless they, too, were listed as ballast. Structural elements did not count as ballast, however.

### 1936: A True Thrash to the Patch

"Ye gods and also ye little fishes of the sea, please so guide and direct us that we shall never again whistle for what it takes to sail a race," wrote Alf Loomis of the 1936 race in a *Yachting* article titled, "An Uphill Slam to Bermuda." Loomis, who sailed in the schooner *Brilliant*, was surprised that there were no serious injuries in the first Bermuda Race sailed entirely in a hard blow.

It began at Newport. For years, sailors had been lobbying for a start there, right on the ocean and free of headlands and tricky tides. The 44-boat fleet—the largest yet, with several European boats that would later race from Bermuda to Germany—got off in a foggy calm and on the second day was smashed by a southeast gale that did not waver over the next four days. Nine boats withdrew, which was not too bad considering that the fleet included 16 untested entries.

A few years earlier this would have been a certain big-boat race, but thanks to the recent intense development of boats in the 45-foot to 55-foot range, the winner and four other boats in the top ten on corrected time were in Class B. In one of the most remarkable performances in Bermuda Race history, the overall winner was the new 53-foot sloop *Kirawan*, owned by Robert Baruch and pressed hard by a crew that included her designer, Philip Rhodes. After finishing dead last in the 1934 Bermuda Race in a schooner, Baruch told Rhodes he wanted a

new boat with a big sail plan for cruising in Long Island Sound, with plenty of headroom (he was six foot, four inches), and with a rating that would put her at the top of Class B in the Bermuda Race, or about the middle of the fleet, as a hedge against the extreme conditions that usually help small boats win (light air) and big boats triumph (a hard blow). Typical of many top-of-the-line cruising-racing boats of that time, *Kirawan*'s construction was both light and strong, with mahogany planking, oak frames, all outside lead ballast, and plenty of Everdur bronze: fastenings, mast step, hanging knees, diagonal strapping, and a ring frame around the after edge of her large doghouse (or deckhouse). *The Rudder* described her as "practically trussed from side to side."

Her all-amateur crew of nine came ashore heaping praise on the boat and especially the doghouse, where the on-watch sat in dry comfort, observing the poor helmsman through a Niagara of spray, and eating hot meals that had been handed up though the ports by the cook, a character named "Porthole Pete" Chamberlain. Richard Henderson, in his book *Philip L. Rhodes and His Yacht Designs*, described Chamberlain as a "Shakespearian scholar, designer of marine fittings, and inventor of a

galley stove." He installed a custom blower in *Kirawan*'s Charlie Noble, the chimney, to improve the draft.

That must have helped, because after five days of hard work—even after taking two hours out to sew up a ripped mainsail—*Kirawan* beat every boat across the finish line except two much larger Class A entries, *Vamarie* and *Brilliant*—and even then she was less than two hours in their wakes. Her corrected time victory margin was almost three and a half hours, and she took home four of the five prizes for which she was eligible (the fifth, for first to finish, was won by the 72-foot *Vamarie*). Her race was memorialized by one of her sailors, Charles Lundgren Jr., in a series of sketches of the sloop putting her shoulder into it under a variety of sail combinations.

Sixty-four years later, *Kirawan* sailed another Bermuda Race under another owner, Sandy Horowitz, who had her trucked east from California in 2000. After two days of fast reaching, a seam opened up near the waterline. It was given a temporary patch. During a subsequent restoration, some of the many cracks found in her frames were thought to have dated to the exceptionally hard 1936 Bermuda Race.

Rhodes sailed in *Kirawan* in one of the few true thrashes to the Onion Patch—the long beat to the island in 1936, which she won by three hours. These dramatic sketches by a crew-member were published in *Yachting*.

Double reefed main
Storm jib

Double reefed main
Large staysail

Full main

Working headsails

Full main
Genoa

Single reefed main
Staysail

COMBINATIONS
of SAIL used on

"Kirawan"

BERMUDA RACE 1936

From a drawing by Charles Lundgren

## The Discomfort Factor

At some dark moment during a race in the 1930s, a sailor in the schooner *Brilliant*, Graham Bigelow, dreamed up a ditty as a tribute to the mixed joys and sorrows of pressing through the Gulf Stream:

*"Fannies wet all day and night,*
  *Brilliant sailing like a kite.*
*Get that damned club topsail set,*
  *Just to make us curse and sweat.*
*Set the guinny on the sprit,*
  *Sheet her down and watch her split.*
*Gulf Stream squalls we drive right through,*
  *Brilliant, here's to you!"*

Most boats then were remarkably simple. Few had radios, house batteries, or power (the few boats with engines were required to seal them before the starting gun). Kerosene provided lights as well as cooking fuel for boats without coal stoves to hold off the damp as far as possible, though wetness was as much a rule as fragile gear. Leaky hulls, shaky wooden spars, natural fiber rope that absorbed water and swelled like a sponge, galvanized stays that seemed to stretch like rubber bands—all those were normal before fiberglass, aluminum, and stainless steel. The cotton sails felt like sheet metal, ripped like paper, and were so stiff they were hard to reef.

And there was the water—water everywhere. A view of the sea might be entrancing, but such a thought passed quickly. "The phosphorus was beautiful and would light up the whole deck," Edward Southworth of *Twilight* observed in his log of the 1932 race. Snapping out of his reverie, he added, "when phosphorus goes down your neck it is nothing more than plain sea water." What did not go down the neck had every good chance of going below. As Southworth put it, the rule was very simple: "In ocean racing in small boats, you cannot have fresh air in the cabin without it being accompanied with salt water." Before 1933, when Rod Stephens invented the miraculous *Dorade* ventilator, with baffles to separate the water from the air, the mix of water and suffocation went hand in hand.

In a vain attempt to keep the cabin at least partially dry, *Twilight*'s skipper, Irving Johnson, slathered waterproof grease around the edges of hatches, covered them with canvas soaked in more grease, and finally cinched down the hatches with wire. This may have stopped water from going down, but it did little about the water in the leaky bilge. When Southworth first tried to sleep in a leeward bunk, he came upon a phenomenon that thousands of other Bermuda Race sailors have shared: "I discovered that lying in six inches of water was not conducive to sound slumber."

The scheduled rotation of cooks through what Southworth called "the hermetically sealed galley"—which like most yacht galleys of that time was located far forward, where the motion was worst—broke down almost immediately. Because Southworth had a strong stomach, he took command of the galley and cooked all the way to the finish using the coffee pot, which he lashed into place on the Sterno stove. In it he boiled eggs, cooked vegetables, warmed up tomato soup, and even brewed coffee. "It would make really a very good and substantial meal," he said with the pride of a man who had learned the art of transforming almost nothing into something.

## Setting Standards

Eager as they were for entries, the race committee was plenty aware of the risks and not afraid to turn away unqualified boats. The list of required equipment was remarkably short. Here is the one for 1930:

  2 anchors, 2 anchor cables
  2 compasses
  1 binnacle light
  lead line
  2 fire extinguishers
  Life preservers
  Stores for 3 weeks, water 12 gal/man
  2 water lights
  12 rockets (pistol)
  1 boat or raft
  Navigation gear: sextant, chronometer, tables, log, protractor, dividers,
    parallel rules, charts, international code book.

Note the absence of sail requirements, lifelines, and a bilge pump, although they surely would have been mentioned by the inspectors, who were instructed to provide personal advice while they formed a judgment as to the boat's and crew's overall seaworthiness.

The first victim of a Bermuda Race inspection was a yawl named *Chaos* in 1923. Little else is known of her except that her plucky crew insisted on sailing anyway and made it safely to Bermuda. When *Gauntlet*, the 28-foot sloop that was in the first race, was brought up from Bermuda by Daniel Stubbs to the start of the 1930 race, the committee told him she was too small to enter. Stubbs and his crew of two turned right around and sailed back to St. George's with an elapsed time comparable to those of some racing boats a dozen feet longer. Another Bermuda-based boat, *Mary Rose*, in 1932, was sailed all the way to America only to be told she would not be permitted to enter because all her crew were professional sailors.

*Mary Rose* also made it to Bermuda with no trouble, which was much more than could be said for a boat that was allowed to start, though with misgivings by the inspectors. When her owner expressed

A pre-race inspector goes over the storm sails. From the Tom Day era to the present, boats have had to pass inspections in order to qualify to sail.

A well set-up ocean racer circa 1946: this New York 32 has a much smaller cockpit than the old boats—meaning less water to drain if the boat is pooped by a wave. The top lifeline is sturdy. Although a bottom lifeline was not yet required, the owner has rigged a line there. The stern pulpit would not be required until the 1960s. (Next page) Class A starts the 1948 Bermuda Race. That's the race winner, *Baruna*, in the right foreground.

interest in entering his 1904 schooner *Curlew* in the 1932 race, people who knew her warned the race committee that boat and sailors were unqualified. Committee chairman Everett Morss Jr., delegated four inspectors to look her over and disqualify her if they had any worry. The inspectors reported back that they could find no particular reason to bar the boat and that, though the crew was inexperienced, they were eager, bright, and prepared to learn. Noting that most Bermuda Race crews had little experience, Morss reluctantly allowed *Curlew* to enter.

When she was not heard from for several days, newspapers began to report the families' worries and an energetic search was undertaken. The Coast Guard (which had already provided three vessels for the start) delegated six ships and a dirigible, while several Bermudian vessels were sent out. When the schooner was eventually found on July 8, 13 days after the start, she was located not near Bermuda, nor in the Gulf Stream, but less than 100 miles from New London, near Nantucket Shoals.

*"In order to encourage the designing, building, and sailing of small seaworthy yachts, to make popular cruising upon deep water, to develop in the amateur sailor a love of true seamanship, and to give opportunity to become proficient in the art of navigation, an ocean race has been planned . . . ."*

(Preamble to the notice of race, 1926, and years thereafter)

# Pushing Hard with Rod Stephens

In 1936, after the roughest Bermuda Race yet, Herb Stone (once again the race chairman) wrote in his report, "the Committee feels that these Bermuda Races and the measurement rules have done much to improve the type of yacht sailing in these long distance events." The average new Bermuda-bound boat was faster, more comfortable, and, with her all-inboard Marconi rig, easier to handle than the schooners of the twenties. Alf Loomis also noticed improvements in sailors and what was expected of them: "A man who can't stand the Gulf Stream blues is no addition to a

crew, however ornamental he may be to a bar."

Leadership came from among a small group of sailors called "the young veterans," the best known of whom was Roderick S. Stephens Jr. A shipmate in *Dorade*'s 1931 race to England characterized Rod Stephens as "the hard-driving mate" who "brought into play those personal forces which figured so prominently in *Dorade*'s success, namely speed, expert knowledge, and a keen determination to keep the boat going at all costs." One of his first lessons in seamanship came during the first of his 17 Bermuda Races, in 1928 when he was just out

of high school. He raced down in the Alden schooner *Teal*, which took second place in Class A and third overall. That success would have been a highlight in any sailor's memory bank, yet when Stephens looked back on this race he said nothing about the silver and spoke only of being taught the buntline hitch by a professional deckhand and learning the importance of securing slack running backstays to keep them from chafing against the mainsail. By his thirtieth birthday, in 1939, he had sailed ten major distance races. The boats he was on won silver in nine of them, including overall victories in two transatlantic races and three Fastnets. Bermuda Race wins eluded him, yet he still enjoyed two class victories.

His older brother, Olin, liked to design boats; Rod liked to rig and prepare them. Among the equipment he created or advanced were the *Dorade* ventilator, the parachute spinnaker, the genoa jib, the aluminum mast, and stronger running and standing rigging. He carried two mainsails in *Blitzen* when she was second overall in the 1938 Bermuda Race, one for light air and the other for a fresh breeze, and he trained his crew until they could change them in a few minutes. (Later, the rules were changed to permit only one mainsail.) Such was Rod's reputation for omnipotence that false rumors arose about him, among them that he was the one who placed toilets on the port side because he was the first to recognize that the typical Bermuda Race was sailed on starboard tack. In fact, John Alden began placing toilets on the port side with *Malabar IV*, the 1923 winner.

Besides seamanship, young Rod Stephens was learning how to race hard. In the 1930 Bermuda Race, one of his shipmates in the Stephens family boat, *Dorade*, was a former Star Class world champion named Arthur Knapp who played the sails continuously. "It was a tremendous education because I don't think we ever cleated the sheet all the way from New London, where that race started,

**Olin (left) and Rod Stephens pose at Bermuda aboard one of the many Sparkman & Stephens boats designed by Olin, with Rod active in construction and rigging. No designer has produced the winners of more Bermuda Races – 14.**

to Bermuda," Stephens recalled. "But his thing was, 'Don't just cleat it and sit down. Play it a little, in a little.'" That became one of his own mantras. The marriage of hard driving and meticulous seamanship became his distinctive mark. His philosophy was nicely summarized in notes that Carleton Mitchell took of a conversation they had in 1951. Here in 103 words is the gospel according to Rod—and not just Rod, but the entire new generation of ocean sailors:

*Rod feels people should sail because of a "true love of the water." On going to Bermuda, enjoy the sail because "for any one boat, there is only a minute chance of winning." Reason why cruising men should ocean race: it increases the efficiency for cruising: "boat well fitted for ocean racing is 90-95% ready for cruising." He also stressed the importance of racing around the buoys – it irons out details of rigging and handling your boat – with other boats close by for comparison, so when making long ocean races and nothing is in sight, the boat is still sailed at maximum efficiency.*

Mitchell continued: "Driving hard at sea, Rod consoles himself by 'thinking what a boat can take.' He looks at a piece of $1/2$-inch wire, and thinks of the strains imposed upon it, but also thinks what it would take to break that piece of wire. For there is 'no real point of strain; the boat relaxes and gives in to the sea.'"

Stephens drove himself as hard as he drove boats (and, for that matter, his crews). A remarkable physical specimen, he was nicknamed "Tarzan." In the 1948 Bermuda Race he shinnied almost 50 feet up the mast of his New York 32 sloop *Mustang* to reeve a spinnaker halyard. Energetic on a boat, he was no less energetic on shore. The march of progress in ocean racing in its formative years was in no small part due to the articles he wrote and to those also written by his brother, Herb Stone, Alf Loomis, and George Roosevelt, the owner of *Mistress*. To read *Yachting* magazine in the 1930s is to be swept up in an enthusiastic seminar on how to race a boat hard and safely at sea.

**Mustang** **drifts toward Bermuda through a gentle dawn in 1946 after almost six days at sea. Nearest the camera are owner Rod (left) and skipper Olin Stephens.** **Mustang** **finished second in Class B.**

# Baruna

The obituary for the racing schooner was all but written in 1938 when yawls and sloops, five of them designed by Sparkman & Stephens, won all top six positions. After a hard beat through the Gulf Stream and then a fast reach to the finish, Henry Taylor's new 72-foot S & S yawl *Baruna* was the first boat since *Memory* in 1924 to be first-to-finish boat and also corrected-time winner. Among the 38 starters were the first boats from California and the U.S. Naval Academy. W.A.W. Stewart's schooner *Santana* had finished second behind *Dorade* in the 1935 Honolulu Race and then was shipped east, where she beat the other seven schooners. *Baruna* won every trophy for which she qualified in 1938. One of only two multiple winners of the race, she was built by the Quincy Adams yard in Massachusetts to a design by Olin Stephens. Her owner, Henry Taylor, wanted a beautiful boat at the maximum size allowed by the CCA Rule that he could cruise and race with family and friends out of beautiful Cold Spring Harbor, Long Island. Having never sailed in an ocean race, Taylor signed on experienced men, including Olin Stephens, to lead the three professional sailors and the young college undergraduate amateurs, who included two of his sons and a pugnacious 150-pound guard on the Harvard football team, John Page. Later, Stillman Taylor would be the boat's skipper during her great duels with *Bolero*, and Page would win Class F in the 1970 Bermuda Race after beating all night into a gale.

**Baruna finishes the 1946 race with a small pack of spectator boats in her wake.**

## The Navy First Races

The entry of the Naval Academy 72-footer *Vamarie*, with a crew consisting largely of newly commissioned ensigns, did not come about overnight. The academy's senior officers had their doubts as to the worthiness of the adventure. One navy captain, who was a stringent teetotaler, offered the very faint endorsement that the ensigns would learn to say no to a drink. "It is my understanding," he complained, "that after the conclusion of such a race a rousing celebration usually takes place in Bermuda and the yachtsmen endeavor to forget the hardships of the voyage." After lobbying by the Cruising Club and Royal Bermuda Yacht Club, the academy was still resisting when a civilian higher-up in the Navy Department, who happened to be a family friend of one of the young ensigns, Robert W. McNitt, allowed as how he thought a race would be a fine way to train young officers. That made the difference.

One of the strangest boats ever built, *Vamarie* was described as a three-masted, main-trysail ketch. In place of a mainsail she carried a trysail under a huge wishbone-rigged topsail. Her mechanical propulsion was an airplane propeller perched on the mizzenmast. This idiosyncratic vessel had performed well in three seasons of ocean racing, including being first to finish in the 1934 and 1936 Bermuda Races. Her owner, Vadim Makaroff, then donated her to the academy as its first ocean-racing boat. *Vamarie* did not like rough weather. A midshipman who sailed in her claimed she rolled so wildly that the milk in the ice chest curdled. The cook for the 1938 race was a submarine veteran who reported with a plug of tobacco in his cheek. On the delivery to Newport into a northeaster, however, the plug disappeared and then so did the cook, who acquired the nickname "Passout." As he staggered onto the wharf, he was heard to mumble, "Submarines never go like that."

Gear problems left *Vamarie* well back in the race standings. When she reached Bermuda the youngsters felt just as far back because their captain was the teetotaler. Fortunately, Makaroff appeared and took the ensigns off to a bar, though his offer of a case of Scotch was rebuffed by the captain.

Despite the disappointing results, the experience was not lost on the navy. McNitt and three of the other midshipmen in that pioneer crew went on to become flag officers. None lost the love for the sea that they acquired while racing to Bermuda in *Vamarie* in 1938. McNitt later wrote in his history of sailing at the Naval Academy:

> *Like human attachments, this romance cannot be taught or forced. It comes gently during a midwatch in the soft warm moonlight of the Gulf Stream, in the crashing roar of a sudden squall, and in the dawn of a new day at sea. It comes most easily and naturally under sail. There is a beauty and a grace in the silent passage of a ship under sail that stirs affection. A healthy respect for the sea and deep affection for the ships which sail upon it become a permanent part of our lives, and we are grateful for having experienced this when we were young.*

Tom Day could not have said it any better.

## The Professionalism Debate

Not everybody believed that constant trimming of sails and the appearance of boats designed for racing were good things. Even Herb Stone and Alfred F. Loomis worried that boats had been taken to extremes. Powerful masthead genoa jibs were overloading rigs and hulls, and some new boats were no longer suited for cruising. Yet, in the late 1930s New England members of the Cruising Club of America were focusing their concerns not on the boats but on their sailors. They complained that "a professional taint" had come upon the Bermuda Race and urged that the CCA should get out of it. Too many boats, the critics said, were not run by their amateur owners but by expert semiprofessional sailors who accepted expense money or were in the boating business.

A CCA committee, which included Stone, considered the problem. The majority admitted that the race had problems, but that no radical change in the rules could solve them. They urged that all-amateur crews should receive prizes, that owners should skipper their own vessels in fact as well as name, and that the CCA's measurement rule should continue to be massaged to encourage able cruising boats. The third member, a Boston cruising sailor named William H. Coolidge Jr., did not agree. "A yacht two months old is considered outbuilt," he exclaimed. "The whole business is like horse racing."

The critics were themselves criticized for not giving due appreciation to the contributions that their targets had made to sailing. "I'll defend you to the last ditch if anybody ever accuses you of handling a boat like a g.d. amateur," Loomis wrote. While it was true that six of the nine postwar races were won by boats with their designers on board, it also was true that yacht design and construction had been advanced significantly.

In 1940, with German submarines plying the Western Atlantic, the Bermuda Race was canceled and replaced with a 455-mile coastal race from Block Island, around Mt. Desert Rock off Maine, and to the finish at Gloucester. Before the start, the CCA race committee barred Rod Stephens, Ed Greeff, and others sailors on a list of "semiprofessionals" from serving as skipper, watch captain, or navigator.

Soon the issue blew away as the racers and the unhappy cruisers were called to more serious duties. When Rod Stephens was elected the CCA's commodore in 1949, peace was declared, though there would always remain a feeling in some quarters that, no matter how much cruisers and racers could learn from each other, the two sides lay at either side of a chasm that would open once again half a century later.

# The Lure of Bermuda

The race's enduring symbol is the light on Bermuda's most fabled island, St. David's. For years the finish line committee took over the keeper's cottage until the last boat had come in. (Opposite) In the usual starboard-tack start, winner dark-hulled *Gesture* crosses the line in the second rank in 1946.

Sailing slowly revived as many of the youngsters who created the new sport in the 1930s returned wearily from battlefields and warships far from Newport. With wartime shortages still in effect, CCA Commodore Ernest Ratsey, head of the country's largest sail loft, Ratsey & Lapthorn, arranged for the club to purchase reels of Manila rope to be sold at cost to sailors. He also made a deal with a shoemaker named Paul Sperry to reserve the first output of his new Topsider deck shoes for Bermuda Race crews. Finding boat shoes and rope was simple compared with the problem of turning up metal alloys, which were still in demand by the military. Still, the Fuller Brush Company got its hands on enough aluminum and dies to produce the first extruded aluminum masts, one of which went into the new 57-foot sloop *Gesture*, owned by the company's head. *Gesture* went on to win the first Bermuda Race in eight years.

## 1946: Shortages and Calm

The sailors headed out with news of a near-tragedy ringing in their ears. The Bermuda-based ketch *Zena*—the first boat built for the race back in 1907, and later a competitor in 1930, 1932, and 1934—was sailing up to Newport under the command of Tom Dill when on June 13 she opened up in a gale. A passing Liberty ship took off the crew and put the old hooker out of her misery by cutting her in half with her propeller. No doubt relieved that *Zena* had chosen to go down before entering their jurisdiction, the committee sent the fleet off in two classes over eight hours. In one of the irregular stabs at keeping the fleet from being too spread out, while providing the crews of the smaller boats a ringside view of Class A sailing through them, the Class B start was at 0930 on June 29 and Class A's gun was fired at 1730. Someone had gone through the records and calculated that the average difference between the two classes was 16 hours, and the committee chose to cut that in half. A weak southerly blanketed the

course for a week, and by the time the first boat drifted to St. David's Head (this was *Baruna*, which survived a bad leak in the early going) 119 hours had elapsed, making this the longest race in 40 years. The final spread was 16 hours.

One of the nicer stories of the first postwar race concerned *Latifa*, a British 70-foot Fife yawl owned by Michael Mason with a crew of military men. She had come over to race in 1938 but dropped out with rigging problems and now she was back again. The crew attracted attention by presenting themselves as a gang of bachelors looking for female company. Their hard-nosed skipper, John Illingworth, one of the finest ocean racers of the immediate postwar era, kept them out of the bars by stripping *Latifa* of almost four tons of gear and fittings, including all the doors in her interior (the rules were quickly amended to require a door to the head). With Bert Darrell of Bermuda aboard, *Latifa* stayed within sight of *Baruna* most of the way and finished fifth. The experience stimulated many other British crews to come across.

The first lighthouse trophy, representing Gibbs Hill Light, goes to A. Howard Fuller (left) in 1946. Later winners received the St. David's Lighthouse trophy. Today both lighthouses are awarded to winners of Cruiser/Racer and Racing divisions.

Two race winners go bow-to-bow after the 1946 start as that year's victor, the 56-foot *Gesture*, struggles to hold off the 59-foot *Niña* (winner in 1962). *Niña* was the race's last successful schooner, and *Gesture* sported one of the first extruded aluminum masts.

**Wrong Way _Baruna_**

As the saying goes, "You never know in a Bermuda Race." The 1948 race was a prime illustration of the race's potential for perversity. "It wasn't the fastest or the slowest or the largest or the smallest," Alf Loomis wrote of this race; "but if a superlative is required the race may properly be called the damnedest." The 36 boats spent the early hours in a familiar fashion almost hard on the wind on the starboard tack in a southwester. By nightfall a northerly had swept in and everybody was contentedly reaching along on port tack, steering for a point in the Gulf Stream 30 miles west of the rhumb line to compensate for the expected northeast crossing.

Then things became messy. As the leaders were sticking their bow into the Stream, the wind clocked into the northeast, dead against the axis, and as it increased into the 30-knot range kicked up such a seaway that even hard-driving boats shortened down drastically. This develop-

ment got everybody guessing about what would happen next. Some boats believed the breeze would continue its swing and end up in the southeast, and so they held high to sail toward the expected header. Others decided there would be no header and went right down the rhumb line or just to the west of it, and did well enough. (One boat had other things to think about. _Stormy Weather_, now from Ohio, became the first Bermuda Race boat to report that it had been bumped by a whale.)

And then there was _Baruna_, the 1938 winner commanded by young Stillman Taylor. Stumbling into a surprising amount of southerly set and almost no easterly set, she came out of the Stream way to the west, booming along at nine knots for 48 straight hours. When it came time to head for the finish, Taylor wasted no mileage feeling his way around the reefs. Instead he kept the island on his port hand (as the rules then permitted) and crossed the finish line from south to north. _Baruna_ therefore became not only the race's first repeat winner but the first of only two

A hard day in the Stream in 1948 for _Argyll_, with her mizzen doused and her owner, Bill Moore (left) keeping a lookout. Carleton Mitchell took the picture and provided this caption: "Keeping _Argyll_ footing, watching for a change in conditions, watching _Stormy Weather_ somewhere out there to windward." _Argyll_ did poorly this year but in 1950 she won the race. Such is ocean racing.

With a send-off by family and friends looking on from the official boat, Class B crosses the starting line in the 1950 race. *Pavana,* nearest the camera, trails the handsome canoe-sterned gaff-headed cutter *Karin III,* which had been sailed across from England. *Karin III,* alas, would finish third from last.

winners to finish in the "wrong" direction. There was no magic in this counterclockwise circuit of the island because the other boat that tried it, the 57-foot yawl *Argyll*, ended up dead last in Class A and thirty-second out of 36 boats overall. All this made people wonder if they would ever understand the Gulf Stream.

### 1950: John Alden Comes Back

The seventeenth Bermuda Race had the most entries yet in the race's history (54), the strongest wind at a start for years, and more calms than anybody feared. The boats that went west, but not too far west, found wind and reached home with great joy. The best example was *Argyll*. After her miserable finish two years earlier her owner, William T. Moore, recruited three of the most experienced and successful Bermuda hands around, Ducky Endt, Ed Greeff, and Jim Mertz, and went ahead and won.

To Greeff, this was the most interesting—and also successful—of all his 24 Bermuda Races. He put it down to skillful wind forecasting. His shipmate Mertz—who sailed a total of 30 races, a record—disagreed. When Mertz was later asked, "How do you win a Bermuda Race?" he decisively answered, "*Luck!* In 1950 we were going west near another boat and then decided to head straight toward the island. We beat that boat in by a day and won the race."

If *Argyll* was lucky, another boat's 66-year-old skipper was living proof of the rule that some people seem to be lucky all the time. John Alden had bought a well-used, 20-year-old semifisherman schooner of his design called *Abenaki* and put a towering Marconi mainmast in her so she could carry a big balloon foremast staysail, or gollywobbler. With that weapon in hand, he then ventured far west of the Gulf Stream in search of a means to use it—a reach. He found it. "We got 90 miles to the westward, put the gollywobbler to her, and roared down to Kitchen Shoals," said her navigator, Bill Anderson. *Abenaki* corrected out to second place in Class C, just under four minutes behind the class winner. This was John Alden's ninth Bermuda Race since 1910, his seventh in command of his own boat, and the sixth from which he went home with a piece of silverware under his arm. He would sail on more as crew in 1954.

### The Year of the Zipper Bows

If the 1950 Bermuda Race could boast of the great duel of the maxis, it could also include the smallest boats since *Gauntlet*. These were the Royal Navy Sailing Association 24s *Samuel Pepys* and *Galway Blazer*, sailed by crews of just four that were commanded by Royal Navy officers Erroll Bruce and Bill King. Just 31 feet from bow to stern, and 24 in waterline length, they were well under the race's 35-foot minimum, yet the race committee allowed them to race in the interest of international yachting amity. Through some confusion, another Englishman, Adlard Coles (the

*Highland Light*'s sail trim woes give *Niña* a green light to move into the passing lane moments after the 1950 start. *Niña*'s owner is DeCoursey Fales, while *Highland Light* (the race record-holder since 1932) is now in the U.S. Naval Academy's fleet.

*Bolero* charges by the old Brenton Reef Lightship, where Bermuda Races were started for years before it was replaced by a tower, which itself gave way to a buoy. *Bolero* was first to Bermuda three times—a record she shares with *Baruna* and a *Boomerang*. (Opposite) A study in cool concentration, Cornelius Shields —known as "the Gray Fox of Long Island Sound"—was *Bolero*'s racing skipper.

# Bolero

The queens of the fleet in 1950 were two great black yawls built to the maximum on-deck length of 72 feet permitted by the CCA Rule. This was the year that the Taylor family's two-time winner *Baruna* began her fabled offshore duels with the slightly larger *Bolero*, whose owner, John Nicholas Brown, had long hosted pre-Bermuda Race parties at his home, Harbour Court (now the New York Yacht Club's Newport clubhouse). *Bolero* and *Baruna* were so well matched that they once finished a 450-mile race almost overlapped.

These big, powerful vessels displaced upwards of 90,000 pounds. Exclaimed one wide-eyed *Bolero* veteran, Bob Smith, "It dawned on me that *anything that flapped on this yacht could kill you on contact.*" During the 1950 race, a Norwegian professional sailor named Arvid Arnheim had an intimate experience with such risks. *Bolero* was charging along at 9 1/2 knots when a wire jib sheet caught him behind the knees and whipped him overboard. He grabbed the flailing sheet and somehow maintained a tight grasp as the helmsman, Olin Stephens, luffed into the wind and the boat's racing skipper, Cornelius Shields reached out, grabbed him, and hauled him aboard. His head bleeding profusely, Arnheim slumped on deck, muttering, "*Ay taut ay vas gone.*" *Bolero*'s crew recovered from the shock and were first to finish and took second on corrected time, just an hour behind the winning *Argyll*.

The duel between the two black Sparkman & Stephens maxis continued over four years, with the two boats always in the running for the elapsed-time trophy and usually for the corrected-time victory, too. Because big boats are

harder to sail to optimum performance than smaller boats, it was unusual for them to do so well on handicaps. If the hard work that went into achieving this record was not widely known, it was due to their owners' sportsmanship and modesty. After the 1950 race, Henry Taylor sent John Nicholas Brown a congratulatory telegram: "Ain't it a grand and glorious sensation to cross the finish line first and get the wonderful welcome which they give you off St. David's Head, and then to be anchored alone in your glory in Hamilton Harbor?" As for Brown, all he could say was that he had lucked into a wonderful boat. "It's a boat one can be proud of. She sails herself."

One reward for the crews' hard labors was the two boats' first-class hospitality, with excellent cooks and well-provisioned larders. Once, however, the high living was self-defeating. In one race, *Baruna* was trailing her great rival and Stillman Taylor did his best to follow in *Bolero*'s track so the two boats would sail in the same wind. Losing sight of *Bolero*, he was getting a little desperate when a trail of green suddenly appeared on the water, heading off in a new direction. On further inspection, the green substance was identified as leaves from artichokes. Realizing that only one boat maintained such high culinary standards in the middle of an ocean race, Taylor altered course and continued the stern chase.

After *Baruna* went to San Francisco in 1953, *Bolero* became the undisputed queen of East Coast yachting and in time set a new course record to Bermuda.

author of the classic *Heavy Weather Sailing*), was led to believe that this special dispensation also applied to his *Cohoe*, and in the end *Cohoe* and Californian Porter Sinclair's Bill Lapworth-designed *Flying Scotchman* were required to install temporary extensions (known as "zipper bows") to make the limit. All these small boats except *Cohoe* were of unusually light displacement, a feature that did not inspire much confidence among Americans until the British boats survived a vicious gale in the Gulf Stream on their way to the start. In the end, they all finished well, and when *Samuel Pepys* returned for the 1952 race with five other British boats, again as the smallest starter, she finished fourth overall.

The lightweight English 55-footer *Gulvain* also did respectably, as did a curious looking ultra lightweight 40-foot cutter from Maine, *Dirigo*. In her crew was an 18-year-old Bermudian dinghy sailor, Kirk Cooper, in the first of his many Bermuda Races—just how many races is unclear. "All these races, they all go like one," Cooper would say. "You forget about it for 18 months, and then you start again." (Another frequent

**Flying a temporary extension (called a "zipper bow") that allowed her to qualify, Adlard Coles's *Cohoe* was part of the large British small-boat invasion in 1950.**

racer, David Vietor, put it a little differently: "They all roll into one big Bermuda Race and all you remember are episodes.")

*Dirigo* was little more than a blown-up centerboard racing boat. "My mother looked at that boat and cried," Cooper recalled. "She said, 'I never should have let you sail.' There was a huge tiller and no external ballast, and it didn't do well upwind, but off the wind it could *move*. There was nothing special in terms of wind, maybe a bit over 20 knots. When we reefed, I was the last guy at the end of the boom. The navigator came on deck to help reef the main and he got seasick and it went right down the boom into my face."

Despite *Argyll*'s victory and the *Bolero-Baruna* duel, the 1950 race pointed toward larger fleets and smaller boats. For the first time in the race's long history, there were almost as many boats smaller than 43 feet (10 boats, or 19 percent of the fleet) as there were ones larger than 65 feet (11, or 20 percent). Eight years later, the fleet would be more than twice as big at 111, and 36 of those boats (32 percent) would be smaller than 43 feet.

And as if to make the same points, the winners themselves would keep getting smaller, until a chubby little 38-footer made a clean sweep not just of one race, but of three.

## The Dreamers

Winning a Bermuda Race is a fine thing, but the fact is that most crews lose races, and they are not all that unhappy to continue to do it so long as they get to Bermuda in one piece and, they hope, with someone astern. In recognition of this reality, in 1938 the race committee began to award a participation plaque for accomplishing something that a great many sailors dream of doing some day, which is simply entering and finishing a Bermuda Race. As an example, consider the story of the schooner *Vega* and her crew of enthusiastic young amateurs.

A 48-foot cruising schooner, *Vega* was owned by Charles W. "Chick" Crouse, a young man in the fish and poultry business in Philadelphia who kept her on the Sassafrass River off Chesapeake Bay. After teaching himself navigation and sailing *Vega* in a coastal race, in 1938 he decided to go to Bermuda. Nobody from his part of the world knew anything about the race other than what appeared in the pages of *Yachting*, but he eventually gathered a crew of five men, and they headed up to Newport with both pluck and a sense of humor, both of which were still lively when they returned home a month later, if we are to believe the narrative that Crouse wrote.

Once he was in Newport and got a good look at *Baruna* and the other goldplaters, Crouse's euphoria mellowed. He was certain that the inspection committee would flunk *Vega*. Another boat's entry had been rejected because, as Herb Stone explained, "the owners are too nice to be permitted to go down between here and the Islands when she opens up."

When *Vega* passed with a few recommendations for improvements, Crouse was certain it was because Stone had seen "the longing in our eyes." That night *Vega*'s crew found themselves in the launch with the most famous of all racing yachtsmen, Rod Stephens, who was cheerfully playing sea chanteys on his accordion. Crouse looked back fondly, "We were sure during that ride through the harbor with the beautiful starlit night as a background that this ocean racing business was something a man could take in his stride."

His heart fell once again soon after they started the race. "We crossed the line, did our best to get the most out of *Vega*, streamed our log, and watched the other boats disappearing over the rim of the horizon." Two days later *Vega* was hove-to under foresail and leaking badly, the one saving grace being that nobody was seasick. The cook's efforts to make a proper meal to celebrate leaving the Stream foundered on the discovery, first, of a thick layer of mold on the baked goods ("not the common garden variety but all the hues and colors of the rainbow," as Crouse

remembered) and, second, of a canned ham so full of botulism that when it was opened, it sprayed all over the cabin.

*Vega* beat on. "We continued on the starboard tack, thinking that the wind would have to change from dead ahead sometime." It finally clocked into the southwest, and *Vega* could do a little reaching. Crouse anxiously awaited his last and most important test: the landfall. When Gibbs Hill Light appeared dead ahead, Chick Crouse's elation knew no limit. He had climbed mountains and piloted an airplane, but nothing in his experience had been as satisfying as that landfall. "For all us novices it was a great moment, our first landfall and right on the button," he wrote in his memoir before corralling his pride enough to add, "even if we were two or three days late." *Vega* finished 87 hours after *Baruna* with a time of seven days, ten hours.

After jogging back and forth off St. David's Island until dawn, *Vega*'s crew enjoyed the beautiful sail into Hamilton. "The smell of the breeze off the land laden with the perfume of trees and flowers was almost too

much. Breakfast was forgotten and never was a sail enjoyed more than that early morning trip through the narrow channel." Greeting them was a cheerful fellow who presented them a pitcher of rum punch, and not long after there appeared a relieved Herb Stone who announced that *Vega* had beaten one boat on corrected time. Only when Crouse read the Philadelphia newspapers did he discover that *Vega* had been considered lost.

*Vega* arrived too late for the big parties, but Crouse and his boys did their best to catch up. Sailors disappeared ashore sometimes for days and nights at a time, their berths taken by anonymous young men from other boats who mumbled, "Paul said I could have his bunk for tonight," and then vanished before breakfast. After several days of this fun, *Vega* weighed anchor and reached to the Chesapeake Lightship in just four days. As she neared home, the sailors realized that they had accomplished something notable. Yes, they were broke, and yes, the salt spray had stripped the boat's varnish clean to a height of ten feet up the mast. But as down and out as they seemed, Chick Crouse had one consolation: "you do not have D.N.F. printed after your name."

## Born into a Yachting Country

"You may be sure we were sorry to see the shores of good old Bermuda gradually fade away," one of *Tamerlane*'s crew, Percy A. Cook, wrote a friend after the first race back in 1906, "and I for one wished we were just approaching them again." To understand the appeal of the Bermuda Race requires understanding the charms of Bermuda. Over a century, the race has started at five American ports—Brooklyn, Marblehead, New London, Montauk, and finally Newport. But it has always finished at Bermuda. Yes, the trip could be uncomfortable. Alf Loomis made the point in this dialogue: "Do you like to race to Bermuda?" "Yes." "When?" "After I get there." But the price is worth it.

After it was first visited in 1505 by Juan de Bermudez and colonized a century later, this archipelago of 150 islands, some 200 rocks, and a long coral reef was so famous for wrecks that it was known as "the Island of Devils." Located near most major British trade routes in the Western Atlantic, for centuries the island survived on shipping, privateering, tobacco growing, vegetable farming, fishing, and providing a western naval and military outpost for the British Empire. The first tourist hotel,

The most successful Bermudian skipper of his generation, deForest "Shorty" Trimingham returns home in 1955 with the Prince of Wales Bowl. (Right) A fitted dinghy with a typically large crew, some of whom might be jettisoned if the wind lightens. (Opposite) It's late June 1946, and ocean racing has returned to Bermuda. The Royal Bermuda Yacht Club honors the guest Cruising Club of America by displaying the CCA burgee on its flagstaff, and much of the newly arrived racing fleet is anchored in Hamilton Harbor.

the Hamilton, opened in 1863 (Bermuda Race banquets were held at the Hamilton more than 40 years later), but tourism did not become a serious enterprise until Princess Louise, a daughter of Queen Victoria, spent a winter on the island in 1883. (The Princess hotels are named for her.) Once it became a tourist and sailing center, Bermuda was no longer the devils' island but a place known as "an Atlantic oasis," "the mid-ocean playground," "the Riviera of the Western Hemisphere," "the isles of rest," "this favored island," "nature's fairyland," and even "lotus land." Such sobriquets may not spring to mind in the middle of the Gulf Stream, or when a competitor who was safely astern on Sunday night turns up ahead on Monday morning. But once an ocean sailor catches a hint of oleander, "lotus land" will seem real enough. "It is Bermuda itself that is the chief factor in the success of the race," wrote Herb Stone. "Without Bermuda after the finish line, the race would lose much of its appeal. A race around a course that brings you back to the starting line may be all

right for some; but as long as the Bermuda Isles lie at one end of the course, we back that race for being the most popular."

There was always sailing. "I was very lucky to be born right here in the lap of sailboat racing," deForest "Shorty" Trimingham has said. "Thank God I was born in a yachting family!" Sailing was as indigenous to Bermuda as the onion. The quickest way to get people and goods around the fishhook-shaped island was to send them by boat up and down the sheltered waters inside the reef. The southwest wind was reliable, and so for many years were the groves of a wonderful rot-resistant wood for boatbuilding, *Juniperus bermudiana*—cedar from seeds believed to have been flown to the island by seabirds during the Ice Age, when much of what is now underwater Bermuda was exposed (cedar stumps have been discovered 20 feet down). Overuse all but depleted the cedar by the 1840s, and a century later came blight.

Bermudians all learned to respect their environment. Kirk Cooper,

one of the island's most successful racing sailors, had a vivid memory of his introduction to the power of nature: "When I was a boy and a hurricane blew through, my father took me outside behind a wall, and he told me to stick my head out so I'd know what a strong wind was."

Bermudians were ingenious boatbuilders and sailors. More than 250 years before *Memory* raced to Bermuda under what was then called the Marconi rig (because the mast seemed as tall as a radio tower), the terms "Bermuda rig" and "Bermudian rig" were being used to refer to a three-sided fore-and-aft mainsail used on many of the island's boats. In other places such a sail would be styled "leg o'mutton" or "jib-headed."

Whatever it was called (and wherever it originated—the West Indies and the Netherlands have been proposed), each was strikingly different from the four-sided gaff-headed rig that predominated in pleasure boats until the 1920s, as well as from the old three-sided lateen rig (like a Sunfish's) that had been around since the Egyptian pharaohs, with its

spars on one side of the mast.

The result was a very close-winded boat. In a history of the rig published in the *Bermuda Journal of Archeology and Maritime History* in 1990, Eldon H. Trimingham II quoted a bit of doggerel by a visitor who admired "the Island Boats" in 1671:

> *To give description of these same Boats*
> *With triple corner'd Sayls they always float*
> *About the Islands, in the world there are*
> *None in all points that may with them compare.*

Another impressed visitor to the island reported, "They lie so near the wind, that they will fetch the same place they took upon close hauled."

What distinguished the rig in its advanced form in Bermuda's fitted dinghies was a remarkably high aspect ratio, with the sail's tack extending well below the boom almost to the base of the mast. Traditionally, the

# Sir Eldon Trimingham

Sir Eldon Trimingham, (below left) helped revive the Bermuda Race and served for years as Bermuda's representative on the organizing committee. He was a partner in the famous family department store with his brother Kenneth (right), served as chairman of the Bank of Bermuda, and was knighted for his contributions to currency stability during World War II. He was mad for boats. Around the time of World War I, when Nat Herreshoff and John Hyslop, the New York Yacht Club's official measurer, spent winters in Bermuda, Trimingham learned some naval architecture. After designing small sailing dinghies, he moved on to fitted dinghies. "He was a great looker ahead, he always wanted to experiment," his son Eldon said. "Particularly on boats, but off boats, too." One product was a fitted dinghy that, because it was built in 1917, was called *War Baby*. The name was carried on by another Bermudian, Warren Brown, in his wide-ranging racing-cruising boats.

Besides playing important roles in small boats and the Bermuda Race, Eldon Trimingham sailed in the international regattas in Six Meters and other classes against leading American sailors like Cornelius Shields, Sherman Hoyt, Olin and Rod Stephens, and Briggs Cunningham, who came down every spring for a week or two of fleet, team, and match racing. Trimingham himself was a skillful racing sailor with, his son said, "a marvelous bloody touch sailing a boat, a magic touch." Someone who watched him on the race course characterized him as "a conjurer with a boat whose bag of tricks is never exhausted" and a helmsman blessed by "some occult faculty" at predicting wind shifts. He usually sailed with his brother Kenneth—Eldon steering, Kenneth calling tactics. One of their boats was a beautiful Six Meter named *Saga*, designed by a young Norwegian named Bjarne Aas. Shields was so smitten that he made *Saga* the model for a new class, the International One-Design.

(Left to right) Ducky Endt, Briggs Cunningham, and Sherman Hoyt pose at the Royal Bermuda YC before heading out for a team race in the 1930s. Hoyt, the greatest racing sailor of his generation, donated the club's premier trophy, the King Edward VII Gold Cup.

boom was an oar that the crew could employ should the wind die.

As these increasingly high-performance boats plied Bermuda's waters, beating upwind to Hamilton and Somerset, and then running home across Great Sound to St. George's, commerce naturally inspired competition until (as Trimingham's father, Sir Eldon Trimingham, put it), "Everybody in Bermuda who was interested in sport was interested in boat designs and performance." By 1844 there were enough sailboat races (and disputes about racing rules) for three dozen men to gather under a calabash tree and found a yacht club with the aim of encouraging "recreation and harmonious feelings, as well as improvement in boat-building and sailing."

One of the very oldest yacht clubs in the Americas, what is now called the Royal Bermuda Yacht Club held its first international race just five years later, when a schooner called *Brenda* came down from Boston and raced a local sloop called *Pearl* on Great Sound (reports of the results are confused). This is a club where the Duke of Edinburgh Cup is named in honor of a son of Queen Victoria who visited the island in 1861, not Queen Elizabeth II's husband. Later came racing by sailors named Gosling, Darrell, and Trimingham in Bermuda's distinctive fitted dinghies: 14-foot, one-inch, Bermuda-rigged keel-boats with a cloud of sail and a crowd of crew sailing under idiosyncratic rules that, among other things,

permitted jettisoning a sailor when the going got light. ("Fitted" here means prepared for a special purpose. Originally general-purpose boats, they were upgraded for racing.) Designed and skippered by Eldon Trimingham and other youngsters, the fitted dinghies raced before spectators in the natural amphitheatres of Hamilton and St. George's harbors, as they still do today.

Trimingham and his friends hosted annual regattas for visiting Americans. Though hard-fought, these Bermudian-American regattas were notable for sportsmanship. After the race committee abandoned a team race when a turning mark went adrift, the two teams unanimously agreed that the positions at the last mark would be official. Still, the Bermudians noticed that the Americans seemed to go at it a *little* more intensely than they did. A writer for *The Bermudian* observed, "American yachtsmen come down to Bermuda not so much to race their boats in the Sound as to resail their races . . . with decanters for marks and bottles of beer and soda for yachts."

One of the most beloved of the Americans was Sherman Hoyt. He had first come down in what Bermudians call the Ocean Race in the winning *Memory* in 1924, and was a member of the heroic crew of *Jolie Brise* in 1932. Enamored of what he called "the usual hectic but always pleasant Bermudian festivities," Hoyt in 1937 donated to the Royal

Bermuda Yacht Club a trophy he had won many years earlier, the King Edward VII Gold Cup. Today it is awarded to the winner of one of the world's most prestigious match-racing regattas, held by the yacht club in International One Designs. Winners have included Russell Coutts, Chris Dickson, and other leading America's Cup skippers.

Since 1952 the club has been running International Race Week, limited to classes with international representation. Mac Paschal, Shorty Trimingham, Bert Darrell, Kirk Cooper, Warren Brown, Jordy Walker, Penny Simmons, Tim Patton, Peter Bromby, Paula Lewin, and other Bermudians sailed in the top ranks of international classes at Race Week and regattas abroad, including the Olympics and in many cases the Bermuda Race. Bert Darrell was famous for his colorful if unrepeatable language when racing and managing his boat yard. He won three straight Gold Cups and represented Bermuda in the Naples Olympics. Shorty Trimingham, one of Kenneth Trimingham's sons, was the first person from outside Britain to win the coveted Prince of Wales Trophy of the International 14s (in 1955 with his cousin Eldon Trimingham II as crew). Penny Simmons won the world championship of the International One Designs six times between 1985 and 2005.

## The Finish Line Club

Sailing fitted dinghies was (and remains) only one of Bermuda's charming customs among many—flying kites on Good Friday, placing cedar seedlings in wedding cakes, hosting festive turtle dinners. On the most remote island in the chain, St. David's, another custom is observed, and that is the finish of the Bermuda Race.

St. David's was separate from the other islands by water, by race, and by the islanders' cultural as well as geographic isolation. "There the people still live in patriarchal simplicity," a historian of the island, Hudson Strode, wrote in 1932 of the St. David's Islanders, going on to describe the "the sun-bronzed inhabitants" as "taciturn, suspicious of strangers," and conversing in Elizabethan English with West Indian accents. Their localism surfaced in the names of the island's bays and coves: Mis' Annie's, Deborah's, Dolly's, Mis' Emily's, Ruth's Bay, and an open fissure known locally as the Orange Hole because, remarkably, orange trees grew there.

Supremely isolated for centuries, the island's culture was first intruded upon in 1876, when construction began on a lighthouse on the high bluff of St. David's Head, near Bermuda's eastern end. First lit in 1878, the light towers 208 feet above sea level and—with the older, taller Gibbs Hill Light to the southwest (built in 1848)—serves as one of the island's two essential aids to navigation. St. David's Island was finally connected to the mainland by a bridge in 1937. Three years later "the last bit of undeveloped and unspoiled Bermuda" (as a Bermuda historian called St. David's Island) began to disappear as the United States Navy built a causeway to the mainland and an airbase (now the airport) on 260 acres

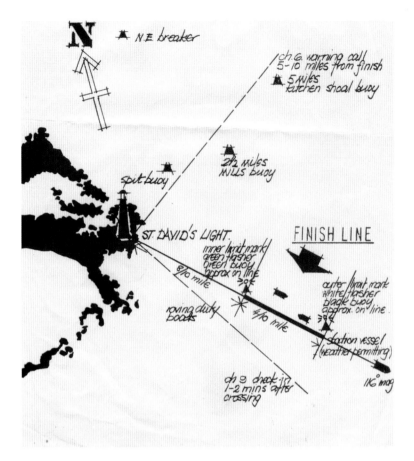

The final approach to the finish around the reef is tricky even in benign conditions. As boats arc southward around the rocks toward St. David's Light, navigators check off the buoys and report in according to schedule.

Her sails illuminated by searchlights, Jakob Isbrandtsens's *Good News* crosses the finish line in 1968 as a crewmember takes a bearing on St. David's Light over the steering compass.

The finish line committee works out of a lookout tower adjacent to the St. David's Lighthouse (left). The official telescope (below, with Tony Siese) sights the line on a bearing of precisely 116 degrees, reportedly because an older instrument was locked into position by corrosion. (Right) One duty of the finish line committee is to present a case of beer to the first boat to finish. CCA Commodore Bill Whitney hands the loot over to *Pyewacket*'s exhausted crew after the rough 2002 race.

of land leased from the British. Some of the old island culture remained. "When I was growing up there were people who had never been off St. David's," said 64-year-old Colin Couper early in 2005.

The Bermuda Race finish line committee has long been based on the island, although in the early days it was to some extent an extension of the St. David's Island pilots. Today, when a race boat nears the finish, it must radio ahead from five or more miles out. Spotters in small boats sent out by the finish line committee provide visual identification, and if the racers cross the line at night, they illuminate their sail numbers with high-powered lights.

In the race's early years, however, the alarm was set off by the St. David's Island pilots. Renowned for their superb eyesight, they were on the lookout for boats, whose appearance brought business. Sometimes in the Tom Day and schooner eras, they were known to take whaleboats out as far as 50 miles. The competition between the pilots became so fierce, in fact, that the Bermuda government nationalized them in 1928.

Usually, nobody would be looking until the race's fourth day because, after the revival of 1923, no boat reached the finish in less than 98 hours.

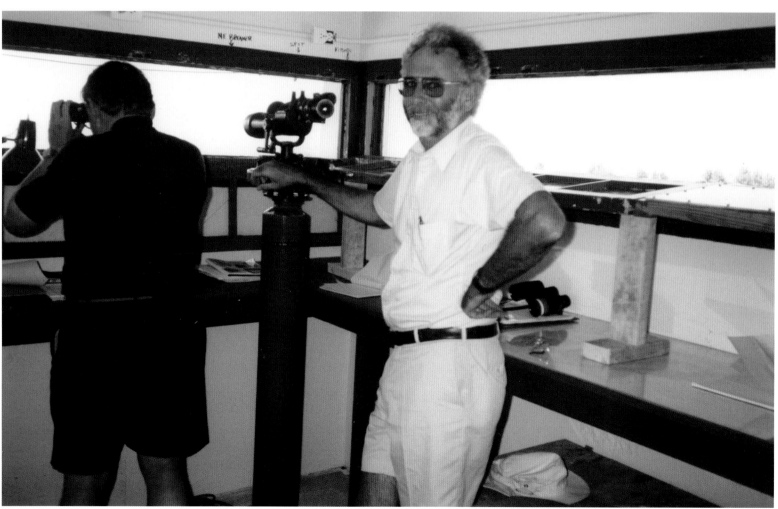

In 1932, however, one of the sharpest-eyed pilots was scanning the northern horizon from high in the lighthouse and spotted what seemed to be a Marconi (or, as they say there, a Bermuda) schooner under shortened sail. He telephoned Eldon Trimingham, who jumped into his powerboat (there were no automobiles on the island then), raced to the St. David's Island dock, clambered up the lighthouse steps—and saw nothing. His son, Eldon, carries on the story: "The pilot aimed his binoculars for him and, sure enough, there was a white speck in sight. As the boat slowly got closer, the pilot saw that wasn't a schooner at all, but a big cutter with the mast in the middle of the boat. From the descriptions by the pilot, my father identified her as *Highland Light*, as she turned out to be, breaking the race record." The stake boat barely beat *Highland Light* to the finish line.

Later finish line committees set up camp on St. David's Head on the day after the start of the race, established round-the-clock watches, and did not abandon their station until the last boat was accounted for. To call this group a committee is a bit misleading. In truth, it was more a men's club, as Jordy Walker testified in his reminiscences of his young days around 1950 as aide-de-camp to his father, Bernard Walker. Before

the race, the lighthouse keeper, Cecil O'Connor, moved his family out of his cottage to make room for the committee members. O'Connor would come back to cook up conch and fish chowders, but otherwise the place was the committee's for the duration. "I'd tell my family and clients, 'I'm on the finish-line committee, so goodbye for a week!'" Nick Dill looked back.

"They'd sit in O'Connor's dining room, all 25 of them, eating together," Jordy Walker recalled with a smile. "In the evenings there would be poker and some other games of chance. As a boy whose weekly allowance was six pence a week, I was amazed by how much money was changing hands. Pound notes! I would bring over the bottles, the rum or the sherry, so the men could recharge their glasses." Somebody was always standing watch, with a telescope and a chronometer at the ready.

After a couple of days, young Jordy Walker was liberated from his onerous duties in the lighthouse keeper's cottage and went back to Hamilton, spending his days on board the Royal Bermuda Yacht Club's launch, captained by Eddie Rance, as it made the rounds of the Ocean Race fleet, which in those days—before the creation of the club's marina

in the late 1960s—were anchored in the harbor, or tied up at the Princess Hotel, or moored over in Salt Kettle at the old Glencoe.

The finish line committee, however, was still at work until they went home at noon on Friday. Anybody who came in later had to take his own time because, said Walker, "They weren't going to win any prize except the Galley Slave for the last place cook." After the light became automatic, the committee stayed in a trailer or a big tent with sides that keep out the blowing rain in the squalls. That ended, too, and the committee camped out or commuted. Walker was not pleased. "It's not nearly the same. *Today, some guys sleep in cars!* A lot of camaraderie has been lost. But," he said with a shrug, "people still look forward to it."

The committee today is not exclusive to the Royal Bermuda Yacht Club. In fact, several members are not sailors. One was the chairman of the 20-member 2004 finish line committee, Eugene Rayner, who took a sailing course 20 years ago but has other interests, among them the island's radio society. When he heard the committee was looking for an

experienced radioman to handle communications with finishers and spotters, he volunteered.

He handled the Marion-to-Bermuda Race as well as the old classic, and knows that difference, too: "The Marion race is a cruising race, the Newport race is a thrash." By custom, the commodore and the chairman of the Bermuda Race organizing committee do not sail in the race but go out with the committee when they assemble near the lighthouse, and the individual known as the keeper of the telescope sets up the instrument in a tower next to the lighthouse. Nowadays, on Sunday, two days after the start in Newport, they usually have a good party to initiate their vigil. In 2004, however, Commodore Jane Correia was concerned that the cant-keel super-maxis in the demonstration division, *Morning Glory* and *Pyewacket*, would arrive in the middle of the festivities and catch the committee in a state of unpreparedness. She put the party back to Saturday so there would be no question about the alertness and competence of the five officials who stood four-hour watches, sighting finishers

through the crosshairs of the telescope, and recording finish times using an atomic clock.

## The Sweet Passage

A finish was just as much a ceremony when looked at from the other end of the telescope. Once a boat crossed the line and made the necessarily abrupt turn to avoid crashing on the rocks, the crew set the yellow quarantine flag and awaited the arrival of the doctor. In the 1920s, the medical inspection was conducted by a Dr. Percy Shelley, a descendent of the poet, whose appearance would set off a round of recitations of "Hail to Thee, Blythe Spirit," by the exuberant sailors. Once Dr. Shelley determined that the boat was not carrying the plague, things lightened up considerably. As a pilot climbed aboard, a boat came alongside carrying a few members of the Royal Bermuda Yacht Club, brandishing liquid presents. As Alfred F. Loomis described one of these moments, "Then Teddy Gosling came alongside with bottles of beer and we knew that we our-

selves were close to heaven." (In fact, liquor is a running theme in Bermuda Race history, both before and after the end of Prohibition. When *Malabar VII* returned from winning the 1926 race, John Alden brought her quietly into Newport late at night and immediately had his crew unload contraband liquor from her bilge and hide it under an old sail in a shed. The Coast Guard inspection team that scoured her from stem to stern the next morning found nothing untoward. After World War II, some of the first bottles of Mount Gay Rum that made their way to America were transported in the bilges of returning Bermuda Race boats.)

Then came the long but sweet passage—under sail, power, or a tow—along the shores of St. George's, Hamilton, and Pembroke parishes into Hamilton Harbor, through a channel just tricky enough to keep one or two people on their toes as everybody else tucked the sails into a harbor furl, and someone whose culinary expertise had been entirely overlooked for the past week scratched up a mountain of cinnamon pancakes, topped with the dark amber Vermont maple syrup that had been secreted at the bottom of the wet locker. On deck, there was the remarkable view, described by a writer who sailed in the 1926 race, Edward Streeter: "Gorgeous aquamarine water, crystal clear, still as a mill pond. Tiny houses, glaring white against green hills. Hanging over all, the now familiar look of fat clouds, ivory colored in the setting sun. Above, a sky of limitless blue."

Once the boats were secured on their anchors or at a wharf, a new round of enjoyment began. "Nobody even thought of living ashore as there was too much fun going on aboard the yachts," Jack Parkinson wrote. While a few senior members of the crew were met by their wives, the younger sailors (almost all of them male) had no thought of permanent female company, except, Parkinson added, for "an occasional tall, blonde Follies beauty who would be waiting for a farsighted crew member, causing envious mutterings among his colleagues." But the colleagues eventually were distracted by the boats and by Bermuda. After 21-year-old Olin Stephens finished his first Bermuda Race, he swam around the fleet to inspect the competition and meet the sailors with such enthusiasm that he completely forgot about the tropical sun and ended up with blistered shoulders. The ever-welcoming Shorty Trimingham would organize dinghy races, there were boisterous crew parties at Coral Beach and other waterfront hotels, and, of course, there were the bicycles and motorbikes, for better or for worse. After the 1938 race, bike accidents put at least 14 sailors into the Bermuda hospital.

For the more sedentary men and women who had found berths to Bermuda, there were more solitary joys on land, as Edward Streeter recalled:

*We felt suddenly tired. Done up in store clothes, pressed like crepe paper from a week in odd corners, we made tracks for the Yacht Club. And now, at last, with one foot on the rail of the Royal Bermuda Yacht Club bar, we might truly be said to have reached our goal. Like all things lived too often in anticipation, however, it had its disillusionments. Not only were we curiously tired, but we were dizzy; sickeningly dizzy. One by one the crew faced about, located a convenient wicker chair, and staggered toward it, to sink into its depths and wait uneasily for a cocktail.*

It would be days before Bermuda would permit anyone to want to feel normal again.

**After the sailors and boats are polished up, they gather in colorful raft-ups for the telling of yarns about surviving the rigors of the Gulf Stream.**

The polestar of sailing records is the one set by the tubby little yawl *Finisterre* and her skipper, Carleton Mitchell. They won three straight Bermuda Races from 1956 to 1960. (Opposite) Time to shorten down in the Stream: two sailors on the bow prepare the new jib for hoisting.

# *Finisterre* Comes Through— and Again, and Again

Any notion that a big boat could not be sailed as hard or as well as a small one evaporated with the 72-footer *Baruna*'s sweeps in 1938 and 1948 and *Bolero*'s second-place finish in 1950. It seemed for a while that the best sailors in boats under 50 feet could hope for were pleasant rides, a few Dark n' Stormies on the veranda of the Royal Bermuda Yacht Club, and dreams of buying one of the 55- to 60-foot mini-maxis like the 1946 and 1950 winners, *Gesture* and *Argyll*. But suddenly the winners began to get smaller. Before 1952, there were only two winners under 47 feet—*Tamerlane* in 1906 and *Malay* in 1930. Yet of the 12 winners from 1952 through 1972, nine were shorter than 47 feet and six were under 40 feet.

## 1952: The Coming of the Small Boats

The names *Finisterre*—winner of the 1956, 1958, and 1960 races—and Carleton Mitchell—her owner—are most closely identified with this trend. At 38 feet, six inches she was three inches longer than *Tamerlane*. Yet relatively small boats were winning when *Finisterre* was just a gleam in Mitchell's eye. Richard S. Nye's Rhodes-designed 46-foot, Class C yawl *Carina* won in a record fleet of 58 boats in 1952, breaking not only the six-race Sparkman & Stephens winning streak but the seven-race run of winners larger than 50 feet since *Malay*'s victory.

Dick Nye and his son Richard would go on to compile one of the most distinguished racing records ever. In their three *Carina*s, from 1952 through 1972 they won two transatlantic races, two Fastnets, and two races to Bermuda. Richard Nye put the first of those victories down to luck. "In 1952 the wind died and the whole fleet was left bunched together in a parking lot two-thirds of the way down the course. That left us with a 200-mile race, and since we were one of the smaller boats we came out on top. The big boats didn't know what to think. A guy

I knew, Breck Marshall, was sailing on a big, new goldplater called *Sea Lion*. He said everybody looked up and saw us. 'Who's that?' They thumbed through the entry list. 'They're not in Class A. They're not in Class B.' When they got to the bottom of the sheet they refused to turn the page." Finishing only three and a half hours after *Sea Lion* and nine hours after first-to-finish *Royono*, a 72-footer, *Carina* won by 45 minutes on corrected time over the Class B winner, Rod Stephens's *Mustang*.

For the first time in four races the elapsed-time winner was not one of the "big black B's." The Naval Academy yawl *Royono*, Alden-designed and Herreshoff-built, overcame three blown-out jibs to make it first to St. David's and win Class A, the best Academy performance before 1992. She was all but willed to the finish by her gruff but heart-of-gold commander, Lt. Frank Siatkowski. "He drove *Royono* as I have only rarely seen an ocean racer driven," wrote Alf Loomis of "Ski," "and never a man to spare his voice, he spent almost his entire waking time telling the nine ensigns, two midshipmen, and an Army captain who comprised his crew, 'This is why I do this, this is how you do that, this is what you learn from a sky that looks like that.'"

British boats kept returning, among them *Bloodhound* with a Royal Ocean Racing Club crew that included four women. Eighteen non-U.S. boats from six countries sailed in the 1952 and 1954 races, 14 percent of the total fleet. Continued international interest led to the Onion Patch Trophy series.

In a good year for navies, Royal Navy Lt. Cdr. Erroll Bruce returned in the little *Samuel Pepys*, despite having to add weight to sink her deeper and meet the minimum waterline length requirement of 27 feet, six inches. Amid concerns that she had no chance to do well, her crew of four made 31 sail changes and ended up third in Class C and fifth overall. This little boat averaged 6.3 knots over a day's run. There were eight other non-U.S. entries, six of them British. Bobby Somerset, the Bermuda Race's undisputed hero, was back in an old yawl called *Iolaire* for his first go since his rescue of most of *Adriana*'s crew in 1932. *Bloodhound* represented the Royal Ocean Racing Club with a crew that included four skilled woman sailors, among them the gifted navigator Mary Blewett. In 1960, Patricia Makin would become the race's first female watch captain when she sailed in her father George Hinman's Concordia *Sagola*.

*Bloodhound* corrected to second in Class A behind *Royono*, giving foreign boats two of the nine class prizes. Foreign interest would only increase. In 1954 *Bloodhound* returned, there was a Swedish entry, and seven boats came up from Argentina to take three prizes. Three of the Argentine boats were designed by German Frers, father and grandfather of two other yacht designers. Both in 1956 and 1958, there were seven non-U.S. boats (including a Cuban entry), and in 1960 15 foreign participants from seven countries.

The formal prize list now stretched to 18, including a Grandfather's Prize for the best finish by an owner-skipper at least 50 years old (which shows how young ocean racing sailors were then). A special prize was awarded to a Naval Academy 44-foot yawl, *Swift*, after one of her crew fell overboard while swabbing the decks. The midshipman was retrieved but not his cleaning tool, and Ernest Ratsey's race committee awarded the vessel a new mop. A stranger and more permanent institution that arose in the 1952 race was Dr. Willi Faraguli. Despite the fact that he was utterly fictitious, his name was frequently announced, referred to, or otherwise acknowledged at race parties and other sailors' gatherings over the next 30 years. One of his creators, Sean O'Connell, explained that Faraguli was a creation of the disrespected port watch of *Blue Sea*, an unofficial entry in 1952. "The starboard watch had two doctors on it, and we had none. So we invented Willi Faraguli, M.D., and he has been paged at every yachting event of any consequence since then." Ocean racing spawns a special breed of characters.

### 1954: *Malay*'s Year

With a total of 77 boats, the nineteenth anniversary Bermuda Race was almost one-third larger than its predecessor. In 1948 there had been just two classes, A and B. Class C was added in 1950; in 1954 came Class D; Class E originated in 1960, with its 131 entries; and class F arrived in 1966, when 167 boats raced. The race had become so big that old-timers were feeling a loss of the old intimacy, when everybody in the race knew each other and social gatherings included only the sailors themselves—almost all of them men—and could be comfortably fitted into one of Bermuda's quaint beachfront hotels. In the fifties, the fleet ballooned as wives and children started coming down for a little vacation and perhaps to sail the boat back.

The 1,200 men and women attending the 1954 prize giving at the Royal Bermuda Yacht Club cheered the smallest overall winner since *Tamerlane*, Dan Strohmeier's 40-foot Concordia yawl *Malay*. Named for the 1930 winner, which had been owned by Strohmeier's father-in-law, she was the first one-design stock boat to win the race. When American custom boatbuilding became very expensive after the war due to rising

Dan Strohmeier won the 1954 race in *Malay* and 24 years later finished second overall in a sistership. A leader in advancing boat design, Strohmeier joined Olin Stephens, Richard McCurdy, and Karl Kirkman in the 1980s for a post-Fastnet Race study of the factors at play in capsizes by modern racing boats.

labor costs, sailors saved money by turning to foreign builders, smaller boats, and boats built to the same design.

Designed by C. Raymond Hunt, the Concordias were mostly built in Germany. *Malay*, Concordia number two, had come out of the Lawley yard in Massachusetts. They were finished off by the class's sponsor, Waldo Howland's Concordia yard in South Dartmouth, Massachusetts. If the Concordia yawls (and a few sloops) were so successful as all-round boats, it was because Howland had engaged in enough thrashes to the Onion Patch to appreciate the demands on a boat and crew before they reached their reward beyond the finish line. He certainly understood the race's purpose and appeals. As he wrote in the first volume of his autobiography, "For a chance to enjoy such pleasures as Bermuda affords, who wouldn't race there, even if he were at heart a cruising man?"

Dan Strohmeier, at heart also a cruising man, was once asked why he did not buy a modern cutting-edge fiberglass boat. In reply, he observed that the questioner probably owned some fine furniture. He did, too: "It is 40 feet long and in it I can cross the ocean." When a hurricane wrecked *Malay* less than two months after her Bermuda Race victory, he had her rebuilt and subsequently raced her to Bermuda eight times, though never as successfully as in her first run. The 1972 race, the roughest in history, was her last. "We shook her up going to Bermuda," was how Strohmeier, in his understated way, explained why he sold her and bought another Concordia yawl, also named *Malay*.

For all the handsome joinerwork and ingenious cruising accommodations in the two *Malays*, her owner was a hard-nosed scientist who had conducted aerodynamic experiments in a wind tunnel and studied naval architecture at MIT. His scientific aptitude helped him win the 1954 race. That was the year the Woods Hole Oceanographic Institution issued the first of its detailed pre-race Gulf Stream reports, and when Strohmeier took a close look at the map, he decided to head as far west as he could. At a time when it was doctrine to enter the Stream about 30 miles west of the rhumb line, he hit it almost 60 miles out, and it paid off. *Malay* found the most favorable current for the longest stretch and won the race by a whopping two hours.

### 1956: *Finisterre*'s Road to Her Trifecta

*Finisterre*'s first victory was in a big-boat race, with a long, fast starboard-tack sprint. She was the only Class D boat in the top ten on corrected time, and ended up first overall (over 88 competitors) by 14 minutes over Bill Snaith's *Figaro*.

The conditions near Bermuda were especially challenging. John Rendel of the *New York Times* reported "A weird concoction of rugged wind, fog with zero visibility, hard rain squalls, and a belt of virtually flat calm." Still, visibility was pretty good at two in the morning when a 45-footer, *Elda*, piled up on the reef between North Rock and Northeast Breakers, making her the second boat lost in the race's history. The crew clung to the rigging for hours before a Bermudian spotted them from shore and came out in a small motorboat to make the rescue.

*Bolero* did not hit the reef, though it seemed to the U.S. Navy escort that she might. Under a new owner, the Swede Sven Salen, she trailed her new near-sistership *Venturer* by only 22 miles from the finish when *Venturer* made two mistakes. Hearing a forecast of lighter winds, the crew shook out the reef. A passing cold front left her in a blow and she sailed on under jib and mizzen. She also made a navigational error and over-

Skirting the reef and with her jib halyards jury-rigged as a temporary headstay, *Bolero* beats toward the finish in 1956. St. David's Light is just visible above her stern. She set a new race record and contributed to one of the most exciting Bermuda Race photographs ever taken.

stood the finish.

With Olin Stephens and Ken Davidson, the director of the Stevens Institute towing tank, in their usual positions as mate and navigator, *Bolero* made no tactical or navigational errors, but she did suffer troubles. Two jibs blew out, the mainsail's reel halyard winch backed off, and the turnbuckle at the top of the headstay broke. The crew quickly doused the headsail, ran jib halyards out to the bow, and set a small forestaysail. Bursting out of the fog at 10 1/2 knots, *Bolero* skirted the reef so efficiently that the commander of the navy escort vessel, furiously announcing that only a "reckless person" would try to make such a landfall under such conditions, signaled, "You are standing into danger." *Bolero* broke *Highland Light*'s old elapsed time race record, as did *Venturer*.

## 1958: Times Square

This race featured the most famous start in ocean racing history. Spinnakers flailing, the fleet careered before a fresh northwester with more than one sailor pulled halfway up the mast by a halyard. "We started under spinnaker and the first night out wrapped the chute," Larry Glenn recalled of his first Bermuda Race at age 17. "Seven of us were on the bow trying to pull it off the headstay and I realized I was hanging out over the water and there were six guys above me." After the breeze faded the 111 entries had a true small-boat race, with the big boats stalled near the island as the little ones roared down on them in a set of line squalls. One hundred boats finished within 12 hours. "That finish line looked like Times Square with all those lights converging," someone said. *Finisterre* finished only four hours behind Jack Hedden's 64-foot *Good News*, the first to finish, and won her second straight Bermuda Race by just over an hour after a bow-to-bow duel all the way with Colin Ratsey's *Golliwogg*.

A lot of light canvas got wildly out of control at the windy 1958 start. (Left) The fellow dangling desperately from *Uomie*'s halyard is Warren Brown, later of *War Baby* fame. (Top) The Naval Academy entry *Fearless* more than lives up to her name.

# Carleton Mitchell

Carleton Mitchell—always "Mitch" to his friends—first sailed as a boy in an uncle's racing sloop off New Orleans. He kept a scrapbook in which he pasted pictures of boats, and when he was 12 he answered an inquiry about his plans for a career by announcing, "I want to sail and write about it." That dream survived college in Ohio and mundane jobs during the Great Depression (for a while he sold women's underwear at Macy's). It even survived a wretched experience in a leaky old ketch that almost sank in the Gulf Stream. When the ketch staggered into Nassau, he began his lifelong love affair with the Bahamas, where he later worked as a writer and photographer.

After wartime service in the U.S. Navy's photography department, he bought one of John Alden's old *Malabar*s, renamed her *Carib*, sailed south to the West Indies, and wrote the book *Islands to Windward*, which introduced the Caribbean's charms to sailing Americans long before the first bareboat fleets. Moving to a 58-foot Rhodes yawl he named *Caribbee*, he won a race to England and wrote a wonderful book about ocean racing, *Passage East*, illustrated with some of his best photographs. His affection for the sea and boats was luminous. "To desire nothing beyond what you have is surely happiness. Aboard a boat, it is frequently possible to achieve just that: That is why sailing is a way of life, one of the finest of lives."

All the while Mitchell was thinking about the dream yacht he would build for himself. He wanted a boat small enough for a couple to handle easily, beamy enough to be comfortable, shallow enough to cruise in the Bahamas, strong enough to cross an ocean, and fast enough to have a chance at winning a race or two. He would describe her as "a small centerboard yawl, orthodox yet unorthodox, dedicated to the personal theory that it is possible to combine in one package speed, comfort, and seaworthiness. . . . [D]espite a worn cliché, a boat need be wholly a compromise between one set of virtues and another." When Rod Stephens rerigged

**"Good admiralship" was his shipmate Bunny Rigg's explanation for Carleton Mitchell's success.**

*Caribbee*, Mitchell was sufficiently impressed to go to Sparkman & Stephens for the boat that he would name for her ability to survive happily far beyond the end of land. Though designed without attention to her rating, *Finisterre* ended up winning three suc-

cessive Bermuda Races, a record approached only by John Alden in three *Malabar*s.

In the vast firmament of sailing records, the polestar is the one set by this tubby little yawl. It is hard enough to win one Bermuda Race. But two in a row? Three? Mitchell gave various reasons. Quoting John Nicholas Brown, *Bolero*'s owner, to the effect that the Bermuda Race is "the great Atlantic lottery," he sometimes credited blind luck. But it was not luck that made *Finisterre* one of the few boats in 1958 to avoid the starting line chaos and later press on to victory through 50-knot squalls. Mitchell credited his crew: "On *Finisterre* we have a basic tenet to keep moving at maximum speed in the wind of the moment. There must be either a trim or a shift in sails every time there is a variation. . . . In no other race in my memory have so many strings been pulled or so many bits of cloth gone up and down the mast. Crew work and helmsmanship have never been more important."

When Dick Nye, the 1952 winner, was asked how *Finisterre* won so often, he replied, "For one thing, she's got everything. And he sails the hell

**With her owner looking on carefully and taking pictures, "the fat little monster" (as Mitchell called her) came to life over several months in Seth Persson's tiny boatyard in Connecticut. She was built strong and heavily of wood and metal.**

out of her." She was a superb boat that was brilliantly prepared and pushed very hard. "My theory was that the time to get everything right is before you leave the dock," Mitchell once said. "And then, once you leave the dock, to be able to drive the hell out of the boat and never have to worry about something carrying away. And if anything did let go on you, the spares were on board with the know-how to put it back together."

If *Finisterre* had everything, it was the best of everything. On the day after Christmas, 1953, he wrote a four-page letter to Ernest Ratsey of Ratsey & Lapthorn laying out his specific expectations for sails. "I realize all these wants of mine add up to a lot of trouble for you and your people," he concluded, "but I want *Finisterre* to be a very special little craft, and to me—as I know to you—perfect sails are necessary for performance and pleasure. And I might add (which I am sure Rod will verify) that nothing short of perfect will match the job the builder is doing." That last sentence was a tribute to Seth Persson, who built the boat almost single-handed of wood, with a strong bronze centerboard trunk and Monel mast step. All that metal helped give her a favorable rating because it was not counted as ballast. The CCA Rule was changed and she no longer had this advantage.

With her 22,000-pound displacement and 11-foot, three-inch beam on a waterline of just 27 feet, six inches—"the fat little monster," Mitchell sometimes called her—*Finisterre* had the inertia and initial stability that add up to sail-carrying ability. In her first race, as she was beating into a hard blow in the company of 50-footers, one of Mitchell's crew, an amiable Bahamian named Bobby Symonette, mused, "I wonder how the little boats are doing tonight." He had forgotten that he was in the smallest boat in the fleet. *Finisterre* did have a problem in light going, but as Olin Stephens, her designer, admiringly commented, "her skipper and her crew maintained an almost magical degree of concentration to keep her moving in light airs." In the long, light-air run that made up the early going in the 1960 Bermuda Race, *Finisterre* cagily played the jibing angles and kept up with lighter boats.

The winning crew in 1956: (left to right) Dick Bertram, Cory Cramer, Ned Freeman, Henry Davis, Carleton Mitchell, Bunny Rigg, and Lockwood Pirie.

Sailing skill had something to do with it, but so did what one of her long-time crew, Bunny Rigg, called Mitchell's "good admiralship." Although Mitchell was a skilled celestial navigator, he signed on at least one more sailor of equal ability so a sight would be taken instantaneously when an overcast momentarily cleared. Once, *Finisterre* got lost near Bermuda. "We didn't know where the hell we were," Mitchell said. "Then with Bunny Rigg holding me, I took a moon sight and we came out right at Northeast Breaker. It was an easy sight." It may have been easy for him. Tell an experienced navigator that an owner sailing near reefs bet the farm on one of the trickiest sights there is, with the moon racing across the sky so fast that an error of a fraction of degree or second can be fatal, and the response is a stunned, respectful silence.

Mitch liked his creature comforts. The navigator and the sailing crew of six were looked after by a full-time cook, and the off-watch was ordered to get their rest. This approach paid off nicely in the final 100 miles of the 1958 race, when the line squalls appeared. "These conditions called for a lot of rugged exertion in the last 12 hours of the race

and many a crew was too fatigued at this stage of the game to do their best," Rigg wrote. "*Finisterre* passed many of her competitors right there, rolling reefs in and out and changing headsails no less than 20 times with the fluctuations of the breeze simply because she had a well-rested crew."

There was more to *Finisterre* than racing. Mitchell estimated that for every mile she raced, she cruised at least ten. After winning the 1956 Bermuda Race, she sailed to the Mediterranean. "It has been a phenomenal trip," Mitchell wrote Rod Stephens from Gibraltar. "I came, basically, because each time I had gone sailing in *Finisterre* we had run out of water too soon. So I figured if I pointed the bow east from Bermuda, there would be plenty of water and plenty of sailing. Now I am not sure there was enough of either." Back home, the boat never finished below third in a major ocean race. Come 1958, with only one new sail she won the Bermuda Race again. She did not sail another race until 1960, which was when she won for the third time in some of the wildest weather in the history of the Bermuda Race.

*Bolero*'s professional captain, Fred Lawton, performs some housekeeping during the 1950 race while wearing a lifebelt with a tether hooked to the boat. A consummate seaman, Lawton had his opinions and was not afraid to express them. When his owner, John Nicholas Brown, carelessly put *Bolero* about without alerting the crew to handle the many sheets and backstays, Lawton half-shouted, "*Commodore! Leave us have no bloody secrets from the foredeck!*" Brown quickly made his peace with the individual without whom *Bolero* could not function. That could well be *Baruna* to leeward.

## Safety Concerns

Mitchell's magazine articles about *Finisterre*, and her phenomenal racing record, set off one of the biggest booms in American sailing history. Mitchell would say that in 1956 there was one *Finisterre*, in 1958 there were many, "and by the third race, the ocean was full of *Finisterre*s. But we still won."

The Bermuda fleet became larger, the average boat became smaller, and the competition became more intense. One night in the 1958 race, 49 sets of running lights were spotted by E. Roddie Williams, the mayor of Hamilton, Bermuda, and skipper of a racing boat. All this spurred the Bermuda Race committee to worry about safety. One issue was visibility. During the 1952 race, a navy task force near the racing fleet was unable to pick up any of the yachts on radar, and the commanders were so wary that they ordered their ships to steam off in the other direction. After this incident, John Nicholas Brown, a former assistant secretary of the navy and then the commodore of the New York Yacht Club, pulled strings at the Navy Department and arranged for a destroyer to try out its radar on the 1952 New York Yacht Club Cruise. There were only a few weak hits at close range until George Roosevelt hung a metal reflector in the rigging of his wooden-hulled, wooden-masted schooner *Mistress*. The destroyer instantly picked her up at a range of five miles. When Brown and a navy officer reported this breakthrough in an article in *Yachting* magazine, many sailors learned for the first time that there was a simple way to take advantage of radar, which soon became an important aspect of normal seamanship, although it was not allowed to be used in the race for many years, except in emergencies.

With the increase in the race's size, the race committee grew from a handful to 16 members, with a paid secretary, a consulting public relations firm, and an advisory committee of yacht designers. In 1956, for the first time in the race's history, an entry fee was charged—it was all of $10. One topic attracted the attention of everybody: boat inspections, which were required even of boats that had qualified for previous races. Because boat owners are proud, the Bermuda Race is prestigious, and inspectors are required to sign their names to statements certifying a boat's and crew's qualifications, the issue of inspection pulled in many directions at once. If a boat were not allowed to enter, the chairman was sure to receive a firmly worded letter from a fellow Cruising Club member complaining about unfair treatment of his good friend with his wonderful yacht. Such pressures honed the committee's sense of mission. Bermuda Race circulars still stated that the purpose of the race was to encourage the creation of seaworthy yachts and develop capable amateur seamen and navigators.

Late in 1954 a member of the race committee, Talcott M. Banks Jr., a Boston lawyer, wrote a firm memorandum predicting trouble. The price of the race's success, he said, was that "Sooner or later a real blow is going to strike in among one of these large present-day fleets, and if a yacht that ought not to have undertaken the course is lost with its crew no amount of stress on the individual responsibility of each entrant will make us feel any better about it. Ocean racing, like mountaineering, has certain minimal risks."

Rod Stephens and others shared that concern. In 1946, Sparkman & Stephens had introduced the British idea of bow pulpits to American ocean racers. In 1958, after three years of discussion, Stephens helped get life belts (the ancestors of safety harnesses) added to the Bermuda Race's list of required equipment. Although *Finisterre* and some other boats already carried lifebelts and required crews to wear them, they were largely unknown. In 1960, the rule limiting cockpit volume (and, there-

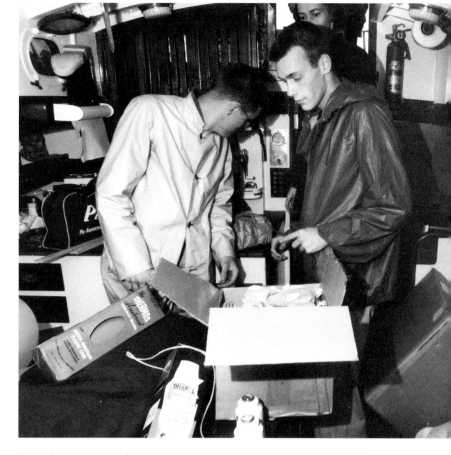

Inspections were meant in part to stimulate crews to prepare their boats with care. Here some sailors aboard *Mistral* in 1958 to find places for all the essentials they brought on board.

fore, the amount of water that could be taken aboard) was tightened. The once skimpy mandatory equipment list grew to 29 items, including emergency tillers and through-bolted stanchion sockets. In 1962, the committee mandated double lifelines and a bilge pump that could be operated from the cockpit.

## 1960: The Year of the Big Blow

Talcott Banks was right: there was a real blow—a horrific one, in fact. Although the 1960 race was the slowest on record, its last 100 miles made it the most exciting by far. Afterwards, *Yachting* sent out a questionnaire to owners that included, "Which gear was most important?" The answer again and again was "lifebelts" (and sometimes "lifebelts!!!").

After three days of light air, the 135-boat fleet was smashed on the nose in the dark of night by an unpredicted tropical storm with high winds and radical wind shifts. On *Stormy Weather* the anemometer showed 70 knots for a while. "We were a little shy about shaking out reefs and setting more sail until daylight," Harry Anderson recalled. "There was a big sea and the easiest sail to set was the mizzen staysail.

We set it all right but after a while someone looked aft and noticed that the transom was lifting right off the boat. We finished the race with our transom lashed to the mizzen mast." Bill Snaith's 46-foot yawl *Figaro II* pounded so hard her water tanks came apart. Charles Ulmer's yawl *Scylla* lost a crew overboard, but one of the very first Guest strobe lights went after him and Ulmer picked him up in half an hour. Two boats lost rudders and three were dismasted. Pierre du Pont's massive 72-foot motorsailer *Barlovento II* suffered no damage to speak of—that would have taken a hurricane—but the mainsail leech shuttered so violently that the hull shook.

If any single incident defined this gale, it was the experience of Henry Morgan's 62-foot sloop *Djinn*. A massive, stiff boat displacing 72,000 pounds with almost half of it in her keel, she was skippered by Morgan's 36-year-old son Henry, a naval officer in the submarine service, with a crew of 12. Taking advantage of a header in the rising wind, *Djinn* came about and was settling down on the port tack. Morgan reminisced:

> By now it was pitch dark, overcast, and raining pretty hard, so the visibility was zilch. At that point we were hit from the starboard (now lee) side by what I now realize was a microburst. The effect was a 70-80 degree right shift and an increase in the wind to about 60. The boat was of course hit flat aback

and went right over on her port side. I know how far over because we found weed in the top of the three sets of spreaders while checking the rig in Bermuda. Since everybody but about three were hooked on the port (old weather) side, they went under, as did I, hanging onto the wheel. The men on jib and main sheets let them go; the boom came over and carried away the old windward running backstay. Just about the time I got to wondering what in hell to do next, she straightened up, courtesy of the released sheets and 18 tons of lead.

There *Djinn* sat, presenting a chilling sight to her young skipper. "The spreader lights were on, and I could see that there wasn't a soul left on deck, whereas I knew there had been seven others when we tacked. That was a bit of a thrill, but very shortly people started appearing over the rail, swarming up their safety harness tethers. One man had a cracked rib and was back under the counter, so we had to haul him up, but everybody was back aboard in a couple of minutes. This was the best lesson in the merits of everybody hooked on I've ever seen."

One of the men who had been on the windward side, David Owen, later swore that as he was shaking the water out of his ears, he heard his shipmate Bob Coulson remark, "Well, I guess they've taken the flowers off the dining room table on *Barlovento* now."

## "One Standard, One Code"

As *Djinn*'s crew picked up the pieces and nursed their sloop to Bermuda, well astern some little boats were still racing hard. Carleton Mitchell's closest competitor was Erroll Bruce in the Royal Naval Sailing Association's *Belmore*, a narrow, light-displacement 36-foot sloop designed by John Illingworth and his partner Angus Primrose specifically for the CCA rule; she had been third overall in 1958 under another skipper. A two-time Bermuda Race veteran in the little *Samuel Pepys*, Bruce was as much a hard-pressing romantic as Mitchell. He wrote in his book *Deep Water Sailing*:

*Racing a yacht hard as part of a good crew is an experience that once felt some will hanker after for ever. Perhaps these feelings are reserved for those that truly love the sea with its ever-changing moods and constant surprises. Racing at sea can bring out the best qualities in people; it gives scope for adventure such as is hard to come by in any other sport. Each haul on the halyard or sheet, every cold douche of discomfort, each long night hour at the tiller, is for the good of the ship. She returns the offering ten-fold with the lasting joy of satisfaction that each individual gains from being part of a team that works together whole-heartedly.*

(Left) Erroll Bruce was philosophical after *Belmore* was edged out by *Finisterre* in 1960. (Right) With a deep reef rolled in, *Cyane* makes time toward Bermuda in the sea left over from the gale.

Also like Mitchell, Bruce was a demon on preparation. He carefully planned the race so his well-trained crew would be rested not merely to carry on in rough weather, but to race at full capacity over the last two days. "It is my belief that the Bermuda Race is usually won during the third and fourth nights at sea," he later wrote in his book *When the Crew Matter Most*; "and it is often lost, particularly by young crews, from over-exuberance and exhaustion on the first two days." Organizing *Belmore*'s six-man crew around this strategy, Bruce found an able navigator who would remove that burden from his shoulders and allow him to get some rest in the early days and then be available, as he wrote, to "put on the boost pressure of hard sailing during the last nights."

But the navigator came down ill before the race. Bruce took over his job and it wore him out. *Belmore* was near *Finisterre* in the early going—a good sign for the British as the Americans had to give them 51 minutes of time (*Finisterre*'s rating had been increased after the bronze centerboard trunk was counted as ballast). When the gale hit, *Belmore* was knocked down more than 50 degrees and as she lay on her side, all but stopped, she took on water—"Life at this time was not comfortable," Bruce dryly looked back on hours of pumping. In time the breeze faded slightly and they set the deeply reefed mainsail, perhaps a little tardily. "There never was a moment's doubt in my mind that this was the critical time of the

race. The gale I had prayed for had arrived, and *Belmore* had come through it very well. . . . Now she was glorying in it, when a few hours earlier she had been shivering and sometimes stopped as too shocked by too violent a jolt. She was certain of herself, and her motion had a rhythm of confident power." Crossing the finish line, Bruce shouted to the stake boat, "'What about the others?' 'There aren't any others,' came the reply across the water. 'You are second in the fleet of course.'"

They had passed 50 boats during the night and beat 100 larger boats to St. David's Head, and still *Finisterre* got away again. She finished in time to take *Belmore* by 25 minutes, 21 seconds. She never shortened down to storm canvas, never shivered to a stop. Erroll Bruce had no regrets: "To be a better man at the game than Mitch is a high standard . . . . To come within 25 minutes of *Finisterre* under such conditions was no failure."

That was one of *Finisterre*'s last races. Carleton Mitchell gave up ocean

racing at the peak of his success to take up cruising full-time. In 1968 he bought one of the first smaller trawler yachts. As he cruised in this floating home (called *Sans Terre*), he wrote articles that brought this new approach to boating to the public's attention. Later he cruised with his wife, Ruth, on the Mediterranean or from his South Florida home. He celebrated his eighty-ninth birthday by sailing in *Finisterre*, which after years of decline in the Caribbean had found a good owner who kept her in Venice, Italy, and took her out on the Adriatic.

An accident called a halt to such pleasures, but in August 2005 Mitchell told a friend who had called to wish him a happy ninety-fifth birthday that he was looking for another new boat—a houseboat on which he could get around in his wheelchair. It was just like Carleton Mitchell to want to get back to the water in something beamy and comfortable.

His fascination with the elusive relationship between the sea and

sailors was the constant through Mitchell's many careers at sea. One of the best reveries in sailing literature is his ruminations about "the somewhat fantastic nature of ocean racing":

> *Here we are, nine men, driving a fragile complex of wood, metal, and cloth through driving rain and building sea, a thousand miles from the nearest harbor; no one to see or admire or applaud; no one to help if our temerity ends in disaster. . . . Our attitude is not even wholly based on the competitive aspect of racing. It is that we all feel there is just one way to do things, one standard, one code, and we live up to it for our own satisfaction. We are driven by our own compulsions, each personal and secret, so nebulous we probably could not express them to our mates if we tried. But in our own way, we are about as dedicated as it is possible for men to be.*

Woman or man, cruiser or racer, who can find fault with that?

1968 winner *Robin* just clears the anchor chain of the frigate marking the finish line's outer end. (Opposite) What it was like on *Dyna* for over 24 hours in late June 1972.

# Controversy and Big Winds

By all appearances, everything was fine with the Bermuda Race. *Finisterre*'s well-publicized hat trick, the regular turnouts of more than 100 boats, the absence of serious damage or injury in the 1960 race — all that and more suggested that the race had reached full maturity and could be run without change for years into the future. Yet the years 1962-1972 saw constant (and often controversial) experimentation as the race committee wrestled with some fundamental issues about the race and its future. While seeing some of the worst weather in the race's long history (including a two-day, hurricane-induced storm), this period also experienced the most dramatic changes since the 1930s' transition out of the schooner era. By 1972, the boats, the rating rule, the race's management, and even the race course had seen changes.

In all her finery, including "the Monster," *Niña* was well prepared for 1962's schooner weather. She was nowhere near as traditional as her 34 years suggested. (Opposite) First-to-finish *Stormvogel* was a new type of maxi, with light-displacement and easily driven.

## 1962: The Commodore

**W**hen a sailor was asked after a one rough Bermuda Race if he had enjoyed himself, he snapped back, "God, no, it was terrible! I'll be damned if I'll do it again until two years from now." So it was that even with the memory of 1960's hair-raising experiences fresh in their minds, over three-fourths of that year's owners expressed interest in coming back. The 1962 entry list peaked at 163 and eventually settled at 131 boats, but in the end most of the sailors were bored silly. Reportedly, one becalmed crew watched helplessly as a Portuguese man-of-war sailed through their lee. When there was wind, it was "schooner weather," on the beam, and the winner turned out to be one of the two schooners in the race, the 34-year-old, 59-foot *Niña*.

Although most Bermuda racers are more adept at answering the question, "How do you lose a Bermuda Race?", everybody prefers to be asked how to win it. Winner or losers, the first answer always is, "Be lucky." To quote Norris Hoyt, who sailed many Bermuda Races, "An ocean race is frequently an exercise in blind luck and comparative ineptitude." Olin Stephens made the point somewhat more positively when he said of one of his most famous boats, "*Finisterre* had the luck that so often follows good handling." The fact is that the credit should at least go to good sails, clever navigation, able crews, or (as we will see in the 1964 race) skilled helmsmen. Another way to at least have a chance at winning a Bermuda Race is to sail a boat that suits the course, treat her well, and take advantage of favorable conditions when they come along.

That last explanation fits DeCoursey Fales's 1962 winner, *Niña*, the first schooner to win the race since John Alden's *Malabar X* in 1932. As schooners go, she was unusual. About all she had in common with a *Malabar* were two masts. Designed by W. Starling Burgess as a rule-beater for the 1928 transatlantic race, which she won, *Niña* was called a "two-masted cutter" because a line drawn from the peak of her towering Marconi-rigged mainmast through the foremasthead to the jib tack was perfectly straight. With her tall rig, fine hull, and deep ballast, she was close-winded and fast in all conditions when sailing on the wind. On a reach, the vast expanse between her masts provided all sorts of opportunities for light sails. By

the time Bobby Somerset acquired her in 1933, she was leaking so badly he cut short a cruise and put her up for sale.

Fales bought her in 1935, and over the next three decades he cleaned up on the Long Island Sound and New England racing circuit. Famously assiduous in his attention to the old girl, over the years Fales lengthened her foremast, upgraded the winches, put her on a weight-saving regimen with aluminum spars (and even aluminum floorboards), and constantly replenished her wardrobe. Among the 24 sails crowding the lockers in her stripped-out cabin were two gollywobblers—balloon mainmast staysails—nicknamed "the Monster" and "the Grand Monster." With one or another of these immense reaching sails set during most of the 1962 race, *Niña* finished within sight of the top-rated boat, Cornelius Bruynzeel's pioneering light-displacement maxi *Stormvogel*. The victory by the oldest boat and the oldest skipper inspired a love fest in Bermuda. "If I couldn't have done it, I'm glad it was the Commodore," other skippers told Bill Robinson of *Yachting*.

At the age of 74, DeCoursey Fales embodied all the ceremonial, companionable, and competitive threads that are the warp and the woof of the Bermuda Race. As much as he loved to win races, he adored the spit and polish of a yacht that had served as his flagship during his term as commodore of the New York Yacht Club. The cooking, cleaning, polishing, and maintenance were performed by a professional crew of three khaki-uniformed sailors, usually Scandinavians, who lived forward of the mast. They stood watches, but most of the sailing and all of the steering were performed by the ten amateurs, friends of Fales to whom, well before each race, he wrote formal invitations with assignments for bunks, lockers, and shore accommodations.

After finishing at St. David's Head, *Niña* was put smart with a harbor furl, her brass was shined, and her brightwork was rinsed with fresh water and chamoised down. Once through Two-Rock Passage and securely tied up, Fales, like Mr. Fezziwig on Christmas Eve, called his boys below for a gathering that was less a party than a ritual. It was founded on the principle that while any other race is merely a *race*, a Bermuda Race is a *voyage*, and any decent voyage can end only with the crew communing over drinks. Some captains preferred rum; Commodore Fales's favorite libation was the martini. "We didn't call for the launch

ashore until the shaker was empty," recalled a former *Niña* crewmember, Rad Daly. The event tolerated no visitors. After my first Bermuda Race, in another former New York Yacht Club commodore's yacht, as the bottle was being passed around the table a powerboat pulled alongside and we heard people clambering on board. Without even turning his head toward the companionway, my able and kind-hearted watch captain, whom I will call Harry Smith, shouted, "If there are any Smiths in that boat, they may go ashore!" There followed the unmistakable sounds of a hasty retreat and the chug-chug of the launch making her way back to the Royal Bermuda Yacht Club's landing.

During the winter, Fales took time from his banking job to draft and distribute an exhaustively detailed, 12-page guide to the boat titled *Niña's Sea Routine for Ocean Racing and Day Cruising, by Her Owner.* Printed across the bottom of the cover was this warning: "All Souls on Board Must Read—No Excuses." On the last page were ten maxims. Most were traditional seamen's rules of thumb like "Hook on a hand for yourself and one for the ship," "Investigate the gear," and "Tidiness is a blessing." But at the tail end of this sobering list came a two-word commandment that said more about Fales the sailor than the sum total

of all the others: "*Let's win.*" For all his love of tradition, DeCoursey Fales was a racing skipper.

He would command *Niña* in one more Bermuda Race, and be third to finish and fifth on corrected time in Class A in 1964. Two years later, after organizing his crew and boat, Fales went into the hospital, where he died while his beloved schooner was working her way out toward the Gulf Stream.

## 1964: The Smallest Winner

For many sailors and race officers, *Niña*'s victory was a temporary distraction from a fundamental problem—entries. While there was some interest in branching out – in the mid-1960s someone proposed a class for catamarans and trimarans—the concern was that there were too many boats, and especially too many small boats. As one race committee member, the yachting writer Everett Morris, commented, in a time of high income taxes the Internal Revenue Service had become "the world's most effective yacht designer." With the boom in fiberglass boats under 40 feet, the entry list might soon top 200. The race committee was regularly asking itself if the new small boats were sound enough to get through the Gulf Stream or another gale, if there were enough inspectors to screen out the unqualified boats and crews, and if the Coast Guard or navy escort vessels could manage communications and rescues.

Dick Nye proposed turning the race into two races, one for big boats and one for small in alternating years. Deciding that one race every two years was labor enough, the all-volunteer race committee opted to limit numbers by making the race an invitational. Eligibility (but not an automatic invitation) was extended to boats that were race veterans, that were owned by members of the two sponsoring clubs, or that represented the service academies or a few foreign yacht clubs. The last window encouraged entries for the Onion Patch Trophy series for national teams of three boats. Inspired by the Admiral's Cup series in England, "Shorty" Trimingham and Edward Greeff launched the Onion Patch series in 1964. In the first series, the United States beat Bermuda.

Anybody who did not qualify under those rules could be proposed by Cruising Club or Royal Bermuda Yacht Club members. If the race committee believed that the boat and crew were qualified, an invitation was extended.

The new system added a layer of control over the fleet, but also considerable weight on the already burdened shoulders of the race chairman. "You realize, I am sure, that the honor that goes with this job is very dubious," Peter Comstock wrote a friend just weeks after taking charge of the 1966 race. "Everyone cannot be pleased even though we try. Sailors (of which I consider myself) are a very outspoken group and most of us have minds of our own. Thank God of that, but it does make the job a little difficult." Among the committee's jobs was issuing penalties for violations of the racing rules. Occasionally the circumstances were painful. In a protest hearing after the 1962 race concerning a starting-line incident involving two boats, Charley Morgan's *Paper Tiger* and William F. Buckley Jr.'s *Suzy Wong*, *Paper Tiger* was found guilty and penalized. During the hearing, Buckley admitted that one of his crew, claiming he was calling from *Paper Tiger* and using a profanity, had asked the escort vessel for a weather forecast. This transmission violated a race rule mandating radio silence except in emergencies, a racing rule against soliciting outside assistance, and the race committee's sense of honorable behavior. Buckley withdrew from the race. The 1964 race committee subsequently voted to not invite *Suzy Wong* back, but recommended that the 1966 committee reconsider without prejudice.

The concern about small boats dated back several years. After the flurry of "zipper bows" and exemptions in the early 1950s, the committee stopped granting favors. John Illingworth, the gifted British designer and sailor who announced in one of his books that the Bermuda Trophy was "the most coveted yachting trophy in the world," tried and failed to get a bye in 1956 for his 24-foot-waterline *Mouse of Malham*. In 1964 the race committee went a big step further by raising the minimum sailing length—the length taken above the waterline—from 27.5 feet to 29 feet.

One victim of the rule change was the second-place boat in 1962, *Burgoo*, a fiberglass Bill Tripp-designed 37-foot centerboard yawl. When her owner, Milton Ernstof heard the news, he wrote race committee chairman Thomas J. Watson Jr. a forceful letter in which he pointed out that several boats her size had been invited back and made it clear he would not give in easily. "Because the *race* is great, the compulsion is great, and I am willing to abase myself to further question as to the possibility of being part of it." Ernstof did not know that the committee believed he already had two strikes against him: he had misbehaved in Bermuda in 1962, and he was a passive owner who did not take part in racing the boat. When Watson discovered that both claims were untrue, the committee issued an invitation with the proviso that *Burgoo* meet the new length rule. *Burgoo* then went out and became the smallest boat and the first fiberglass boat ever to win a Bermuda Race.

She won because Ernstof had put together a "crew of skippers"— almost all of them prize-winning small-boat sailors—who concentrated on steering well on the long starboard-tack leg to the island. "When someone innocently cracked a joke or offered the helmsman a Fig

**Burgoo**, the smallest Bermuda Race winner ever, creeps to the finish. Her owner was willing to abase himself in order to be allowed to compete.

Newton, the compass would swing more than the critical two degrees and the speed would drop three-tenths of a knot," one of them, Geoff Spranger, later related. "The poor distracted chap at the tiller then had the chore of getting the boat moving in the groove again before someone noticed, or his trick was over." Even owner Ernstof was relieved from the helm. "That's the way we work," he explained to Alf Loomis. The *Burgoo* crew's approach paid off during the last 20 miles in a light-air beat to the finish. "For six painful hours *Burgoo* ground her way toward the smell of oleander," Spranger looked back—and toward the Bermuda Trophy.

### 1966: The Year of the Curve

Another new idea was tried in 1966. The chairman of the CCA's measurement rules committee, Arthur Homer, proposed that the best way to avoid "small-boat races" and "big-boat races" was to replace the Herreshoff time allowance tables with an innovative computerized system that would gauge a boat's performance against her rating. The results were displayed on a graph, with the boats as dots clustered around a curve representing the fleet's average performance. The boat whose performance (or average speed) was farthest above the curve was the winner in the 167-boat fleet.

It took a long time to identify the winner. Three-fourths of each class had to finish before the curves were drawn, and then the data had to be double-checked and, in that technologically Paleolithic age, sent by telex to IBM's headquarters in New York for computation. To nobody's surprise, the overall winner turned out to be the 40-footer that was twentieth boat to finish, only six and a half hours after the 72-foot elapsed-time winner *Kialoa II*. This was Vincent Learson's *Thunderbird*, one of the six light-displacement, fin-keel Cal 40s in the race. There were at least 40 stock boats this year, including the 1954 winner, *Malay*, and 10 other Concordias. By 1972 well over half the fleet would be moderate-displacement, separate-rudder, fiberglass stock boats—Swans, C&Cs, Tartans, and others—that looked a lot more like a Cal 40 than a Concordia.

*Thunderbird*'s crew included the able navigator Chick Larkin, her sailmaker, Lowell North, and her designer, Bill Lapworth, five of whose designs were in the top ten. It turned out to be a small-boat race after all, with the big boats stalled for hours near the island. The second-place finisher was the Class F winner, the light-displacement *Nike* from Argentina, designed by German Frers Sr., with a relatively shoal draft of five feet so she could sail in the shallow River Plate. *Thunderbird*'s corrected time margin was 19 minutes. Under the old time-allowance system, it would have been three hours, one of the biggest ever.

The key to the 1966 race was playing the multitude of vicious squalls (and the occasional waterspout) just right. Wind was everywhere, from all directions. In the 58-footer *Caper*, the wind came and went with a

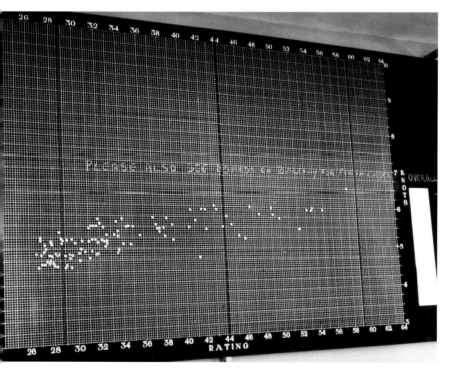

This is the display board for the ingenious but not entirely practical performance curve system used in 1966. The speedy lightweight Cal 40 *Thunderbird* won easily— and not because her owner was an executive at IBM.

suddenness that sometimes was hilarious. We watched with amazement as Dick and Richard Nye in the smaller *Carina* negotiated a line of anvil heads as gracefully as an Olympic skier managing a mogul field. *Carina* was almost hull-down ahead within two hours; she won Class B for the third time in eight races. *Thunderbird* was even with another Cal 40, *Illusion*, sailed by America's Cup winner Bus Mosbacher, but got away when her crew spotted a squall and got the spinnaker doused before *Illusion's*.

## Safety Concerns

There were 11 withdrawals in the rough going in 1966, by no means all of them among the small boats. The biggest boat in the fleet, the 75-footer *Big Toy*, dropped out after losing a spreader, and *Royono*, the Naval Academy's old warhorse, came apart with broken rigging, a 300-gallon-an-hour leak, and a burned-out starter motor (Ski Siatkowski got her to Bermuda under sail). Other wooden boats withdrew because of leaks, and there were several dismastings when the new low-stretch rod rigging failed, in some cases because it was not set up properly. There were just two withdrawals in Class F, perhaps due to more careful inspections, perhaps to raising the minimum sailing length again, this time to 29.5. That effectively established a 38-foot minimum overall length and kept out *Burgoo* (she sailed down anyway and survived a pasting in the Gulf Stream).

While the dropout rate of 11 of 167 boats was nothing like the one in 1936, when nine of 43 entries quit during the 600-mile beat to Bermuda, the attrition was far larger than in any other race. In the brutal blow in 1960, just three boats withdrew. The sport was obviously at a turning point as yacht design and construction turned toward lighter, faster, higher-tech boats that were having teething problems. Race officials agreed to further increase emphasis on inspection and to add new safety rules. For a while there was a movement to bar all boats that had withdrawn due to damage from future races. Saner heads prevailed. When the yacht designer James A. McCurdy was appointed by the Cruising Club to head its Design and Construction Committee, he insisted that it would be impossible to eliminate all failures on all boats through regulation alone, and that the only sensible strategy was to combine inspections, race rules, and an education campaign that publicized gear and boat failures.

The sustained public effort to make boats safer was prescient and effective. No string of races in Bermuda Race history has experienced as much rough weather as the four between 1966 and 1972. Squalls, fronts, depressions, and, in 1972, the tail of a hurricane staggered these fleets. A total of 44 boats did not finish. Damage was spread across the fleets. Twelve of the 44 were in Classes A and B, yet smaller boats were most vulnerable. Classes E and F (boats smaller than about 44 feet) accounted

for 20 withdrawals. The most common reason for dropping out was rigging failure: 13 boats were dismasted and several boats withdrew with broken spreaders or stays. A large number of other boats with damaged rigging, meanwhile, staggered to the finish under jury rigs. This was just as stretchy rope-luff jibs in grooved-rod headstays were coming into use so sail shape could be changed by adjusting the halyard. When the yawl *Inverness's* rod headstay broke at a weld, one of her crew, Tom Young, recalled, "It sounded like a cannon shot. We raced on deck, let go the mainsheet, and got all the halyards out to the bow as quick as we could." They added support by setting a jib with a wire luff; Bermuda Race rules required that storm sails be capable of being set independent of grooves.

Among the new rules in the late 1960s and early seventies were requirements for life rafts, permanently rigged main boom topping lifts, radio telephones, stern pulpits, safety harnesses with chest attachments for tethers, and crewoverboard rescue drills. If an entrant had withdrawn from any race in the previous five years, the owner had to explain why in writing. Sailors complained about the expense, the paperwork, the race committee's paternalism, and the limits on small boats, but every time a big blow came along the grumbling quieted. After the catastrophic 1979 Fastnet Race in England, Richard Nye would point out that almost all the losses of life and serious damage occurred in boats smaller than 38 feet, the Bermuda's Race's de facto minimum size.

## Handling the Crowd

The big new fleets packed Bermuda's anchorages and marinas. Many boats moored at St. George's, but the bulk of them crowded into Hamilton Harbor at the hotels or anchored near the Royal Bermuda Yacht Club. Before 1968, when the first piers of its now-large marina were built, the club had just a small wharf. At race time it was looked after by the volunteer unofficial dockmaster, Bobby Burcher, a Bahamian who flew in before every race and, in his white uniform, greeted sailors and sold them the avocados and coconuts he had carried up with him. The biggest demand was for the club's showers, which were kept in business night and day for a week. "Even cold, slightly lukewarm showers are an invaluable thing," said one race veteran, Stephen Thing, speaking for thousands of formerly grungy sailors. "Every time I get in a shower, I remember my first one at RBYC."

Non-sailors awaiting the arrival of boats did not need showers. They required assurance, which was provided by the club's manager, Tony Marsh. Described as "imperturbably cheerful" by Bill Robinson of *Yachting*, Marsh was once confronted by an anxious woman who demanded to be told *right now* the location of the yet-to-finish boat in which her husband was racing. Peering out a clubhouse window in the general direction of St. David's Head, 15 miles away, Marsh assured her

## Bermuda

*"For a chance to enjoy such*

*pleasures as Bermuda affords,*

*who wouldn't race there,*

*even if he were at heart a*

*cruising man?"*

—*Waldo Howland*

**Much of the fleet is tied up at the Royal Bermuda Yacht Club marina around 2000. A comparison of this photo with the one on page 75 reveals how at least one aspect of the race has changed.**

that he spotted the boat's running lights.

Bermuda's kindnesses continued through the week. On the Sunday after the finish, one of the island's charming churches would hold a service for the yachtsmen. The commodores of the two sponsoring clubs read Psalm 107 ("down to the sea in ships") and other relevant passages from Scripture, and the congregation sang "Eternal Father, Strong to Save," "The Star Spangled Banner," and "God Save the Queen." With those tunes ringing in their ears, many of the sailors wandered back to the yacht club for a last Planter's Punch, and then boarded their boats for the return sail to America.

## 1968: Ted Hood's Race

Judged too complex, slow, and error-prone, the performance curve system was dismissed after one try. *Thunderbird* came back and won her class in 1968, but the race was dominated by medium-size boats. The winner was the Class C 52-foot yawl *Robin*, whose skipper, designer, and sailmaker all were Ted Hood. While not the sport's first man for all seasons, none came closer to being so successful since Nat Herreshoff retired. As a young man in Marblehead, Massachusetts, Hood had pioneered in using Dacron in sails. From there he moved into yacht design, creating the first of 39 racer-cruisers for his own use, all called *Robin* or something like it, as well as an America's Cup defense candidate, *Nefertiti*. When Hood was skipper of the 1974 cup winner *Courageous*, he became the second sailor after Harold Vanderbilt to win both classics.

Very much an exception to the new trend toward light displacement, this *Robin* was a hefty steel-hulled whale, with a round-bottomed hull displacing 47,000 pounds and a roomy four-cabin cruising interior. Everything else about her was sharply cutting edge, though it had taken Hood a while to hone his blade. On the drawing board, *Robin* had been a 50-foot centerboard sloop. After the Dutch builder misread the plans and made her two feet too long, Hood merely shrugged, explaining, "As designed, she was probably too fat." Her poor performance in her first racing season was more worrisome. Hood tore out the hinged centerboard and replaced it with an eight-foot deep, buoyant daggerboard (like one in a Laser dinghy), and then installed a high-aspect-ratio yawl rig on two aerodynamically clean masts. John Alden and Olin Stephens had altered boats, but nobody had gone so far so quickly.

This was Hood's first Bermuda Race. Although he had been racing for well over half his 41 years, until then, every June in an even-numbered year found him busy fulfilling sail orders. He came into the race fully aware of how complex the task was and signed on a talented crew that included a meteorologist who was not a sailor, and a navigator who very definitely was: Robert N. Bavier Jr., the son of the 1924 and 1934 Bermuda Race winner and the helmsman of the America's Cup winner *Constellation* in 1964, when he beat Hood in the defender trials.

The winning skipper in 1968 and, as a sailmaker, rigger, and yacht designer, Ted Hood is one of the more significant figures in Bermuda Race history.

According to Bavier, sailing *Robin* successfully was not all that hard: just get her in the right place and then "let *Robin* go." She had plenty of opportunity for that. After some upwind work the first day, the wind shifted to the southwest, blew hard at times, and gave *Robin* a long, fast sleighride to the island, where she finished with boats rating much higher.

There were two unprecedented events this year. One was the postponement of the start for a day because of a threatening early-season hurricane. Starts had been delayed before, but only for a few minutes for fog (although in recent years the race committee fired the guns on time on the assumption that it was less dangerous to send 150 boats off than to have them milling around a huge spectator fleet). The other was the withdrawal of the third-place boat in Class C. The owner of the yawl *Guinevere*, George Moffat, was fooling around with his new Loran set one day and had confirmed his position when the navigator reminded

# Alf Loomis

It was a time of transition in yacht design, and also in the faces seen at Bermuda Race gatherings. Herb Stone, who revived the race and made it an institution, died in 1955. John Alden, whose boats provided a rationale for the revival and who won the race three times, passed away in 1962. Yet some founders and first-generation sailors were still around in proxy or in person. The Baviers were well represented. So were the Morsses, who won trophies in the schooners *Dervish* and *Grenadier* in 1907, 1908, and 1932. In 1958 and 1964, Wells Morss won his class in *Legend* and *Carillon*. After Charles "Chick" Larkin II first came down from Buffalo, New York, to take a berth to Bermuda in 1930, he became a sought-after navigator (and, with his ukulele, a regular member of the improvised orchestras that were features of post-race celebrations). When he guided *Thunderbird* to her win, Larkin got his fourth Bermuda Race victory, a

record for navigators. One of the last active survivors of the race's formative days was the writer-sailor-navigator Alfred F. Loomis. After an incomplete formal education, he fell in love with boats and writing about them. His initial interest in powerboats led him into submarine-chaser duty in World War I. He later taught himself how to sail while cruising in a yawl to Panama, and, after going to Bermuda in 1923, he became an ocean racer for life. Over the next half century, he sailed in every important race right through his seventeenth Bermuda Race in 1966, two years before his death at age 77. He usually navigated, and was on board the schooner *Brilliant* in her first race, in 1932, and in 1954 he helped *Circe* win Class B.

Once Alf Loomis reached Bermuda, he went back to being a journalist. Relying on interviews, inspections of logs, and his own experience, he methodically chased down each race's turning points and compiled tracks of boats' positions. His lengthy histories of the races were published in *Yachting* magazine and in pamphlets and became valuable sources for skippers and navigators. One of the first sailors to recognize the importance of the Gulf Stream research by the Woods Hole Oceanographic Institution, he kept his readers up to date on the new theories about the Stream's currents.

For all his importance as a serious race analyst, Loomis probably was best known for what was called the "tactful acidity" with which he wrote about the sport. In an article titled, "Are there Any Sailors in the Navy?", in 1932 this contrarian provoked the Naval Academy to found a sailing program. The uprising against semiprofessionals in the 1930s simulated him to declare, "If they are to be excommunicated, ocean racing will suffer." When traditionalists assaulted the Marconi rig and later light displacement, he defended modern boats. Appalled by displays of bad sportsmanship and

general acrimony, he invented an organization for bad actors called the Lee Rail Vikings and, in his column, named its members.

Alf Loomis also was the patriarch of one of the Bermuda Race's great families. He, his sons Worth, Bob, and Harvey, and his grandson Alfred raced down a total of 52 times, covering more than 33,000 miles under racing canvas. In 1970, Bob, Harvey, and their brother-in-law Ward Campbell formed the backbone of John Page's crew when they won Class F in *Pageant*.

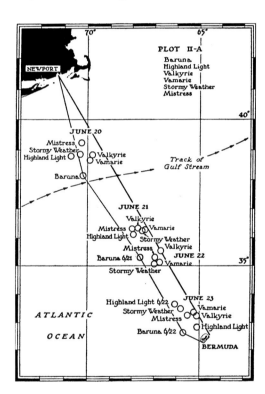

**For 40 years, Alfred F. Loomis provided Bermuda Race sailors and the race's many fans with contrarian opinions, humorous commentary, and a level of serious analysis (like the above plot of the 1948 race) that the race deserved.**

# The Bermuda Race Song

**L**ike any extreme activity, the Bermuda Race has long been the butt of jokes, some of them set to music on long wet (or long calm) watches by crews seeking relief from the miseries at hand. All the Loomis family's Gulf Stream experience, coupled with Loomis humor, led Worth and Harvey over a period of many years to compose a sardonic ditty about the race and its occasional trials. (They did not take their own advice; Harvey Loomis was still racing down ten years later.)

## The Bermuda Race Song

Verse 1, Worth Loomis, 1932

*Oh, I don't want to race*
*To Bermuda on my face,*
*I've never felt like this before.*
*All I do is wet my tail*
*Trimming sheets down to the rail —*
*Bedroom sheets have never made me sore.*
*So next time the wind is dead ahead*
*I'll be sleeping with my red-a-head,*
*You can take your ocean racing,*
*And by accurately placing,*
*You can shove every rail,*
*Every plank and every sail*
*Right up where they won't bother me no more.*

Verse 2, Harvey Loomis, 1970

*Oh, I have had my fill*
*Of that bloody foredeck drill,*
*I've changed too many jibs in the Gulf Stream sea.*
*So it's time to close the hatch*
*On the dear old Onion Patch —*
*The rum is fine but the rhumb line's not for me.*
*So next time the bunks are cold and wet,*
*I'll be sleeping you know where, you bet.*
*And it would be no surprise*
*To find that all those other guys*
*Would trade their sheets, large and small,*
*Main, jib, spinnaker, and all,*
*For the sheets beneath my red-a-head and me.*

him that electronic navigation was barred. Moffat crossed the finish line, came in, and withdrew. It would take a dozen years before Loran became legal for an entire race.

## 1970: Searching for the Tower

Many American sailors were supremely content with the CCA Rule. Besides inspiring three generations of capable dual-purpose cruising-racing boats, it had a good track record for fairly rating different types of yachts. Since 1950, the Bermuda Race had been won by boats between 37 and 59 feet, including narrow keel sloops, beamy centerboard yawls, a lightweight Cal 40, and a schooner. Three of those ten winners were relatively inexpensive stock boats. Yet the rule did not always accurately gauge performance, it was onerous for the CCA to manage, and the many boats it encouraged were too different from those produced by the Royal Ocean Racing Club rule to allow for fair international competition. After several years of discussion, the International Offshore Rule came into effect in 1969.

In the meantime, the 1970 race committee headed by Walter Flower changed the Bermuda Race course by adding a turning mark. The aim was to provide what Flower called "a kink to the usual starboard tack close reach" to allow a beat to windward. "The Bermuda Race used to be called 'the thrash to the Onion Patch,' but there was no windward work," explained Richard Nye. Members of the committee believed that a true upwind course in the frequent southwest wind would increase the race's international standing while discouraging entries by the new breed of light and presumably fragile boats. After considering several alternatives, the committee chose the Nantucket Lightship as a turning mark because it would set the rhumb line six degrees farther west. The Royal Bermuda Yacht Club strenuously objected. The 100-mile leg along the southern New England coast to Nantucket violated the principle that this was an ocean race, and it seemed that Nantucket Shoals was too shallow, foggy, and tidal to be safe in a strong wind. The Bermudians also declared that they had not been properly consulted. Too often they had learned about new Bermuda Race policies from press releases.

They liked the idea of adding a turning mark but proposed that it be the tower on Argus Bank 25 miles south-southwest of Bermuda. As an added appeal, the now 679-mile race would end with a leg running down the back side of the island, within view of competitors' families and other spectators on the island's south beaches. The approach to the finish line would be safely clear of reefs. After several strongly worded exchanges, the race committee adopted this course in late April 1970.

The string of rough weather continued. After a fast reaching start, on the evening of the second day the 149-boat fleet was hammered by thunderstorms sweeping in from the west with hurricane-strength gusts. In John Page's *Pageant*, Harvey Loomis noticed "a particularly heavy

One or another of Sumner A. "Huey" Long's world-traveling *Ondines* twice had the best time to Bermuda. One broke the record in 1974. In 1970, however, this *Ondine*'s sprint to the Onion Patch became a long, agonizing search for the tower that served as a turning mark in that year only.

cloud that we wishfully hoped was not doing what it appeared to be doing: moving against the wind, toward us. . . . The leading edge was blacker and sharper than any squall I'd ever seen. Reminded me of the thin black mustache on the upper lip of the villainous landlord in the old melodramas. And low. And spitting straight down out of it were occasional blasts of lightning. Altogether a very much more than ordinarily imposing piece of nature's work." The crew doused all sail. Ten minutes later *Pageant* was sailing again.

"I've been in 13 of these races and have never seen one like it," Peter Comstock of another small boat, *The Hawk*, told a journalist. "There were long periods when we drifted with no wind at all, and long periods

also when it blew hard. We registered up to 62 miles an hour for a while the second night out, and on Thursday it blew hard all day long and there were big seas that built up very quickly." As the little boats banged into that last blow, a freak wave knocked a 38-footer, *Promessa*, upside down and loosened her bulkheads and cabin sole.

Far ahead of Class F, the four maxis were approaching Bermuda at night. Leading them, and possibly winning the race on corrected time, was Huey Long's *Ondine*, the most recent of the boats that Long had been campaigning in most of the world's ocean races. The problem was that nobody in her crew of 22 could find the Argus Tower's light. When Long tried to home-in on its beacon with the radio direction finder—

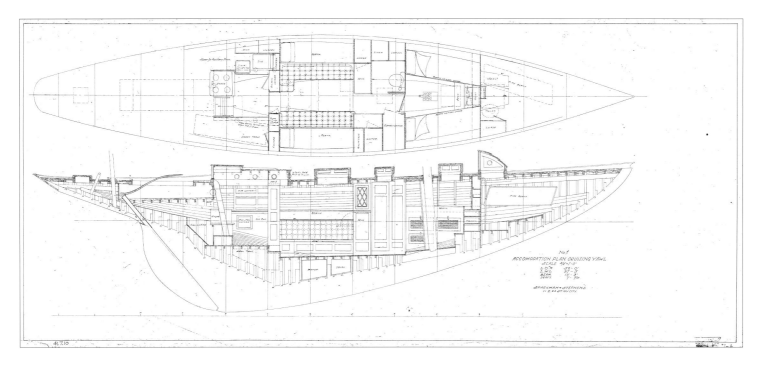

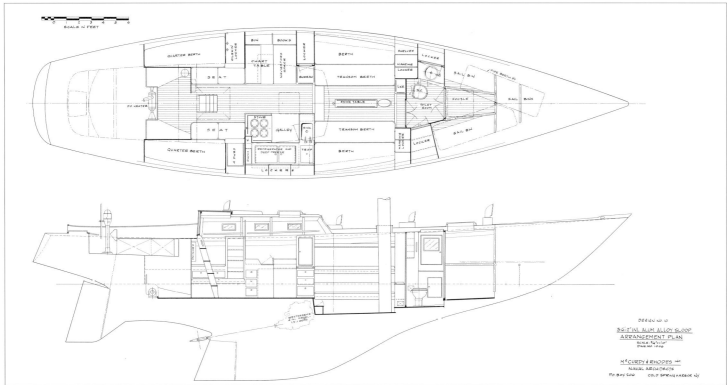

(Opposite) The Nye family's new, third *Carina* won the 1970 race, the first sailed under the IOR. (Above) A comparison of her plans with those of the 1929 *Dorade* (top) indicates the evolution of ocean racing yachts. Long keels gave way to fins with detached rudders, and beam increased. Later IOR boats would be far wider and more skinned out. *Dorade* is 52' LOA, 37'3" LWL; *Carina*, 48' LOA, 36'2" LWL.

one of very few electronic navigation devices allowed—the signal was drowned out by a much stronger one. Long later estimated that he lost five hours, 13 minutes searching for the tower. Only slightly more fortunate was the 72-footer *Windigo II.* "We just *couldn't* find the tower," her navigator, Larry Glenn, remembered. "There was some sort of anomaly that drowned out the radio beacon with one from San Juan, Puerto Rico. We sailed on and on and finally decided we'd sailed too far, so we turned around and set a spinnaker. That was when Dick Sykes came on deck and spotted the tower, so we sailed for it and *Ondine* passed us. They'd been looking for it, too, so they followed us in."

As the big boats hunted around for the tower, Dick and Richard Nye were rapidly gaining on them in their new 48-foot Class C aluminum sloop *Carina*, designed to the IOR by Jim McCurdy and Philip Rhodes Jr. "It was a beautiful night, that last night, with a moon, but we weren't sure where we were," Richard Nye remembered. "When the RDF found the tower beacon frequency, the call sign was SJU, San

Juan, Puerto Rico. We didn't know what to do. 'Do we sail on?' we asked ourselves. So we tacked. When we found the tower we were only 50 yards off. The light was a 100-watt bulb but otherwise it was as advertised. We saw *Ondine* running back to it under spinnaker." *Carina* ran up the backside of the island, finished just 29 minutes behind *Ondine*, and won the Nyes' second Bermuda Race in 18 years.

## 1972: The Year of the Gale

What everybody who sailed the roughest of all Bermuda Races remembered best was the true thrash, if not thrashing, to the Onion Patch over the old course. (The Argus Tower had been torn down, and while the 1970 course had its admirers, few were willing to stake the race on a temporary buoy.) The 172 boats—the biggest fleet in race history—were lashed for the last two days by a 30-to-50-knot southeasterly running dead into the teeth of a 3-knot Gulf Stream meander and kicking up terrific breaking seas. Stillman Taylor, *Baruna*'s former captain and now a

At first dominated by schooners, then by yawls, the starting line in the IOR era became crowded with sloops. One of the few two-masters in the 1970 Class D start is Arthur Wullschleger's *Elske* (foreground). She finished fifth in class in the one "race to the tower."

watch captain in *Windigo*, said that while the 1960 blow was briefly worse, "I've never known it so stormy for such a sustained period of time. It was a damn good test of men and material." On the smaller boats, crews felt close to the edge. "It was like driving a truck into a stone wall three times a minute for two days," one sailor said afterwards. On board Bob Bavier's 40-footer *Witch*, somebody noted in the log, "The watchword for today is survival."

The big test came on the approach to the finish. Warren Brown, of *War Baby* fame, ranked the difficulty of 1972's landfall with the one in 1960. Even in the best weather, finding the finish line requires the closest possible coordination between navigator, helmsman, and crew as the buoys guarding the reef are located and checked off—North Rock, Northeast Breaker, Kitchen Shoals, Mills Breaker—on the gradual but anxious arc toward St. David's Head. When mistakes are made here, they generally go carefully unpublicized, but every now and then a horror story leaks out. The midshipman skipper of *Royono* in the 1954 race, Stan Keck, watched with amazement as his boat's autocratic commanding officer—a navy captain who, Keck said, "always seemed to be carrying those steel balls in his hand which you could almost hear"—defied his navigator and insisted on steering straight across the reef for the British frigate posted at the finish line. "The net result was dropping all our sails with the exception of the mizzen and setting a small forestaysail, and with bow lookouts, steering hard starboard or port to dodge coral reefs for quite some time."

That close call was in fine weather. The 1972 fleet approached its landfall after three days without sextant sights (Loran was still not allowed), and with a two-knot north-setting current, erratic RDF bearings, and so much flying spray that visibility was a matter of yards. Few if any navigators would later admit to having known anything close to their exact positions near the island.

We in the Swan 55 *Dyna*, owned and navigated by two superb seamen, Clayton Ewing and Dick McCurdy, respectively, approached the island just at sunrise. Our race until then had been plenty eventful but without excessive anxiety. After almost hitting a whale west of the Gulf Stream, we watched the barometer plummet at dawn on the third day, and soon it was blowing a solid 35 under a black sky. Shortened down to the number three jib and four rolls of reefs in the mainsail, we were regularly taking solid green water. One wave was high enough to reach the cowl of a ventilator rising two feet above the cabin. Like a firehose, the vent redirected the water down into the cabin, right onto McCurdy as he was engaged in cleaning his sextant. Insecure navigators might take this as a personal insult, but McCurdy let out a loud guffaw.

Navigating solely on dead reckoning, McCurdy told us to start looking for the island before dawn. Luckily, the low cloud cover briefly opened up to show Gibbs Hill Light. Our depth sounder and other elec-

tronic instruments had shorted out, leaving us to find the finish line by eyeball and feel. We held in on port tack until the waves became shorter and steeper (a sign of shoal water), tacked out quickly, and when the seas lengthened again, tacked back. In this way we felt our way around the reef, yet without knowing exactly where we were until we could find and identify one of the dimly lit buoys through the gloom. After what seemed like an age of fruitless searching by our watch, the other watch captain, a burly Australian fisherman named Sid Brown, stuck his head out of the companionway, looked around, and, pointing almost abeam, announced, "There it is." We had no idea which buoy this was until McCurdy and Ewing instructed us to circle it and read its number. It was Northeast Breaker, and from there our path to the finish was relatively straightforward.

Meanwhile, there were 14 withdrawals—three due to dismastings, some to other damage, and many due to the seamanlike caution of their owners. Approaching Bermuda with rigging problems, Stanley Livingston in *Wailele* found the radio bearings unreliable. An escorting Royal Navy frigate that was nearby hailed, "Are you satisfied with your position?" Livingston looked up, saw rocks, and promptly anchored. When he could not start his engine—he later found the fuel tanks full of salt water—he decided to accept a tow. When the 68-foot ketch *Equation* reached the vicinity of Northeast Breaker at midnight, the crew spotted the buoy but quickly lost it in a squall. She drew 12 feet with her ballasted centerboard down, so her owner, Jack Potter, sailed around for six hours until he decided that with his boat and crew at risk he should use an Omni aircraft navigational device to find the finish, even if it was illegal. *Equation* was disqualified from the race.

Other boats simply stopped. *Ondine* hove to until dawn. When *Carina*'s radio direction finder bizarrely showed danger on one tack and safety on the other, the Nyes became cautious. "We hove-to for a couple of hours and watched other boats go by," Richard Nye said. "My father was beside himself. He wanted to call ashore and say he was safe. He asked how to use the radiotelephone but we had a unanimous memory lapse and forgot how to work it."

Afterwards, except for complaints that flat-bottom new IOR designs tended to pound more than older boats, for once there was little handwringing over modern boats and sailors. Despite boats' fractured frames, several sailors' fractured ribs, and a great many torn sails, almost 160 boats survived the roughest race and the riskiest landfall in the Bermuda Race's history. One of them was the light-displacement ketch *Windward Passage*. She led for two days, but when the wind came in she commenced to fall apart. "Everything was all right, good sailing, plenty of wind on the way down," said her navigator, Peter Bowker. "Then we neared Bermuda, and everything happened at once." His shipmate, Kirk Elliott, continued the story: "During the next 24 hours we saw the wind velocity increase, and

remained on the wind. During this time we blew out our mainsail and genoa. After setting the storm trysail, and storm genoa staysail, we were able to make slow progress towards the finish. We crossed the finish line early the next morning, broad reaching at speeds between 15 and 18 knots, in the pitch black."

With *Passage* limping, and *Equation* and *Ondine* essentially hove-to, the C&C 61 *Robon*, from Newport Beach, California, became the smallest first-to-finish boat since 1928 and also won Class A. According to one of her crew, Taylor Grant, although the electronic instruments and even the compass light failed, the legendary California navigator Ben Mitchell kept everything in order. "Everyone on board were dinghy sailors," said Taylor Grant. "We just sailed the boat, went fast and found the finish line. The rain was blowing horizontal and it was hard to see anything anyway."

*Robon* was just one of the many fiberglass stock boats that came through it well. Besides her elapsed time and Class A win, stock boats took four of the other five classes and the Bermuda Trophy. The overall winner was *Noryema*, an English Swan 48 that had been slightly modified with beefed-up winches and a cutter rig that one of her crew, Paul Antrobus, would refer to as "our race-winning weapon." Another candidate for that label was a diving mask that the helmsman wore to keep stinging salt water out of his eyes. *Noryema* suffered no damage to speak of in the wild conditions. As Antrobus said, "We sailed through a hurricane and only broke an ornamental oil lamp glass which popped off its wall light as we fell off another cliff."

The first and (as of 2004) only winner of a Bermuda Race from outside the United States, *Noryema* was owned by Ron Amey, one of the lucky few who can produce a pretty name by spelling his own name backwards. He had raced to Bermuda before; in 1966 he was fifth overall. He could not race this time due to business obligations, and the boat and crew of nine were in the charge of the very able and genial Ted Hicks. *Noreyma*'s success was celebrated from Somerset to St. George's, Antrobus recalled. "We got a tremendous reception from the locals as Bermuda was then still an outpost of the British Empire, and to have a Brit boat win the trophy was feted by all and sundry, with endless invitations to parties in the following few days. My wife had to become social secretary."

By then the Bermudians were more than a little relieved. As the first news of the storm had filtered in, Kirk Cooper, the Royal Bermuda Yacht Club's commodore that year, started getting calls at three in the morning with some startling information. "The race committee chairman woke me up and said there were three dismasted boats, *Windward Passage* was down to storm trysail and storm jib, and a Royal Navy frigate was reporting they had lines over the side. That's when I decided I should go over to the finish line, and there I found a police commissioner who was hot as a mackerel, which in Bermuda means he was extremely angry." Down at the yacht club, in the pouring rain, hundreds of wives and girlfriends were keeping a long watch of such desperate anxiety that even Bermudian kindliness could provide only small relief until boats checked in by radio as they neared the island.

There was a race, and it was won by the unusual tactic of sailing east. The Woods Hole Oceanographic Institution prerace forecast indicated that the Gulf Stream would provide a favorable boost 20 to 80 miles east of the rhumb line. The boats that reached fast for that gate (dodging some whales and Russian trawlers along the way) came out of it as much as 100 miles east of the rhumb line. When the wind conveniently backed into the southeast, they tacked and aimed at Bermuda.

Some of the more colorful stories came from the 27 non-U.S. boats from six countries. Although the American team won the Onion Patch Series, foreign boats took five of the 18 class cups, including two victories.

In the English *Crusade*, recalled Scott Osler, "We were surfing in the mid-teens with a storm jib and a storm trysail. The wave troughs were deeper than our spreaders were high." Domestic life, meanwhile, became a little unhinged: "Our second sunrise at sea showed a gray sky

and rising wind. We had breakfast on cold leftover chicken which was stored in the galley oven. As the wind and seas rose, we kept making good progress toward Bermuda. I was off watch during a pretty terrific fall into a wave trough which broke the oven gimbals and door. All of the chicken carcasses flew out and several of them climbed into our foul weather gear on the floor. As we were asleep, we didn't realize this until we tried to put them on."

Australian Alan Bond's *Apollo* had been the first Bermuda Race entry from the southern hemisphere in 1970 and finished sixth in Class A. She returned in 1972 and had the same result. Ron Packer recalled some incidents from the storm's second day:

*The breeze got quite strong and we ended up beating to windward with a fully reefed mainsail and storm jib. By late afternoon the wind appeared to be moderating slightly and Trygve Halvorsen in his very low key style said to us "Boys, if we were really trying we would have the number four jib up." Well, by this time the sea was quite rough and the two forward hatches were regularly under water and were battened shut. The number four jib had to be manhandled from the fo'c'sle aft through the cabin to the cockpit, and then forward along the weather deck to the bow to be hanked on. In order to keep the sail under control we recruited Doc Phillips to come forward of the mast, out of his usual territory, into what was known as Marlboro Country, i.e., a man's world.*

*Just as we had finished hanking the new sail on below the storm jib, Trygve ordered the sail change to be delayed for a few minutes while another squall passed through. At this stage we had four crew on the foredeck trying to control the new sail while the bow plunged through rather than over each wave. The foredeck was going up and down like the proverbial department store lift and there was a considerable quantity of water cascading across the deck. On one occasion as the bow slammed into the next wave, John Longley put his hand down to cushion the landing and found a flying fish in his hand. Not wanting to miss an opportunity, he merely pushed it into his oilskin pocket and continued with the sail change.*

*We eventually got the number four jib up and the storm jib back into the main cabin via the cockpit, at which Doc Phillips turned to the rest of the crew and said "Wow, that was pretty hairy," to which John Longley replied "What do you mean? I had time for a spot of fishing!", and produced a flying fish out of his pocket.*

And so the Aussies discovered the mixed joys of the Gulf Stream.

The first of several chances *Brigadoon III* took in 1982 was to squeeze between the committee boat and her competitors. She won the race. (Opposite) Long, easy sleighrides down the rhumb line lost their luster when pinpoint electronic navigation allowed clever navigators to hunt down favorable Gulf Stream meanders and eddies.

# Taking Risks

"Are all Bermuda Races different?" someone asked Jim Mertz.

"Yeah," he replied. Having sailed in 30 of them, he should know.

That was as true as ever between the mid 1970s and the late 1980s, when the race was reinvigorated by new types of boats, more aggressive sailors, and innovative technology that transformed the part-art, part-science of navigation from a long-range target shoot into a chess match.

In 1974 *Scaramouche* (sporting an early Kevlar mainsail and the powerful new IOR flush-deck look) became the first freshwater boat to take a Bermuda Race. She also was the first winner designed by German Frers, who after Olin Stephens is the most successful designer of Bermuda Race winners (six).

## 1974: The First Frers Winner

Only half the boats that raced in 1972 came back two years later. This unusually high attrition rate was understandable considering the violence of a storm that left at least one boat so brutalized that she was shipped home on a freighter. But in the end there were 166 entries, only 12 fewer than 1972's record fleet. For the fifth race in a row there was a fresh to strong breeze, with a steady southwester providing a fast 630-mile starboard-tack close reach all the way to Kitchen Shoals before the brief turn to windward to the finish.

Although everybody likes to believe those are typical Bermuda Race conditions, if that were true the elapsed-time record would be broken far more often than every ten or 12 years. A study of historic sailing conditions made before the 1980 race showed that, with the exception of the usual nasty Gulf Stream squalls and the less frequent calms and gales, the average true wind speed in a Bermuda Race is between eight and 16 knots, and a boat typically is close-hauled for 18 percent of the course and otherwise is reaching. This year it was mostly reaching in good breeze, and S. A. "Huey" Long's new *Ondine*, a 74-foot ketch designed by Britton

Chance Jr., broke *Bolero*'s 1956 elapsed-time record by over two hours.

Astern of *Ondine* came a small, triumphant fleet of Great Lakes boats. After decades of winning only the rare prize, boats that usually sailed in drinkable water took five of the top six places on corrected time. Lynn Williams, who first raced to Bermuda in 1928 as a 19-year-old in an Alden schooner that his father brought east from Chicago, corrected out to fifth place overall in *Dora IV* and won Class A over Frank Zurn's *Kahili II*, from Erie, Pennsylvania. The other three top Lakes boats were in Class B: Chuck Kirsch's *Scaramouche* from Michigan, Jesse Philips's *Charisma* from Ohio, and Joseph Wright's Chicago-based *Siren Song*. The top dog was *Scaramouche*, which match-raced *Charisma* most of the way down to the island but had the advantage because her navigator, Peter Bowker, found a helpful meander in the Gulf Stream more than 40 miles west of the rhumb line.

*Scaramouche* was designed by the young naval architect German Frers Jr., who also produced the only saltwater boat to break into the top six, Class C winner *Recluta III*, from Frers's home country of Argentina. (Frers's father and other Argentines had been knocking at the door to the Bermuda Trophy for almost 20 years.)

(Above) With *Scaramouche* tied up in the place of honor at the Royal Bermuda Yacht Club marina, owner Chuck Kirsch and navigator Peter Bowker pose for the camera. (Left) A new course record was set by Huey Long's new Chance-designed *Ondine*, with a mizzen set in different wind than the mainsail.

## 1976: The Year of the Biggest Calm

And then the wind died. After an entire week of sailing, 28 boats—almost 20 percent of the 150-entry fleet—were still out there. For the first time the last boats were instructed to switch on their engines and spare themselves and the finish line committee any more misery.

There were three reasons why Al Van Metre's *Running Tide* became the first Class A boat to win a Bermuda Race since *Niña* in 1962. First, this seven-year-old, 61-footer was fast (her designer, Olin Stephens, described her shape as "close to ideal"). Second, her strategy was perfect: to avoid the flats of a high-pressure system that had plunked itself down near the rhumb line, she sailed 200 miles east, found a header, tacked for Bermuda, and came barreling in. By contrast, *Ondine* took an initial stab to the east, had second thoughts, headed way west, and eventually reached St. David's Head a full day behind first-to-finish *Tempest*. Long estimated that his wind-hunting had added 175 miles to the 635-mile course.

But the chief reason why *Running Tide* won was that her closest competitor made a dumb mistake. The race instructions clearly direct boats approaching the finish line to sail on the seaward side of the buoys marking the north and east sides of the reef. The Australian 53-footer *Bumblebee 3* was reaching to the finish with the Bermuda Trophy comfortably in her pocket when she sailed inside Kitchen Shoals buoy. Her crew caught on too late and, in the resulting confusion as they rewound themselves, they succeeded in tearing up two spinnakers and blowing 35 minutes. In the end, she lost to *Running Tide* by a mere seven minutes.

Later, Harry Macklowe's *Unfurled* approached the finish line in the dark, with the next boat in Class F far astern, and cut one of the flashing buoys. Her crew failed to correct their error. *Bumblebee 3* went home with the trophy for winning Class B. All *Unfurled* got out of it was a disqualification.

No Bermuda Race entry has ever experienced a calamity on the order of *Bumblebee*'s. Still, every Bermuda Race crew experiences its ups and downs. Take, for example, the reversal of fortune experienced by *Windance* in Class F in 1976. Starting ahead of 1968 winner Ted Hood in his *Abino Robin*, her crew made their way down the course with little

sense of how well they were doing until their spirits were lifted by the sight of a press helicopter coming out from Bermuda and circling her, not once but twice. The tension ended as they approached the yacht club marina, as owner George Eddy remembered: "The band began some loud and crazy British march, the big boats alongside the dock turned their bright spotlights on *Windance*, every horn in the harbor was honked in our honor, and there was a special space reserved for us. Once we tied up, girls in party dresses and ice-cold drinks appeared by magic. We all were hugged and kissed, like we'd sailed around the world to get there." Lo and behold, *Windance* had won Class F.

It seemed too good to be true—and it was. *Unfurled* was not a problem; the race committee had already settled her fate. But out of the crowd stepped Ted Hood, cleanly shaved and in a blue blazer and tie. When *Abino Robin* had come into Hamilton several hours earlier, Hood, not the sort of man who likes to make a show, had quietly skirted the yacht club and tied up elsewhere. Eddy was left with third place in Class F, an honored spot in the marina, and thoughts of what might have been.

*Bumblebee 3* (upper left) would have been the first Australian winner if she hadn't cut a required buoy near the finish. She still won Class B. *Abino Robin* (right, Ted Hood steering) won Class F because another boat made the same incredible mistake but, unlike *Bumblebee*, did not correct it and was disqualified.

A rare port-tack start gets the small boats away in the light-air 1978 race. The Brenton Reef tower is just visible in the background. Bow and stern pulpits, full lifelines, long-and short-range radios, and life rafts are now mandatory, and though masthead wind instruments are not required, most boats have them.

## 1978: Two Fleets

Blending features of the CCA and Royal Ocean Racing Club rating rules, the new International Offshore Rule (IOR) broke down national barriers while making many CCA Rule boats noncompetitive. New boats built to the IOR sailed faster, rated better under the new rule, and had some characteristics that not everyone considered desirable.

Some of the old guard's criticisms of the IOR were unfair. Many boats (including the Swan, Tartan, and C&C lines) were able and comfortable as well as fast. The IOR did not invent fragile masts, crews had been riding the windward rail rather than sleeping below since the days of *Finisterre*, and some of the centerboarders from the 1950s and sixties were not particularly stable at high angles of heel. Yet some IOR boats were big dinghies more suited for day racing in protected waters than for going to sea—flat-bilged, over-canvassed, lightly built, prone to broaching, and uncomfortable below in skimpy, poorly ventilated cabins. More worrisome yet was a pattern of poor stability due to a combination of unusually wide beam, light displacement, and a practice of carrying external ballast high in the keel to improve the rating.

John N. Newman and Justin E. Kerwin of MIT proposed a research project aimed at developing new ways to measure and handicap boats. Encouraged by the possibility that older cruising boats could win races again, some American yachtsmen (many of them members of the Cruising Club of America) supported the work that led to the Measurement Handicap System, with its ingenious Velocity Prediction Program (VPP) method of evaluating boats. After taking the lines off the hull with a special instrument, technicians "sailed" it in a computer to simulate the boat's sailing performance on different points of sail in different conditions. Out of this came a set of ratings.

The MHS's initial major test was in the 1978 Bermuda Race, when for the first time there were two fleets. The 162 entries—90 sailing under IOR, 72 under MHS—suffered an unconscionable amount of fluky, shifty, upwind sailing. The first boat to finish was an ultra-light-displacement 67-foot downwind flyer, *Circus Maximus*, that conducted an 890-mile search for breeze and finally found a nice easterly. Though Burt Keenan's Frers-designed Class B *Acadia* took half a day to cover the last 35 miles, she was the seventh boat to finish and won the IOR division.

In the brand-new MHS division, the top two boats were two near-ancient wooden Concordia yawls, Arnie Gay's *Babe* and Dan Strohmeier's second *Malay* (his 1954 race winner had been beaten up in the 1972 storm). When Gay said, "We've set yacht design back 30 years," he was both underestimating—the Concordias were designed in 1938—and oversimplifying. The ten boats that finished first and second in the five MHS classes cut across four decades, from the Concordias to three boats built to the IOR. "It would be hard to find a more diverse group of winners," Kerwin and Newman concluded with satisfaction.

Critics of the MHS claimed the new rule unduly penalized fast boats and, because no other country used it, was sabotaging international competition. Critics of the IOR muttered darkly about death traps. The consensus about the race's identity and goals that had survived many transitions and the debate about professionalism now seemed to be reeling. As Bill Robinson, the race committee's former secretary, observed in *Yachting*, the Bermuda Race had become "a split race with a split personality and a distinct split of opinion on what the future should hold."

The gamble on another rating rule was disorienting, but gradually people became used to a diverse fleet. The challenge was to make the race available to several types of boats and crews without straying from the foundational goal dating back to 1906, which was to encourage amateur sailors to go out in seaworthy cruising-racing boats.

## The Onion Patch Trophy

The founders of the Onion Patch Trophy Series, Shorty Trimingham and Ed Greeff, were especially concerned about the effect of the split fleet on international entries. From a peak of teams from six countries in 1970, Onion Patch Trophy participation was declining, they believed, due to the two rating rules (though others blamed crowded racing schedules and the unsuitability of IOR racing boats to cross oceans).

DeForest Trimingham was a young Bermudian dinghy skipper when he sailed his first Bermuda Race with Briggs Cunningham in *Brilliant* in 1946 and discovered the charms of going to sea. Convinced that "the comradeship of ocean racing is fantastic," he went on to own a series of boats with names like *Whistler of Paget* and *Flirt of Paget*. (Bermudian boats have such long and often elegant names in part to honor their owners' home parishes but also to satisfy an English law requiring every vessel to have a distinctive name). As a brilliant small-boat and ocean racer, as a retailer with a far-flung clientele, and as Bermuda's Minister of Tourism, Trimingham—with his friend Ed Greeff, a New York investment banker—had a broad vision of the Bermuda Race as an important international event. They developed the Onion Patch series and labored hard and long to recruit foreign entries to the race.

MHS had only a small following abroad at that time. The de-emphasis of IOR so frustrated Trimingham that it influenced his decision to resign from the Cruising Club. He exchanged his passion for sailing for photography. Greeff pressed on. After the return of a one-rule race in 1990, the Onion Patch series recovered to something like its old vitality, though with teams representing geographical regions or yacht clubs.

## The Navigator's Lot

At the time the new IOR rating rule was changing boats, the Bermuda Race's foundations were also being shaken by a shift in the role of the navigator.

Bromley Stone takes a sight from *Argyll* in the 1948 race. The sextant was the essential tool of Bermuda Racer navigators from 1906 through 1978. (Lower) In the same race Carleton Mitchell operates an early seagoing radio. (Right) Navigators spent much of their time below making calculations. Here is Ken Davidson in *Bolero*'s simple 1950s-era navigator's station.

## The Navigator

*"The Navigator, crawling from the main hatch like a strange, subterranean animal, created a welcome diversion. With eyes red and bleary from peeking through a sextant all the afternoon, he examined the sky critically and then dove below for his instruments."*

—Edward Streeter

Navigating a Bermuda Race boat before 1974 required exactly the same equipment as in 1906: a sextant, an accurate clock, a speedometer, and some tables. Because many sailors had used a sextant but were out of practice, each race was preceded by a flurry of refresher courses. Before the 1972 race, the Mystic Seaport Planetarium offered programs showing the morning and evening stars that would be visible during the race, and the Corinthians sailing club sponsored a seminar at Larchmont Yacht Club on "The Problems and Techniques of Navigating the Bermuda Race." *Sail* magazine, meanwhile, was sending out a packet of pre-computed sun altitudes.

Two electronic devices were permitted, but they were far from decisive. A radio direction finder had to be within about 40 miles of Bermuda in order to get a compass bearing on one of the island's two beacons, and even then its accuracy could not be relied on. Consolan had much longer range, yet because the transmitter sending signals to onboard receivers was located on Nantucket, the bearings so closely paralleled the rhumb line that a fix with cross bearings could not be plotted without a celestial sight.

As three new long-range electronic systems, Loran-C and Omega (both for maritime use) and Omni (used by aircraft), became less expensive, pressure built to end the race's absolute dependence on sextants. Among the converts was the 1960 Bermuda Race Committee chairman, Fred Adams, who soon after stepping down wrote his successor, Pierre S. du Pont III, "Personally, I think it's a darn good idea for us to make use of the most modern available (and practical) navigational aids." No doubt

Adams was one of many sailors who were still having nightmares about the hair-raising landfall in the 1960 storm.

Yet throughout the 1960s and early seventies, the same Bermuda Race committees that were throwing their considerable prestige behind making boats and crews safer—requiring owners, for example, to install better lifelines, buy life rafts, undergo rigorous inspections, practice crew-overboard rescues, and explain in detail why they had dropped out of previous races—were shooting down every proposal to permit modern instruments. Celestial navigation was too closely identified with good seamanship for them to do otherwise.

The old policy finally gave way in 1973 when James Michael, the Cruising Club's commodore and a lawyer, advised that the ban on up-to-date navigation equipment exposed the CCA to lawsuits. Michael found a sympathetic ear among the navigators who had struggled through the 1972 race with few if any celestial sights. One was Peter Bowker, who had homed *Windward Passage* in on Bermuda by following a cruise ship. Bowker would express the governing principle this way: "I imagine it would be rather difficult explaining to your insurance company that you had wrecked your vessel on Kitchen Shoals because the sailing instructions forbade the use of devices that would have prevented such a mishap."

In 1974 use of Loran-C and Omega was permitted within 50 miles of the start and finish. Neither system was perfect. Signals from Loran transmitters were sometimes non-existent near Bermuda. Omega worked better near the island, but its accuracy depended on keying-in a precise

Nav stations became more crowded until the arrival of the laptop computer with satellite phone connections to the Internet. Electronic charts replaced paper ones.

known point of departure, which meant the instrument had to be kept running throughout the race with its readout taped over until the navigator deemed that the boat was 50 miles from Bermuda.

By 1980 Loran was legal throughout the race. Some experienced navigators were a little sad. "Navigation's a lot easier now," said Edwin Gaynor, who navigated in 22 races beginning in 1960. "With celestial, you were always up there, taking sights. But there was something wholesome about doing the navigation the old way. It was a more challenging thing. But it was slower." And slower was not good for the new kind of racing that was developing.

## The Target Shoot

The navigator's main problem is obvious: find Bermuda. A cumulative uncorrected steering or navigational error of only two degrees either side of the rhumb line of 164 degrees will leave a boat as far as 20 miles off the island—enough to make St. David's Head and Gibbs Hill lights invisible from the deck of a small boat in hazy weather.

Boats missed the island all the time, and all the time crews offered bizarre explanations why. Soon before the start of the initial Bermuda Race in 1906, a shipmaster who had failed to locate Bermuda advised that it had been swallowed up by the volcano on which it sat. After the 1924 race, the owner of a schooner explained why he finished almost a day and a half after the first boat. It seemed he had been winning by such a huge margin that he thought it only sporting to circle around for a while to give the other boats a break. "The rumors of beam and quarter landfalls were as many as the denials were vociferous," Alfred F. Loomis reported after another race.

Bermuda is so small on the chart, one sailor speculated, that a navigator might easily confuse its markings with a fly's turd. On a related subject, Jack Merrill has told a strange story of navigating *Gray Lady* (ex-*Circe*) in the 1960 race. Sitting in the navigator's station with a cup of coffee, he noticed that the lid of an egg carton on the chart table was pulsing. The lid flew open, and out stepped a small bird that proceeded to make a bowel movement on the chart. Merrill was so astonished that he spilled his coffee. As he was mopping up the mess, the owner appeared and asked for a position report. Merrill was far too rattled to say anything except that *Gray Lady* was "somewhere between the bird crap and the coffee stain." (Merrill recalled that the owner "was not particularly pleased.") Merrill later learned that the bird had flown into a sail and bounced on deck, where it was rescued by a thoughtful crewmember who stowed it in the egg carton for a rest cure.

Even without such hazards, navigating in the traditional way could be a trial. The foundation of all navigation is the record of compass courses steered and distances run called the dead reckoning, or DR. Before the Kenyon company came up with the first speedometer in the 1930s

The radio direction finder (seen here on *Cyane*'s cabin in the 1960 race) came into play near Bermuda, but only an unwise navigator depended on it entirely. Note the analog Kenyon instruments and the note reminding helmsmen of the course to the finish.

(some older sailors still say "Kenyon" when they mean "speedometer") distance run and speed were determined by streaming a taffrail log (sometimes called a patent log or Walker log). A spinner was towed astern at the end of a line attached to a calibrated dial mounted on the stern. To figure speed, navigators took log readings at regular intervals and did some short division. The problem with a taffrail log on a Bermuda Race was that the log line was constantly fouled by the dense weed drifting in and near the Gulf Stream. If the on-watch was distracted by sail handling or by cockpit chatter and failed to notice that the log line was not spinning, log entries became guesstimates.

The single most valuable instrument in traditional navigation was the sextant. It made a slave of the navigator. Edward Streeter, the writer who sailed the 1926 Bermuda Race, described the navigator as "crawling from the main hatch like a strange, subterranean animal" and, "With eyes red and bleary from peeking through a sextant all the afternoon, he examined the sky critically and then dove below for his instruments." Returning, the navigator handed a wrist watch or stop watch to the designated timekeeper, took some sights of the sun, a star, or the moon, and—reciting the times and angles of the sights like a mantra in order to hold them in memory—slid back below to compare the time with the chronometer (the boat's holy of holies, stored in a special padded box) and painstakingly calculate the fix using thick printed tables.

That was the routine for the first 70 years of the Bermuda Race, with only a few advances. "When I started out in the 1950s the difference between the normal boats like us and the hotshot boats is that the hotshots had Zenith Transoceanic radios," said one long-time navigator, Larry Glenn. "That was the first transistor radio and it picked up a time tick so you didn't have to depend on a watch or ship's clock that might be wrong. Then quartz crystal watches came along."

The skills and equipment were so important and arcane that navigators were perceived as precise machines. "They are supposed to be scientists whose two-times-two is four," said Chick Larkin, who, with four wins, was the most successful navigator in Bermuda Race history. That perception was wrong, Larkin continued. "In navigation two-times-two is seldom four. Sailing produces an unknown plus or minus factor, especially for eight-knotters eight feet above the sea. Ask any man who has been there." Good navigators covered up these ambiguities with a veneer of brazen confidence. "Before Loran came in, the navigator was like a priest," said Larry Glenn. "People were always asking, 'Where are we?'", and when you blindly put your finger on the chart, they'd believe you and say, 'Ahhh,' in a respectful way." A little authority can go a long way—sometimes too long, as Mitchell Gibbons-Neff (known as Mitch Neff) made clear about the 1976 race, which saw the worst calm ever in the Bermuda Race:

*We sailed with six people in my family's 40-footer,* Prim—*"four Neffs and two refs," we used to call it. In '76 I'm the cook and also the navigator. We sail into the Stream, hit every current wrong, and after 24 hours of staying in the same place I'm getting pretty tired of everybody asking me when we'll reach Bermuda. I'm in the galley cooking corned beef hash and eggs and announcing, "The next guy who asks me how many miles we have to go is going to get it."*

*Well, my older brother is in the head and doesn't hear me. He comes out of the head and says, "How many miles do we. . . ." That's as far as he got before I put a plate of corned beef hash and eggs right in his face. When we finally reach the island, one of my brothers burns up his foul weather gear and seaboots right there on the RBYC lawn.*

Rare tantrums aside, the navigator usually is a bastion of cool confidence even when engaged in the most anxious part of the job, which is the landfall. Henry A. Morss, who won his class in the 1907 and 1908 races, was famous for telling his crews exactly when to go aloft to spot Gibbs Hill Lighthouse. But Bermuda usually does not appear on command. "There was always trouble coming into Bermuda," said Glenn. "In the usual rough water, in a small boat, it was very hard to get star sights so sometimes you just didn't know where you were. Someone would ask you, 'Where are we?' and you'd have to say, 'I don't know,' and then he'd say, 'Well, I'm going to sleep with my feet forward in case we run into the reef.'"

The landfall was the moment of truth. Nick Nicholson, who navigated to Bermuda in 18 Newport or Marion races, wrote in an article in *Practical Sailor* magazine, "All the self-doubts about what you had done for the last three or four days piled up at once: Were my sights accurate? Do I really have a clue? The first time Bermuda popped up in front of the boat approximately when and where it was supposed to be, it was a divine revelation. There was meaning to the universe. The celestial clock was still God's timepiece, and it still ran with eternal perfection."

A landfall could involve the use of many senses, as Ed Greeff recalled:

*We were approaching the island from the north, the wind was about south with heavy squalls, rain, and wind. Visibility at times was zero. We never shortened down, just feathered through. As we were in the vicinity of North Rock and Kitchen Shoals, RDF bearings on Gibbs Hill were not much help—not enough angle. We had to rely on DR and the fathometer. As we stood in to the reefs on the port tack another heavy squall came down on us, the Fathometer went below 20 fathoms, and an almost overpowering smell of flowers hit us. I said, "This is close enough boys, hard alee," and we came over onto the starboard tack to clear the reefs. For a moment there I thought we were in Shorty and Dot Trimingham's garden.*

Such risk-taking may seem appalling, yet there are always people who like living on the edge. George W. Mixter was in middle age and cooking in a boat in the 1926 Bermuda Race when he "caught the germ." He bought his own racing schooner and became a student of navigation. In 1940 he published the first of many editions of his authoritative *Primer of Navigation.* A member of Mixter's crew was a young man from Buffalo, Charles ("Chick") Larkin II. When Mixter's eyes were injured, Larkin became navigator under the expert's tutelage. Larkin went on to navigate four of the eleven race winners between 1946 and 1966, each time winning the George W. Mixter Memorial Trophy. No other navigator has won more than two Mixter trophies.

Given the stakes, the relationship between navigators and their skippers can be a complex one, which is why some skippers prefer to do

# Jim Mertz

One believer in the DR was James M. Mertz, a laconic and to all appearances age-proof individual who navigated boats in 17 Newport-Bermuda Races and sailed in a total of 30 before his death in 2006. "Once, we had a Loran expert on board and didn't keep up the DR. When we got near Bermuda the Loran coverage ended. I learned two things from this experience. Number one, keep up the DR. Number two, don't let the navigator stand watch. It takes a lot of energy to keep up a DR."

Other sailors have navigated more races—Edwin Gaynor did 22, for example—but nobody comes close to Mertz's record of 30 races sailed, or 70 percent of all Bermuda Races. (Ed Greeff held the previous record of either 24 or 25 races—he could not remember which.) Counting eight "cruising" races from Marion, Mertz raced to Bermuda 38 times for a total of almost 25,000 miles, enough to get him around the globe.

Raised as a sextant man, Mertz remained one all his sailing life. "In *Argyll*, which won the 1950 race, I don't remember instruments at all. Bill Moore usually kept an RDF in his cabin, but when I took a close look at it, I discovered it was half full of water from a deck leak." Although Mertz would not turn down the opportunity to exploit Loran and GPS, his old reliable was a Navy-issue Bendix sextant (bought by his wife, Allegra Knapp Mertz, in a surplus store in 1950) that was identical to the one he used on a submarine chaser and a destroyer escort during World War II. In 2005, at the age of 93, with the help of this instrument Mertz skippered and navigated his Beneteau 42, *Allegra*, to third place in the Marion-Bermuda Race's 15-entry group for boats that used only celestial navigation.

Mertz was not after cups. "I've never been very competitive. I just go for the experience. I really don't care how we do in the race. I've even dropped out of a couple of races when it's Wednesday and we're out there slatting around." Where one or two other race veterans might say the best crew is the one that sails fastest, Mertz begged to differ: "The best crew is people you get along with. The trip is shorter if it's a happy boat."

**"I just go for the experience,"**
**Jim Mertz said after sailing**
**in almost three-fourths of all**
**Bermuda Races through**
**2004. He helped win one of**
**them, in *Argyll* in 1950**
**(he's on the side deck, left).**

Built for cruising, *Holger Danske* was sailed hard, found her ideal conditions, and won in 1980. Her victory stirred controversy in the debate over rating rules between traditionalists and grand prix racers.

their own navigating. But Chick Larkin believed in designated hitters. "These are days of specialists," he wrote in 1958. "If you want a navigator's berth, go after it. Don't be the fair-haired boy with the eight-blade jackknife in his pocket." It was more than a full-time job. Sextant sights had to be taken and calculated. The DR had to be kept up. The RDF had to be operated and interpreted. Through all that, someone had to be sharp enough in mind and judgment to recognize which information was garbage and which was a gem.

Good skippers learned to give navigators their due—eventually. Richard du Moulin was the skipper of the Naval Academy's *Rage* in the 1970 race with a German submarine officer navigating. With her chief opponent, *Carina*, comfortably astern, *Rage* was sailing toward the Argus Tower, the turning mark that year. Taking sights on the moon, the navigator warned that the current was setting *Rage* to the east, away from the tower. Nobody was inclined to believe him. "What did a U-boat navigator know about sailboat navigation?" Du Moulin remembered thinking. "But come the dawn, we found ourselves ten miles east of the tower. Meantime *Carina* hit the tower dead on. We crossed paths, she running to the island and we beating to the tower. She won fleet and we finished fifth in fleet—pretty good, but I will never again ignore advice from navigators, even if they come from under-the-sea boats."

## 1980: The Year of the Cruising Boat

The technological revolution came full-time to the Bermuda Race in 1980 when Loran was permitted from start to finish. The initial equipment of choice was the Texas Instruments 9000 Loran-C set, with a $2,100 price tag (the equivalent of more than $5,000 in 2006, and 10 to 12 times the cost of a hand-held GPS device). Over the next 15 years came weather faxes connected to the boat's single-sideband radio, satellite navigation, Global Positioning System navigation, onboard laptop computers programmed with charting software, and satellite phones providing Internet access to weather and Gulf Stream reports.

Old-timers scoffed that navigation had become merely an exercise in pushing buttons. True, what Nick Nicholson called "that little speck of land in the middle of the ocean" was much easier to find. Yet as beam and quarter landfalls became rare, the challenge shifted to what another navigator, Mark Plough, called the "navigational chess game." Among the people who understood the many potential uses of Loran was the skipper of the least-likely winner in the long history of the Bermuda Race. This was 30-year-old Richard Wilson, son of the owner of the wooden, 16-year-old, 43-footer *Holger Danske*. Her story is like a tale spun by Hans Christian Andersen, whose story of a Danish folk hero provided her name. A heavy, long-keel, bluff-bowed cruising ketch, *Holger Danske* was designed in Boston by one Dane, K. Aage Nielsen, and built in Denmark by another, Aage Walsted.

Her only previous Bermuda Race, in 1970, had come up very short thanks to the combination of an unfavorable IOR rating, a flat calm, and a long upwind slog. Giving up on racing, John Wilson put in 50,000 miles of cruising. As Rich Wilson was sailing *Holger Danske* from the Canaries to the West Indies in 1978, he found himself speculating that a boat that sailed so fast might do well under a crew of skilled small-boat racers. At least the boat rated well enough under MHS to be competitive. (As it turned out, MHS was the only rule for the 1980 race. After dozens of boats designed to the IOR had capsized in the 1979 Fastnet Race gale, the race committee eliminated the IOR division.) Wilson upgraded *Danske* with a new Loran set and a digital speedometer, though he retained the old apparent indicator—a windsock that his sister had sewed—and the anemometer—which he called "the traditional, highly calibrated wet finger."

Sure that the crucial factors were pushing hard and steering well, Wilson organized his young crew ("we had one old guy, in his fifties") into three-hour watches balanced between top one-design sailors and veterans of *Holger Danske*'s offshore passages, and designated the most gifted helmsmen to stand 15- to 30-minute tricks at the wheel. As navigator, he tracked each steerer's effectiveness by calling up a set of Loran lines of position that paralleled the rhumb line. If a helmsman tended high or low, it was immediately obvious and he adjusted the course a couple of degrees. When the Loran was not policing the helm, it was guiding him to three X's on the chart that got him into favorable currents that he had been tracking for months with the help of an oceanographer, Jenifer Clark. "As we edged up to the good side of a big warm eddy, we saw a lot of other boats footing off and sailing away from it. 'Well,' I thought, 'all those boats just took themselves right out of the race.'"

Even before then, *Holger Danske* had found her best conditions. After several hours of windward work in a choppy sea, the breeze clocked into the west for a fast reach all the way to Bermuda. I was sailing in another hard-driving, split-rig Class F boat with an imaginative, assiduous navigator. This was David Noyes's 38-foot yawl *Elixir*, with a sleepless Ted Bilkey hovering over the Loran set. After one of the most thrilling races I can remember, we corrected to second place in class and fleet behind *Holger Danske* by a few seconds over five hours. Rich Wilson not only was the youngest winning skipper in the race's history to date, but he had the largest margin of victory since the race's revival in 1923.

His win was not taken kindly in all circles. Many tongues wagged loudly and long about the unfairness of it all: so many new, expensive, aluminum IOR racers whipped by an ancient wooden ketch that (some people preferred to presume) had merely cruised down across the Gulf Stream. Critics seized on the fact that though it was overwhelmingly a reaching race, the time allowances were based on a pre-race prediction

Things got a little out of control after 1982's downwind start in the usual crowded quarters. Spinnakers are set infrequently in Bermuda Races, and rarely right away.

that almost one mile out of five miles would be sailed hard on the wind. (As Lynn Williams, the chairman of the CCA's technical committee, put it, *Holger Danske* "had the benefit of a handicap for her worst sailing condition and sailed the race at her best.") The boat's defenders pointed out that favorable conditions had never *not* been a factor in ocean racing— for example, when *Niña* won in 1962—and that, in any case, *Holger Danske* had beaten several dozen larger boats on elapsed time.

The best and most generous take on the race take came from Burt Keenan, winner of the IOR division in 1978. He came up to Wilson after the race and told him this: "I don't know that you should have beaten us by that much, but you certainly did beat us and you deserved to win, and don't let anybody take anything away from it."

## 1982: Playing the Stream

The next race went back to the two-division, IOR-MHS format, with the Bermuda Trophy going to the boat winning her division by the largest margin. For the second time in the race's history, the start was delayed due to a storm in the Western Atlantic (the first was in 1968). The postponement held for two days amid widespread complaints that Jim McCurdy's race committee was oversensitive to worries about legal liability. The critics were silenced by reports of 70-knot winds, 40-foot seas, and the capsize (with the loss of a crew member) of a cruising boat that had departed Newport for Bermuda the day before the scheduled start.

Once the weather settled down, the 178 starters—matching the peak of 1972—got off the line quickly on a spinnaker reach. The wind gradu-

Marvin Green's maxi *Nirvana* took more than five hours off *Ondine*'s old course record in the 1982 race, averaging 10.2 knots despite carrying a full cruising interior. It appears as though her crew of 20 will soon change jibs.

ally came ahead until, in the middle of day two, the boats in the 45- to 60-foot range were hard on the wind on starboard tack, almost laying Bermuda.

One of those boats was the 48-foot Class C, McCurdy & Rhodes-designed sloop *Carina*, Dick and Richard Nye's 1970 race winner. The on-watch was settling down for a long leg to the finish when Richard Nye poked his head up through the companionway, rubbing sleep from his eyes, and took a look around. Way up to windward, a lightning bolt flashed down to the water.

"Tack," Nye ordered.

The crew looked at him incredulously. Someone told him they were only 10 degrees off the layline to the finish.

"Tack. There's lightning to windward. The Stream's up there." *Carina* tacked away from the layline and sailed away from Bermuda for a couple of hours until she was well into hot water and a three-knot current bound southeast. Nye then tacked back and won the IOR division by a comfortable 34 minutes.

Another boat that forked off from the rhumb line was Bob Morton's 57-foot, Sparkman & Stephens-designed, Class B sloop *Brigadoon III*. Like *Carina*, she was an aluminum boat built in the first year of the IOR, 1969. When *Carina* won the 1970 Bermuda Race in the year of the tower, *Brigadoon* (then named *Equation*) was second. Now in 1982 they were in separate divisions, *Carina* in IOR and *Brigadoon* in MHS. Once again they would finish 1-2.

As *Brigadoon III* sailed fast almost at Bermuda, Morton worried that she was not in the best current. According to the pre-race briefing by Jenifer Wurtha-Clark, the oceanographer who had helped Richard Wilson win in 1980, the Stream was making a hard right turn to the southeast well upwind of *Brigadoon*. In other words, *Brigadoon*'s course paralleled the Stream's. Morton, himself an oceanographer and not one to make seat-of-the-pants decisions, gathered his afterguard. "We huddled over the chart table and thought, 'Why keep heading this way on starboard tack, when if we went on port tack for a couple of hours we would be in the Stream and could tack back onto starboard and have a three-knot push to weather?'"

*Brigadoon* tacked, but nearby boats held on. One was a Class A boat, *Siren*, that owed *Brigadoon* about four hours. The next time Morton saw *Siren*, she was coming into the Royal Bermuda Yacht Club marina where *Brigadoon* was already tied up.

Because boats at that time did not provide position reports, the eager crews of *Carina* and *Brigadoon* were unaware that well ahead of them, Marvin Green's maxi *Nirvana*, with Bermudian Warren Brown as first mate, was on her way to breaking *Ondine*'s elapsed time record by almost five and a half hours. Each crew did know, however, that its 13-year-old boat was sailing fast and in the running for silver.

As *Brigadoon* heaved her way through the fast, rough, close reach to the finish, Morton was in a state of bliss:

> That day we had two rallying cries that came from Geoff Ewensen, with his Australian accent. As we rolled along with Geoff behind the helm he would yell out, "Eight and a quarter to please your daughter!" or "Eight and a half to make you laugh!" Pretty soon everyone who drove that day would be yelling it out and we really kept the boat going all morning and afternoon. That day is something I'll never forget. We were on the verge of achieving something great, that few people experience. It was such a beautiful day; with the blue ocean and the white caps, a great crew all working together, and a fantastic boat that, if she only held together for the next six hours, would fulfill a boyhood dream and win the biggest ocean race in the world. I knew that if we did it, our lives would never be the same, and I still think of that day as what life is all about and how ocean racing reflects the greatest parts of life.

When all the numbers were in, *Brigadoon* won the MHS division by 50 minutes, and *Carina* won IOR by 34 minutes. That 16-minute difference meant the Lighthouse Trophy went to *Brigadoon*.

Dick Nye prepares for the start in 1952 with one of his usual young crews recruited by his son Richard (standing, right). (Opposite) Nye in *Carina* heaven: a good blow, and a cigar.

## The Nyes: Swinging for the Fences

In their eighteenth and last race to the Onion Patch, the father-and-son team of Dick and Richard Nye just missed tying John Alden and Carleton Mitchell for the most wins, three. Over those 18 races, the three *Carina*s finished in the top five in their class nine times, and in the top three—winning trophies—seven times. A .388 batting average for taking home silver over such an extended career is an astonishing record in an event in which most sailors dream of winning even one cup.

The Nyes were accidental sailors. When Dick Nye acquired a company in 1945, along with it came a 40-foot Rhodes cutter. He decided to take a chance on sailing. After two years of cruising, he and his young son decided that racing might be fun and bought their first *Carina*, a Rhodes-designed 46-foot yawl. They finished respectably in their first distance race, from Newport to Annapolis, and won the next one. "My father somehow remembered DeCoursey Fales saying. 'My boy, you've

got to have a good reason not to go to the Long Island shore,' and when the sun came up in the morning, there was *Djinn* right to leeward."

A year later, 1948, they entered their first Bermuda Race with a young crew. "One of the secrets of our success was that my father didn't have friends who were yachtsmen, so we sailed with my contemporaries. We sailed harder than the boats with older crews, especially at night." The old man kept up with the kids, though. One of the most famous anecdotes in the history of ocean racing concerns the second *Carina*, a 53-foot Rhodes centerboard yawl. As she staggered across the finish line at the end of the rough 1957 Fastnet Race with three broken frames, a deck that was threatening to part company from the hull, and most of the crew manning the pumps, Dick Nye shouted, "Okay, boys, you can let her sink." They won that race for their second-straight Fastnet Race victory, and it came on the heels of winning the 1957 transatlantic race to Spain.

The Nyes discovered that while some of the common wisdom worked, much of it was too cautious. Many crews used an upwind strategy known as "the Illingworth ladder" (one of its proponents was the English sailor John Illingworth) that called for tacking up the middle of the course on ever shorter legs as the turning mark or finish line got closer. Richard Nye looked with disdain on the Illingworth ladder. "It's very safe—and it's sure to end you up in the middle of the fleet. We used to swing for the fences quite a bit." Yes indeed. In 1972 *Carina* was drifting along in a race to Spain when Richard heard a radio report indicating more wind to the north. Instead of slowly easing up there he abruptly turned 90 degrees to port, violating the fundamental rule in sailboat racing, which is to sail the most direct course to the next turning mark. "When the other watch came on deck, they were so mad they wouldn't talk to me." Nye sailed north for 23 1/2 hours, found better wind, turned east, and won the race.

Of course, there is nothing new about sailors betting on the weather; sailing by definition is one big wager on the wind. What may be surprising is that the sailors who take the biggest bets often are grizzled, gray-haired characters who have been wringing salt water out of their socks for many decades. After his twelfth Bermuda Race, in 1954, Ed Greeff summarized his navigational choices in the yawl *Windigo* this way: "We took a nine-to-one gamble and went 90 miles east of the [rhumb] line, hoping that for once the weather reports might be correct. After 24 years of this race I should have known better, but I guess we're all gamblers at heart and sometimes come up with pearls." Although Greeff found no pearls (*Windigo* was thirteenth in Class A), there was always another year.

Besides weather, an owner can bet on the boat herself. Though the third *Carina* finished second in her class in 1978, the Nyes went to a yacht designer who specialized in updating existing boats, Scott Kaufman, and had him design a new keel. At 79, Dick Nye was not getting around the boat as spryly as he once had, but with a crew that now included Richard's son and his friends, this rebuilt *Carina* almost won him his third Bermuda Race in 1982.

## 1984: The Misery Rule

One of the fundamental tensions between the two rating rules, the IOR and what became the IMS (after the American Measurement Handicap System went global as the International Measurement System), concerned the extent of the tradeoff between speed on one hand and comfort and seaworthiness on the other. The comfort question took on new meaning in 1984 when 115 boats—the smallest Bermuda Race fleet since 1958—beat almost all the way down to the island. There was plenty of hard going west of the Gulf Stream, but when the boats found the predicted long arm of southbound current the misery only increased. The top boats carried favorable current for 12 to 16 hours not by study-

ing a chart of the Stream or checking the water temperature every 15 minutes, but by gauging the roughness of the ride. As Alex Bruno, the navigator in Jack King's IOR winner *Merrythought*, explained, "You could feel when you were getting out of the southerly flow. The sea would flatten out and the ride would become much more comfortable. That was when you had to get back into it." Whenever the on-watch was lounging about, or the off-watch was getting some sleep, it was time to tack and look for a rougher sea. *Pamir*, a Sparkman & Stephens Swan 48, won IMS the same way and took the overall trophy because her division victory margin was greater than *Merrythought*'s.

In the Frers 51-footer *Toscana*, regular wave-jumping at eight to nine knots brought much water below through deck openings. It spread so far around the typical IOR shallow bilge that the electric bilge pump gave out and my shipmates and I jury-rigged a hand-operated pump from the one used to drain the galley sink. We made it to Bermuda in one piece, but we were still vibrating a day after we reached shore.

## 1986: More Light Air

The debate over rating rules took on added urgency when the Royal Bermuda Yacht Club—eager to attract more foreign boats—told the

Glowing, Don Robinson (standing, right), navigator Frank Bohlen (steering), and the crew of *Puritan* accept congratulations from shore as they approach the dock after winning the IMS division in 1986.

CCA that as of 1986 the Lighthouse Trophy for overall victory would go to the winner of the IOR division. The RBYC also wanted to exempt IOR boats from compliance with special Bermuda Race equipment regulations because they appeared to discourage foreign entries. (Several Americans also felt that these regulations and pre-race inspections were unduly onerous and, because some rules were changed from race to race, confusing.) After months of negotiation, the race committee agreed to award two first prizes of equal merit. Safety regulations remained in place, some in simpler formats.

That debate was much more exciting than the racing. After starting in a near calm, Bob Bell's *Condor* split with the seven other maxis, found a little breeze, and, though averaging just seven knots, was first to finish by a large margin of three hours. The wind finally came up in time to make this a small-boat race and the winners of the two equal Lighthouse Trophies came from the bottommost classes—David H. Clarke's *Silver Star* in IOR Class E, and Donald Robinson's *Puritan* in IMS Class F.

### 1988: Another Kind of Misery

In 1988, when Beven Koeppel's 77-footer *Congere* won both on elapsed and corrected time (in the IOR division), she became the first double victor in 40 years, since *Baruna*'s second win. It was a big-boat race all around, with Charles Robertson's 73-footer *Cannonball* taking the MHS division on corrected time.

In an excruciating upwind drifter—*Congere*'s elapsed time was a full day short of the record—it was good to be in a big boat; *Cannonball* ran her air conditioner much of the race. Lazy boat speeds prevented most boats from following their pre-race strategies of chasing down the favorable wind and eddies shown on the weather and Gulf Stream charts. Robertson and his navigator, Arthur Ellis, concentrated on sailing as fast as they could by trying to match the boat's target speeds—the velocity predictions (VPPs) calculated during IMS measurement. Other boats, like Edwin Gaynor's *Emily*, approached this decisively non-thrash to the Onion Patch as a very long small-boat race, sailing up the middle and keeping moving. *Emily* (designed by Aage Nielsen, who had created *Holger Danske*) won Class E and was third overall in the IMS division.

Another Nielsen design was *Saphaedra*, owned and skippered by Queene Foster four years after she almost lost her thumb in the 1984 race. She was the first woman skipper in the race's history. (Women sailors were no longer rare in the Bermuda Race. Of the 1,600 people in the published crew list before the 1982 race, 70 were women, 40 identified as cooks.) *Saphaedra*'s race was a bore. Over one 37-hour period, she averaged less than three knots.

In Foster's crew was a writer, Doug Logan. His report of the tedious drifting match of 1988 (titled "Stalking the Elusive Onion") ended with a witty and wise benediction recognizing ocean racing's occasional ago-

nies while simultaneously skewering the notion that nature can be outsmarted by VPPs, electronic aids, weather maps, and Gulf Stream charts. "If you think about these things too much," Logan advised, "you can easily get to the point where all you really want around you are a bottle of Jack Daniels, a flannel blanket, and a Chinese acupuncturist. Better to forget about it for a couple of years, then head to Newport and start over."

As usual, many people did just that.

Queene Foster came back from a serious injury to be the race's first woman skipper.

# Two Emergencies

About one out of every two Bermuda Races experiences enough severe weather to remind sailors that what Tom Day romantically referred to as "the smell of the sea" can be accompanied by some risk.

In rough conditions, someone may be heaved across a cabin or cockpit and strain a muscle or break a tooth or a bone. And there is always mal de mer. Among the many known treatments for seasickness, the most outrageous may be the one set out by a veteran Gulf Stream racer, Jack Parkinson, many years before the TransDermScope patch. Writing with utmost seriousness, he claimed that the best way to treat seasick shipmates is to distract them by either threatening physical violence or calling attention in humiliating language to an incipient risk to life and limb. Parkinson predicted that sufferers would be so relieved that they would quickly forgive any insults or slurs.

But only rarely is major medical attention required due to injury or illness. Bermuda Race sailors and organizers prepared themselves for such an eventuality.

## Six Centuries under Water

Following a family tradition, Bob Gunther started racing to Bermuda when he was 13, in 1962, and by the 1980s he was regularly racing down in his own boats. One night during the rough 1984 race his 58-footer *Bagheera* was knocked down by a wind gust just as a sea swept her deck. Under the shock load of these two great forces, the jib sheet block broke at the shackle. Queene Foster was holding on to the lifeline directly above the block, which tore into her left hand, almost severing her thumb. As she was looked after by the boat's medical officer, John Schutz (a former medic in Vietnam), the boat was put about onto the other tack, and, with water flying everywhere, Doug Logan and the rest of the on-watch got to work replacing the block and leading a new jib sheet. Logan picks up the story:

*I landed the job of running the new sheet around the mast and down to leeward. The sprint through the dark went well, and I got down to leeward, clipped my safety harness to something, and got the bowline out of the old sheet without incident. But then began the trial of trying to get the bitter end of the fat sheet through the undersized clew of the number 3 jib.*

*Much of this operation took place underwater, lit by rushing phosphorescence, and I had a welter of thoughts during the six centuries it lasted—how there had been tons of tension on that block, and that Queene might be in real trouble; how inconvenient it would be for the crew if I were to be torn off the boat at that point; and how things can go quickly from fun to unfun.*

*I spent the first couple of centuries trying to push the end of the sheet through the clew. I always sailed offshore with a belt pack that had a knife, marlinspike, and mini locking pliers. The pliers came into their own that night. Pulling the sheet a bit at a time in a circular way for the remaining four centuries finally got the job done.*

Schutz meanwhile was immobilizing Queene Foster's damaged hand and administering painkillers. Since *Bagheera* was already sailing fast toward Bermuda, Gunther decided to keep racing. When the breeze temporarily died the next day, Foster (who was standing her watches and even steering) insisted that they not turn on the motor and power in.

On shore, she was taken to the King Edward VII Memorial Hospital, where a surgeon set two pins in her thumb. Within a few days she was sailing her yawl, and four years later she raced *Saphaedra* to the island with Doug Logan in the crew.

## An Evacuation from *Denali*

One of the most striking boats in the Bermuda Race fleet in the late 1980s was a ketch-rigged 44-footer with her mainmast perched so far forward that she was unable to set a jib, and with a crew so tall they looked like members of a championship basketball team. She was named *Denali* because her owner, Larry Huntington, and his sons Matthew, Stewart, and Christopher, had climbed the Alaskan mountain.

The Huntingtons often raced together, too. Always strong, the Bermuda Race's family tradition was even more pronounced (and successful) in recent races. When we in *Elixir* finished second in the 1980 race, almost half our crew of seven were named Noyes—skipper David Noyes and his sons

David and Bob (navigator Ted Bilkey would soon become their son- and brother-in-law). When *Carina* almost won her third Bermuda Race in 1982, three generations of Nyes were in her crew. That same year seven of the ten sailors in the ketch *Adele* were named Burnes. In 1986, according to a veteran of Bob Stone's *Arcadia* (second place in IMS Class B that year), "Everyone aboard was related to someone else aboard in our 13-member crew, except for Stoney."

As Larry Huntington was going through *Denali*'s medical kit before the 1988 race, he debated whether he should renew the prescription for the antibiotic Methoxin until his wife, Caroline, told him that if the drug was ever needed but not on board, he would never be able to live with himself. Several

weeks later, *Denali* was 250 miles from the finish when 23-year-old Matthew Huntington complained of nausea and began vomiting. A first-aid book indicated it might be appendicitis. Consulting the schedule for the race's required rotating single-side-band radio watch, and also the list of doctors sailing in the race, Huntington found Dr. Peter Stovell on board *Kittiwake*. Stovell diagnosed appendicitis and instructed Larry to inject his son with the Methoxin every four hours. Stovell also urged that Matthew be hospitalized as soon as possible.

The options for evacuation were limited. *Denali* would need over a day to sail to Bermuda. An aerial pickup was a remote possibility. Even if it were safe for someone with abdominal distress, *Denali* would not be within the maximum 100-mile helicopter range from Bermuda for several hours.

That left evacuation by boat. When Huntington called the largest race entry standing radio watch, the 70-footer *Karyatis*, to request a radio relay to shore, her owner, Christos Kritikos, did not hesitate to offer to drop out of the race and carry Matthew to Bermuda. Kritikos joined a long roster of Bermuda Race skippers who offered assistance to vessels in trouble, usually by forwarding a message or by standing by a disabled boat until the arrival of a tow. Among them were Shorty Trimingham, Pierre du Pont, Huey Long (who interrupted *Ondine*'s record run for 16 minutes in 1976), and Emanuel Greene, whose *Circe* stood by a dismasted boat in the 1976 race for nine hours, 55 minutes. The race committee deducted assisting vessels' times on station from their elapsed times (*Circe* ended up second in Class F), but in the case of the generous Christos Kritikos there would be no elapsed time because he was dropping out of the race entirely.

At 0100 *Denali*'s well-padded bow nudged alongside *Karyatis*' after quarter, and Matthew stepped aboard with his brother Stewart. By the time *Denali* tied up at the Royal Bermuda Yacht Club marina late the following afternoon, Matthew had been operated on and was ready to head out and risk much more than his abdomen on a motorbike.

These two boats define the range of a centennial-era Bermuda fleet. *Snow Lion*, a high-tech 50-foot racer, finished fifth in the Racing Division in 2004. At the helm is owner Larry Huntington, with 18 Bermuda Races under his belt (he won in 1990). (Opposite) *Dame of Sark* is a varnished wooden 40-foot Concordia yawl designed in 1938, built in 1961, and owned by Steve Donovan. Fulfilling a lifelong dream, he sailed *Dame of Sark* in the 2002 (start shown here) and 2004 races, finishing twentieth and then second in the Cruising Division. She is also shown on page 3.

# Sporting Character

A typical Bermuda Race is four races in one. After the start, the crew plays the wandering warm eddies west of the Stream and hunts down a favorable meander. Then there is the squally sail through the Stream and among its adjacent cold eddies. After that comes the approach to the island, when the crew tries to predict the next wind shift. The fourth race within the race is the hard press to the finish. The race may be won—or lost—on any of those legs.

## The Always Restless Gulf Stream

"It is the Stream which imparts on the Bermuda Race its sporting character," Alf Loomis observed of the challenges posed by the Gulf Stream. Even today, half a century after detailed observations of the Stream's structure first became available, many competitors may find themselves agreeing with the sailor who wrote in 1903, "The Gulf Stream is something like the sea serpent, in that all of us have seen it, but no one has yet been able to locate it."

For all the doubts about predicting the Stream's location, there are none about its power. Erroll Bruce, the ocean racer and Royal Navy officer, described a gale he encountered there as "one of the most magnificent and frightening spectacles in all the ocean." He went on: "The waves seem too impatient to form into ranks with long crests, instead the sea becomes a mass of separate steep crests, each moving independently, and breaking haphazardly."

That is a classic description of the Stream when a strong wind runs against the current. Yet the Stream can seem threatening even when windless, as Bruce also observed: "On a calm day, without enough breeze to flicker a match flame, the Gulf Stream simmers in irregular patches, some perhaps only 50 yards across. It is always restless, and the first gentle breeze kicks up a sea out of all proportion to the wind force." The Stream has a remarkable ability to breed nasty weather as warm, moist air

rises from its 80-degree water into cold fronts sweeping in from elsewhere. A Gulf Stream squall can seem especially fearsome at night when its clouds (as Tony Gibbs noted) are "reduced to half-seen negatives—places in the sky where there are no stars—except when they are momentarily silhouetted by lightning."

Besides intimidating, the Stream also is perverse. Five hundred years ago, Ponce de Leon and his shipmates discovered "a current such that, although they had great wind, they could not proceed forward, but backward." Those two- to six-knot currents that only sometimes ran straight to the northeast provided cover for navigators; when a voyage or race went poorly, the skipper blamed the navigator, who blamed the erratic Stream. No wonder, then, that cautious Bermuda Race navigators hugged the rhumb line to Bermuda like a lifeline. They obsessed about how far west they should enter the Stream so as to compensate for the easterly set and come out on the rhumb line. Some swore by 30 miles, others by 20. After it was rumored that Carleton Mitchell and *Finisterre* entered the Stream 15 miles west of the rhumb line, navigators drew an "X" there and called it "Mitch's Buoy."

Meanwhile, the Stream's secrets were being uncovered by Henry Stommel, Valentine Worthington, and other oceanographers at the Wood's Hole Oceanographic Institution. As they monitored it with ships, aircraft, and buoys beginning in the 1940s, WHOI researchers learned that the

A midshipman scrambles to shorten sail in a Naval Academy sloop before a black squall hits in the Gulf Stream. (Opposite) As knowledge of the Stream was disseminated, thermometers became standard racing equipment. Illustrations evolved from sketches to satellite images. This one (enhanced by oceanographer Jenifer Clark) shows the 2002 race's alignment of doughnut-shaped eddies and the deep meander, plus the winning boat's route.

Stream is never still. It is, as oceanographer and Bermuda racer Frank Bohlen put it, "thoroughly turbulent and displays significant variability in space and time." It meanders violently, and even turns back on itself. Four of the first nine times that the Stream was tracked at the time of a Bermuda Race, it made a hard right turn in a southerly meander that paralleled the rhumb line. Then came the discovery of eddies pinched off from meanders to form slow-moving, fast-rotating "cold core rings" if south of the Stream, and "warm core rings" if to the north—or, as they were commonly called, "cold eddies" and "warm eddies."

By 1954 Jan Hahn at WHOI was providing navigators a pre-race Gulf Stream briefing and a pamphlet titled *Rules of Thumb for Crossing the Gulf Stream.* The Basic Rule read, "When the water is getting WARMER, you are being set to the left of your course. When the water is getting COLDER, you are beings set to the right of your course." Thermometers joined the list of essential racing equipment. Sailors could not use these theories or even water temperatures with precision because celestial and dead reckoning navigation was

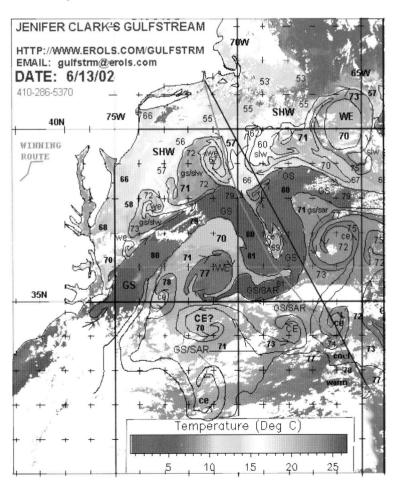

## Alfred F. Loomis

Over some 2,500,000 miles of racing by 4,200 boats and more than 40,000 sailors, there have been countless opportunities not just for winning—and losing—a Bermuda Race, but for advising people how (and how not) to sail it. Everybody has a different theory. This humorous mock pre-race interview between Alf Loomis and a typical race veteran in 1938 reveals the ample room and opportunity for second-guessing.

Question: Do you feel yourself qualified to give any advice about how the race should be sailed?
Answer: Yes and no.

Q: Answer the last part first.
A: I've sailed it wrong so many times I ought to know how to sail it right.

Q: What weather do you expect this year?
A: Average weather, anything from a calm to half a gale.

Q: Ahead, or abaft the beam?
A: Oh, definitely.

Q: Now, with a falling barometer and the wind in the east southeast would you get well to westward of the base line so that you would be sitting pretty when a southwester came in?
A: I didn't last time, but I certainly would this.

Q: With what anticipated result?
A: That the wind would stay where it was and throw me for a loss.

Q: Do you have any opinion concerning the Gulf Stream?
A: I disapprove of it.

## In the Stream

*"On a calm day, without enough breeze to flicker a match flame, the Gulf Stream simmers in irregular patches, some perhaps only 50 yards across. It is always restless, and the first gentle breeze kicks up a sea out of all proportion to the wind force."* —*Erroll Bruce*, Deep Sea Sailing

unreliable. "I can conclude that you can win Bermuda Races by getting into a southward-running meander," Alf Loomis complained in 1952, "but that you have no way of knowing how to get into one or stay there if accidentally in it." He looked forward to the day when precision long-range navigational devices could help him and other navigators exploit the new understanding of the Gulf Stream.

When that day finally came in 1980, the practical effectiveness of the Gulf Stream revolution advanced one very long step. Later came GPS and communications systems linked to an ever-growing library of Gulf Stream and weather data, which the new type of navigators were allowed to use so long as the information was available to all competitors.

## Gulf Stream Guru

When Richard Wilson was preparing to race *Holger Danske* to Bermuda in 1980, he was having no luck finding out about the Gulf Stream because much information then was closely held. Then he found "this amazing young woman deep down in NOAA. "Jenifer knew *everything*. All winter before the race she was faxing me weekly analyses." Though she was not a sailor, Jenifer Clark may well be the most influential figure in the race's recent history.

After studying oceanography at Johns Hopkins, Clark, in her twenties, became an oceanographic features analyst at the National Oceanographic and Atmospheric Administration. As she analyzed images of the Gulf Stream, she became good at predicting currents. When she began conducting the pre-Bermuda Race briefings in 1980, she discovered that sailors were starved for data and for advice about how to exploit the race's crucial feature. She provided both with clarity and personality.

Frustrated by government restrictions, Clark retired from NOAA in

"Taking a risk is what wins most of the time," says Jenifer Clark. Once sailors understood the Stream and had the tools to help them get where they wanted to go, tactical risk-taking came of age.

1995 and, with her husband, a meteorologist, formed a consulting service. In 2004 she was still briefing the fleet, over half of which retained her to provide Gulf Stream interpretation. "I work 15 or 20 hours a day all spring, go up for the briefing, and then go out and watch the start. When I watch them sail away I get the postpartum blues. Later, when people tell me they sailed faster and safer because of what I told them, I have a lovely sense of gratification." Asked to identify the most important thing a sailor should know about the Gulf Stream, Clark's first thought was of safety: "Take your thermometer and take an EPIRB," she said emphatically. "The Stream's all about water temperature, and the Stream's dangerous, especially when the wind is against the current." Only then did she mention racing tactics: "Most crews make the mistake of staying within 30 miles of the rhumb line. But the boats that win *get away*. Taking a risk is what wins the race most of the time."

## 1990: *Denali* Gets Away

Coming into the 1990 race, the forecasters were telling crews not to stray from the rhumb line. That was where the wind, the meander, and the best eddies would be found. But an eddy is no good if a boat can't get to it. Sometimes frustration leads to a fruitful risk.

The early going was a beat to windward in a flimsy south wind—the worst conditions for *Denali*, Larry Huntington's jibless cat ketch that two years earlier had evacuated Huntington's son Matthew. Originally an English Admiral's Cup sloop owned by British Prime Minister Edward Heath, she had been given this extremely unusual rig by Huntington in part because he had seen the wisdom of a second mast when his previous boat was dismasted in the 1982 race, but also because it provided both a low rating and the reaching ability long associated with a schooner. But here she was struggling to climb to windward to get to a meander when a weather fax arrived saying that the meander had moved farther upwind. "That meant more beating for poor old *Denali*," Huntington looked back. "So we decided to tack to port, crack off a little, and foot to the west in search of a wind shift." It was not too wild a wager. At the pre-race briefing that morning, the Royal Bermuda Yacht Club commodore had reported that, while flying up from the island, he had looked down from the plane and seen a good southwesterly.

Huntington's gambler's instincts were well honed by 14 previous Bermuda Races, five of them in *Carina*s with those high-stakes sailors, Dick and Richard Nye. Yet even he had something to learn about taking chances. "We sailed for a while on the port tack but there was no southwest wind, so I said we should tack back to starboard. That's when my son Chris said, '*What are we doing? We're chickening out!*' So we kept going until we were more than 120 miles west of the rhumb line." That was where the southwesterly finally found *Denali*, and she tacked and sprinted to Bermuda while almost everybody else, way to the east, was pounding

# Warren Brown and *War Baby*

"That was the only time I'd been frightened at sea," Warren Brown was saying about a moment in the 1990 race. "I've been worried. I've been nervous. I've been in hurricanes. But that was the only time I've ever been truly frightened."

There had been plenty of opportunity for fear. In the early minutes of the 1958 Bermuda Race the spinnaker got out of control and left Brown dangling aloft from the halyard. Near the finish of the 1960 race, the boat stumbled inside North Rock (the crew somehow extracted her without damage). Coming up to Newport for the start of the 1964 race, his 40-footer *Force 7* was overtaken by a hurricane. Brown later hit a trifecta of great gales: the 1972 Bermuda Race, the 1979 Fastnet Race, and (near New

Zealand) the 1994 Queen's Birthday storm, which knocked his *War Baby* so flat she put her mast in the water.

A Bermudian, Brown called his later boats *War Baby* because that was the name of a champion Bermuda fitted dinghy that Sir Eldon Trimingham built during World War I. The last *War Baby* was the Sparkman & Stephens 61-foot sloop that, as *Dora IV*, had won Class A in the 1974 Bermuda Race and as Ted Turner's *Tenacious* won the 1979 Fastnet. Deciding to sail to the ends of the seas, Brown bought her in 1982, reinforced her bow for ice, and launched a legendary 22-year, 200,000-mile cruising career in the Arctic, the Pacific, and Europe.

The fourth night out from Newport in 1990, in a

35-knot blow, *War Baby* was under three reefs and a small jib when a crewmember's safety harness tether accidentally unhooked and he went over the side. *War Baby* quickly turned back, her searchlight found the reflective tape on the man's foul weather jacket, and three shipmates hauled him on deck. Preparation and good teamwork helped. So did the warm water. Whenever *War Baby* headed out into high latitudes, Brown told his crew, "If you go over— let's say, if you're not hooked on when you come up the companionway—I want you to do one thing. I want you to wave goodbye. And we'll wave goodbye to you, too."

A regular Bermuda Race competitor under three owners, as Bermudian Warren Brown's *War Baby* this Sparkman & Stephens 61-footer compiled an extraordinary cruising resume. She also made a superb rescue of a crew who fell overboard in the rough 1990 race.

upwind through squalls and a steep sea. She won the race by two hours—a huge margin at a time when a ten-minute lead was considered comfortable.

## 1992: The Youngest Winner

An unusually straightforward test of boat speed and pinpoint navigation produced an unusually surprising winner. The winning skipper, at 22, was just two years older than his boat. U.S. Navy Ensign Kyle Weaver commanded the Swan 48 *Constellation*, one of the Naval Academy Sailing Squadron's ocean racers and a sistership to the 1972 overall winner, *Noreyma*, with a crew of young officers and midshipmen. Supervising them was the head of the Academy's sailing program, Commander Chip Barber, who had taught the crew the tactic of sailing the boat to target speeds as laid out in polar diagrams by the IMS's velocity prediction program.

This victory was a boost for the Naval Academy's sailing program. Since 1938, the academy had sent 157 crews on the race as a training exercise and had taken home a few cups. But it had not come close to winning. *Constellation*'s only difficulty was that she spent so much time with her rail down on starboard tack that her water intake (on the starboard side) was clear of the water and the engine could not be run to

Ensign Kyle Weaver commanded the U.S. Naval Academy's *Constellation* when she won the 1992 race with a crew of midshipmen and officers. For almost 60 years American and foreign service academies had been entering boats enthusiastically but with modest success.

charge batteries. She sailed the last miles with no electronics, not even a compass light, and navigated by a battery-powered GPS.

*Constellation* owed her victory to consistently good sailing. At least one other boat did well because two factors went her way. In Tom Josten's *Taniwha*, a New York 40, we were fortunate to sail the first fourteen hours and the last three alongside well-sailed sisterships that pushed us hard—an advantage enjoyed by all one-design classes. And then we had brilliant crew work. On the second night, when black squalls were roaming the Gulf Stream, *Taniwha*'s crew shortened sail and then piled it back on with no hesitation or problem while (as we later learned) some of our competitors were running off before it or even dragging jibs out of the water. Later we suffered a rigging failure and the boat had to be nursed for a while before a jury rig was effected, but we had enough of a lead to finish third in our class and fifteenth in fleet.

## Keeping Everyone Honest

Before the four races within the Bermuda Race, there is a fifth race that takes place on shore—the sprint to qualify for the race and prepare the boat and crew. Warren Brown justified that effort when he compared the Bermuda Race to the Fastnet Race: "As for being rough, if you take the 1979 Fastnet out of it, the Bermuda Race is a more demanding race, year in and year out. But if that storm had hit the CCA fleet, we wouldn't have lost a boat. The qualifications are much tighter than the Fastnet's old come-one-come-all spirit."

Gaining the privilege of sailing in the Bermuda Race can be compared to simultaneously applying for a new job, undergoing army basic training, and submitting to a colonoscopy. After the entry form is submitted, if the race committee has doubts about the boat, it can reject it out of hand. More likely, it requests changes by, say, instructing the owner to sign on a more-experienced afterguard.

Then comes the mandatory pre-race visit by one or more official inspectors. "It used to be amicable, and afterwards, you'd go have lunch with the inspector," recalled Edwin Gaynor, who first raced to Bermuda in 1960, and whose own *Emily* was first inspected in 1978. "It's a more regulatory process now. Rightly so. You've got to keep everybody honest. It's a matter of conscience. You owe it to your crew. Maybe the professionals cut corners, but we're taking our friends and children out there. They're not signing up to sail with you because it's dangerous."

Amicable or not, inspections were always taken seriously. Years ago an inspector tested a boat's lifelines by employing them as a grabrail to haul himself on deck. He ended up flat on his back in the launch, and the boat was excused from the race. When a sistership named *Prim* entered her first Bermuda Race two years later, the forewarned race committee assigned three inspectors to scrutinize the boat. She passed the lifeline test and all the others until water was sprayed on the mast boot, the rubber seal around the mast at deck level, and the inspectors saw that it leaked. "*All* mast boots leak," said Mitch Neff, the son of *Prim*'s owner. "They just had to say something." *Prim* passed the inspection and ended up racing down a record 14 times.

Serious sailors welcome inspections in much the same way a good military commander looks forward to an exercise with blank ammunition. "Inspection is a grand thing. It really forces you to prepare to go to sea," said Kaighn Smith, the 1994 race winner. According to another experienced skipper, Tom Young, "The most impressive thing about my first Bermuda Race as an owner was the inspector. There was a very short list of rules then, but he took the time to go over everything very carefully. He found no problems until he got to the bilge pump. It was in the sail locker, which meant that to use it we had to open the locker, which was open to the bilge. The inspector told me I had to be able to pump without opening the locker, and that meant putting the pump handle up through the seat through a seal." Making the change entailed bother and expense, but Young was extremely grateful for the advice.

He went on to be an inspector and then the race's chief inspector. As he examined a dozen or more boats before every race, he learned how to read an owner. "You got suspicious if the owner seemed less than forthright, or if you learned indirectly that the mast wasn't insured. My successor as chief inspector, Frank Snyder, rejected a well-known Admiral's Cup boat over her mast." The famously scrupulous Snyder made a training video for novice inspectors with Henry Strauss, a filmmaker. Today there are 30 inspectors, all experienced offshore sailors, and all members of the Cruising Club of America (more than 10 percent of whose 1,150 members help with the race in one way or another).

As they worked through an ever longer list of required equipment, inspectors offered advice about nonregulated concerns. Peter Millard, for example, peered into on-deck chain lockers to check if they had drains, frowned on slippery hatch covers, and gave lectures on flimsy buckets ("You don't want your cheap JC Penney car wash bucket").

Inspection did not end in America. After a boat crossed the finish line, a team of Americans and Bermudians came alongside in a powerboat to ask some pointed questions about the boat. If the answers seemed evasive, if the boat had a shaky reputation, or if something looked out of place, the team would climb on board and conduct an on-the-spot inspection. "Loose lifelines so the crew can hike out further—now there's something that we've been known to notice. Some of the owners think we'll go away, but *we will apprehend suspects*," said Jordy Walker, a member of the large team of Bermudians handling details at the race's end, from inspecting and finishing boats to managing immigration and customs. Inspectors may ask a photographer to take a picture to present to the race judges. "We want to be sure the prize winners are really prize winners," Walker continued. "One year we called a boat's paid captain in,

## HOW TO WIN A BERMUDA RACE

### Larry Huntington
(*overall winner*, Denali, *1990*)

*I don't sleep well until I stop thinking about*

*anything that's left undone. Everything you can think*

*about is fair game. If the preparation is as good as you*

*can get it, then your mind's free to think about how you*

*can sail the boat and where you can take the boat.*

*When shortening sail is no longer a safety question, it*

*becomes a boat speed question.*

showed him the photographs, and gave him a 15-minute penalty. He got so mad he put his fist through the wall. We called him back and knocked him back another half hour and reported him to the national sailing authority in the U.S."

Although boat inspection and preparation tend to be conducted under a somber cloud of life-or-death concerns, humor sometimes emerges. Edward du Moulin was examining a sail locker before one Bermuda Race when he noticed a small hole in a sail bag. He dumped out the sail and found a hole in it, too. Soon all the sails were spread out on deck, and all had holes. The sailmaker who patched them up suggested that the boat had become a haven for a rat. With that, the crew's state of alertness increased exponentially. "The first night, when we turned in we could hear scratching in various parts of the shelving," du Moulin reminisced. "At daylight we found that the stowaway had chewed into the cereal containers. We were unable to capture it, and it was still scratching until we arrived back home and exterminators finally took care of the problem. By then the crew had arranged to print up a newspaper headline, '*Xanadu II*'s Rat Races to Bermuda.' Had the rat survived, we planned to propose it for membership in the Storm Trysail Club."

## 1994: An Old Controversy Revives

When the International Measurement System became the race's only rule in 1990, it hardly ended controversy. The issue of professionalism, which had been divisive in the late 1930s, reappeared when some owners hired sailors for racing. The CCA commodore in 1994, Kaighn Smith, made his convictions clear when he stated that "nobody should think they could buy the Lighthouse Trophy." Initially, the 1994 race committee barred professional sailors (with the exception of a tiny class for large racers), but when the U.S. Sailing Association issued new rules distinguishing amateurs from professionals, the race created two divisions—Grand Prix for boats with professional crews or minimal accommodations, and Cruiser/Racer for amateur sailors and dual-purpose boats. The Lighthouse Trophy would go to the top Cruiser/Racer. After the race, an owner won a protest that the conditions were changed too late for him to alter his boat to qualify for the Cruiser/Racer Division, and the results were recalculated with little effect on the original standings.

In 1994 the winner of the Grand Prix Division was a crew of middle-aged amateur sailors in the new Bruce Farr-designed 36-footer, *Conspiracy*, one of the shortest class winners in the race's history. The Lighthouse Trophy was won by a 20-year-old Swan 38, *Gaylark*, owned

Several members of the 2004 race's 30-person organizing committee meet at the Royal Bermuda YC. In the front row (left to right), CCA Commodore Truman Casner, RBYC Commodore Jane Correia, chairman John Winder, and former RBYC Commodores Les Crane and Jordy Walker.

by Kaighn Smith. The first CCA commodore to win the race, Smith was a medical doctor and had been racing *Gaylark* down for years with some success. He rode a Gulf Stream meander for 60 miles into what he called "Happy Valley"—the semitropical region of usually easy breezes between the Stream and Bermuda. Laying Bermuda on starboard tack, he noted a weather forecast calling for the wind to back from southwest to southeast near the island, so he eased sheets and reached to the east until the new breeze arrived. The rest was easy: "Port tack, close reach all the way to St. David's Head and victory." *Gaylark*'s corrected time was almost three and a half hours faster than *Conspiracy*'s.

Professional and amateur divisions were with the race to stay, although beginning in 1996, professional sailors were allowed to make up a certain proportion of the crew of a boat in the Cruiser/Racer Division.

## 1996: Chasing Jason's Fleece

One of the more striking recent developments was the return of maxi boats in large numbers, with eight entries in 1986. Designed to the maximum IOR rating, these 80-footers were sailed by crews of about 25. All boats had cruising accommodations, though some were removed before races. The contrast was noticed by one sailor, Jeremy Gordon Walker, who in 1986 raced down in Marvin Green's *Nirvana*, side-by-side with Bill Koch's *Matador*:

> We retired below in watches to Nirvana's sumptuous teak and holly-floored saloon, to dine on a full roast dinner, piping hot vegetables, and roast potatoes, prepared by our full-time chef in the Dutch-tiled galley. Back on deck, and sitting like ducks on the rail digesting our feast, it was only natural to discuss our gastronomic dinner experience with the Matador crew just across the narrow stretch of water. This camaraderie was met with stony silence as Matador had recently had her equally splendid Huisman-built interior stripped right out, and the crew were subsisting on trail mix, or worse.

Racing against each other several times a year on an international circuit in which owners were required to steer, these maxis were honed to a point where they were often competitive on corrected time with smaller boats. The most consistently successful maxi was George Coumantaros's first *Boomerang*, a blue, aluminum, masthead-rigged Frers sloop that was first to finish three times. No other boat had more elapsed-time victories, and only *Baruna* had as many under one owner. When newer IMS boats caught up, in 1996 Coumantaros built a white carbon-fiber *Boomerang* with a shape optimized for reaching.

"George could have had a boat designed for beating to do well anywhere else in the world," said his long-time watch captain Jeffrey Neuberth, "but he wanted to win the Bermuda Race, and it's usually a

reaching race. The Bermuda Race is closer to George's heart than anything else he did sailing. He started racing down there in 1952 and did every one through 2002. That's 26 races." Coumantaros's first boat was a 52-foot yawl, *Baccarat*, which he bought with his winnings after breaking the bank at Monaco. Later came a 73-footer, *Baccara*, in which Coumantaros, in one simple, noble gesture, made his respect for ocean racing and his competitors clear. After finishing second on elapsed time, *Baccara* towed in the lead boat, *Windward Passage*, which was unable to make speed under power due to engine problems. But as they approached Two Rock Passage, Coumantaros ordered the tow line cast off so that *Passage* could be the first boat into Hamilton Harbor.

After the second *Boomerang* was launched early in 1996, Coumantaros, now 72, and his afterguard spent two months breaking in the boat and her new, mostly amateur crew so she could qualify for the

## HOW TO WIN A BERMUDA RACE

### Peter Bowker

(navigator, first to finish *Windward Passage*, 1970,
winner *Merrythought*, 1974)

1. Ensure that Lady Luck is one of your crew. Use witch-craft. Rubbing chicken bones together with suitable incantations might work.

2. Pick a good boat and ensure you sail with a good crew who know the boat.

3. Ensure the skipper, the watch captains, and the navigator have studied the Gulf Stream satellite photos and have a plan of action before you leave Newport. Negotiating the Stream is of course the crucial part of this race. Get it right and you can be on the prize list. Get it wrong and you're toast!

4. If conditions change during the course of the race, especially when approaching the Stream, don't be afraid to wake people up for a tactical discussion. As a navigator I have had serious qualms when left to my own devices when it came to making strategic and tactical decisions.

Cruiser/Racer Division. Powerful enough to sail in an apparent wind of 40 knots without being reefed, she found her conditions. "That boat was just flying," Neuberth remembered. When she finished at 11:30 Sunday night, she became the first boat to complete a Bermuda Race in a long weekend and broke *Nirvana*'s 1982 record by almost five hours. Most important to her owner, *Boomerang* won on corrected time. When Coumantarous was presented with the Lighthouse Trophy in the award ceremony at Government House, he told the crowd, "We've been like Jason chasing the Golden Fleece.... I'd like to give all who sail for the Lighthouse Trophy some advice: don't despair, keep trying, and if you don't win it by the time you are 75, withdraw."

### 1998: Improvising

The 1998 winner was another experienced captain searching for his first Lighthouse Trophy. In his initial Bermuda Race 30 years earlier, Llwyd Ecclestone sailed into the Gulf Stream under a bright orange sky and was promptly knocked flat by a squall. Undiscouraged, he returned many times. This was his sixth race in his Frers 66-footer *Kodiak*, in which he had cruised widely and which he optimized for this race with a new rudder, a new keel, and a new bottom. Ecclestone and his navigator, Dan Dyer, spent the winter and spring watching the Gulf Stream and developing a race strategy. After the start, the strategy promptly blew up in their faces, leaving *Kodiak* drifting toward the wrong side of a cold eddy. There was nothing to do but head the other way, far to the east. Navigators had come to call that side of the course "the Death Zone" because it had paid off only twice since the 1960s—first in the windiest of all Bermuda Races in 1972, and then in the calmest in 1976. But now in 1998 there did not appear to be an alternative to going left.

*Kodiak* was not the only boat to improvise. "All the forecasts were wrong," Ed Adams, navigator on the maxi *Alexia*, later said, "but we had tools that allowed us to get good satellite images, so we began routing ourselves." Adams became so wrapped up with prognosticating that over the last three and a half days, he spent only three hours on deck ("The rest of the time I was below trying to figure out what to do"). He did poke his head through the hatch long enough to spot a fog bank ahead, which meant that *Alexia* was being sucked into a cell of high pressure and calm. So, like *Kodiak*, *Alexia* sailed east. Thirty miles beyond the rhumb line they both found a northeast breeze that pushed them toward Bermuda while everybody to the west lay almost dead in the water. In the twelfth slowest Bermuda Race in history, *Alexia* was first to finish, and Llwyd Ecclestone got his Lighthouse Trophy.

### 2000: Just Their Luck

There was fog again early in the next race, and a little danger, too, as the 175 boats reached fast off the starting line in a 25-knot southwesterly and a rough sea. The fleet was now extremely diverse, with 13 classes (instead of the old six). Beginning in 1990 the organizers had gradually broadened the race's appeal, first adding classes for cruising boats sailing without spinnakers, and then classes for classic boats, for the popular J-44 class, and for doublehanded boats sailed by a crew of two. These classes used the Americap Rule, a measurement rule built on the Velocity Prediction Program and other foundations of the International Measurement System, but without some of the IMS's complexity and cost.

Less than an hour after starting in the Doublehanded Division, the 54-foot *Strella Encore* was charging along at hull speed when Louis-David Mangin was working his way forward on the leeward deck to clear a line. A wave washed him over the side. As he was towed underwater at nine knots by his safety harness tether, the helmsman (who was his father, Charles-Henri Mangin) adeptly headed off to push the rail under and scoop up his son. They kept racing.

On the first night, with the fog thick, the captain of a fishing boat that happened to be on the rhumb line with his nets out was alarmed to see his radar monitor light up like a Christmas tree. When he went on the radiotelephone's emergency channel to ask what was going on, the Coast Guard instructed him to clear the channel because there was no emergency. To that he replied that it certainly is an emergency when 60 boats are coming out of nowhere. "Not 60 boats, 160," commented one of the sailors who were listening. "Just my luck," answered the fisherman. He turned on his lights and slowly inched across the fleet to safety.

I was in *Kirawan*, the 54-foot Rhodes sloop that, after winning the 1936 race, spent many years on the West Coast before her owner, Sandy Horowitz, undertook a partial restoration and trucked her east to take part in her second Bermuda Race in 64 years in the Classic Division.

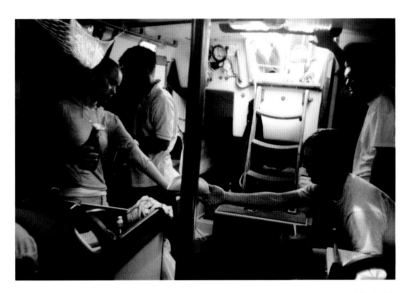

Even in moderate weather, life aboard a hard-driving racing boat at sea like this Naval Academy 44-footer can be uncomfortable, with meals often eaten on the run. (Above) When a seam opened up in the wooden *Kirawan* (the 1936 winner back for another race), Tom Adams went over the side to fill it. (Left) *Kirawan* made it to Bermuda. In a lineup of modern bow shapes, she's the fifth boat from the left, with red sail bag on her bow.

# Trophies

With the proliferation of classes and enthusiasm for the race, ever more tables were required to support the race's trophies. From 35 in 1962, the trophy list grew to 59 in 1976, and 87 in 2004. With trophies named for Thomas Fleming Day, Herbert L. Stone, Alfred F. Loomis, *Malabar*, *Dorade*, *Edlu*, and other major figures and boats of the race's past, these lists offered a compact history lesson. The Argentine Trophy reflected the keen interest that Argentineans have taken in the race since the early 1950s. In 1978 the winner of the IOR division, Burt Keenan's *Acadia*, received a gold representation of the first winner, *Tamerlane*, her bow lifting to a quartz whitecap. More would come. In 2005 Carleton Mitchell donated a *Finisterre* trophy for the Cruiser Division to add to recently dedicated prizes recognizing special accomplishments—for example, the top boats with family crews.

Names on some other trophies were more obscure. For example, there is the Ray Graham Bigelow Memorial Trophy, first presented in 1948 to the winner of Class B and now given to the winner of Class 7. After their beloved former shipmate Graham Bigelow died in 1946 when the schooner he was in was run down by a freighter, his friends donated funds for a perpetual Bermuda Race trophy in his name. Bigelow, who had provided Rod Stephens his first berth to Bermuda, was an able and enjoyable sailor (he wrote the song that began, "Fannies wet all day and night, / *Brilliant* sailing like a kite"). The donors insisted that the prize have a nautical theme, but for one reason or another a perpetual did not exist until the late 1990s, when Stanley Livingston Jr. donated a silver sextant in a box with sterling silver nameplates for the winners.

The overall winner's prize was called the Bermuda Trophy because it was presented by the government of Bermuda. After it was first presented in 1926, it was a silver bowl, although a sterling sil-ver replica of the Gibbs Hill Light was presented in 1946 to *Gesture*. After another three years of bowls, in 1954 Bermuda awarded *Malay* the first St. David's Lighthouse Trophy, which has been awarded in every subsequent Bermuda Race to the overall winner or, beginning in 2002, to the winner of the Cruiser/Racer Division. Since 2002, the top boat in the Racing Division has won the Gibbs Hill Lighthouse Trophy.

In the 1960s there were worries about the safety of perpetual trophies. At least one trophy was dropped overboard during an over-exuberant celebration. When a winner refused to return his trophy before the next race, the race committee retained a private detective to retrieve it. Eventually the race committee decided to take back the perpetuals after they were awarded and keep them in a case at the New York Yacht Club between races.

(Left) This representation of *Tamerlane* was awarded Burt Keenan after his *Acadia* won the IOR division in 1978. (Right) Presented only once, in 1946, the elegant Gibbs Hill Lighthouse Trophy returned to duty in 2002 as first prize in the Racing Division. It and the St. David's Lighthouse Trophy (awarded since 1954, and now going to the winner of the Cruiser/Racer Division) are keeper prizes presented by the Government of Bermuda.

She made 400 miles in the first 48 hours before a seam opened up on the windward side. Tom Adams got into a bosun's sling, was lowered by a halyard over the side, and, steadied by guy lines, moved fore and aft, squeezing polysulfide sealant into the seam. (For this feat, Adams was later awarded the Cruising Club of America's first Rod Stephens Seamanship Trophy.) With our collective foot off the pedal, we sailed into an immense parking lot around Bermuda. On the last night I counted 50 sets of running lights.

Although *Kirawan* lost her 30-mile lead on her classmates, it was a triumphant race for the late Phil Rhodes. The overall winner was Eric Crawford's Rhodes fiberglass 41-footer *Restless*, which had held high to the east, while second place was taken by a tiller-steered, wooden Rhodes sloop built in 1930. This was Carvel Tefft's 43-footer *Bangalore*, which had been racing against modern boats for ten years and was thoroughly updated with Kevlar sails.

## 2002: No Happy Valley

There was no great surprise that *Zaraffa*, a 66-foot Reichel Pugh sloop owned by Huntington Sheldon, won the St. David's Light Trophy for the Cruiser/Racer Division, and that Bob and Farley Towse's *Blue Yankee* took the new Gibbs Hill Trophy for the Racing Division. Both boats had been doing well for years. The big news was the astonishing sailing conditions that vanquished all thoughts of Happy Valley. The wildest ride since 1972 opened with a cold northeaster pushing the record fleet of 182 at high speeds under control. In the Stream the usual lines of squalls were punctuated by waterspouts, and the seaway was incredibly confused. Sheldon's crew credited their victory in part to their good luck at sailing through the worst of it in daylight, when they were able to pick their way around the worst waves.

Already rough, the conditions only deteriorated. Thanks to a perfect alignment of a warm eddy, a deep meander, and then a large cold eddy, the fleet found itself in a powerful, 400-mile-long arm of four- to six-knot southbound current. When the northeast wind gave way to a 25- to 30-knot southwesterly blowing right into the teeth of this phenomenon, the sea was of the sort that Erroll Bruce referred to as "a mass of separate steep crests, each moving independently, and breaking haphazardly."

Despite the appalling conditions there was little damage. The one broken rudder and one dismasting are testimony to the skills of modern boatbuilders and also to the caution of sailors, who nursed their boats through the chaos. One boat that took it easy for a while was the 75-foot "turbomaxi" *Pyewacket*, a Transpac Race record-holder that Roy Disney had brought east for this Bermuda Race. In the worst going she jogged along at a mere eight knots under deeply reefed mainsail and with no headsail up. She suffered no damage, but there was great discomfort. "You would not have wanted to be on the boat," Disney somberly

## HOW TO WIN A BERMUDA RACE

### Stan Honey
(navigator, first-to-finish *Pyewacket*, 2002)

*My impression of the Bermuda Race is that an analytical approach to course selection can work pretty well. I think this is because the Stream is such a large influence on tactics in that race, and the forecasts of the Stream tend to be far more dependable than weather forecasts. This is because the Stream location and direction change slowly and relatively predictably. So for the Bermuda Race, the optimum route that you can compute from accurate polars, forecasts of the Stream, and weather forecasts often turns out to be a pretty good choice.*

The 70-footer *Trader* lost her mast when a huge wave pitchpoled her in the 2002 race.

informed journalists after the finish. He and his crew had fought not only the extraordinarily rough conditions but also the flu, which had come aboard with a sailor and quickly became a contagion. "We had people throwing up throughout the race, even when we were powering to the dock after the race," said Disney's right-hand man, Robbie Haines. "Family members waiting for us said they have never seen such a sick group."

Still, *Pyewacket* was first to finish. Averaging 11.8 knots, she shattered *Boomerang's* six-year-old elapsed time record by almost four hours, at 53 hours, 39 minutes. When *Highland Light* set a new course record of 71 hours, 35 minutes in 1932, people marveled that a sailboat could reach Bermuda in less than three days. Now the race was within sniping distance of two days. Second behind *Pyewacket* (and also breaking the old record) was *Boomerang*. In his last Bermuda Race, George Coumantaros was attempting to win the new Gibbs Hill Light Trophy for the Racing Class to put alongside the St. David's Light Trophy she had won in the Cruiser/Racer Division in 1996. She led *Pyewacket* handily until her mast was damaged while she was being reefed.

This race had several scares. It was known for a fact that four men went over the side of three boats in the Racing Division (including *Boomerang*). None had secured themselves to the boat with safety harnesses. All were back on board within minutes; the crews gave credit to the race requirement for a crewoverboard drill. Besides those four accidents, the race committee had information about another five crewoverboard accidents, all of which also had happy endings.

The only known major injury occurred when a block exploded near the face of Dave Frazer, in *Clover*, gashing his mouth and knocking out teeth. As a shipmate who was a state trooper stabilized the wound, the emergency procedures that had been planned by the race organizers sprang into action. The race had a communications boat, *Geronimo* (on charter from St. George's School), but thanks to satellite telephones and a list of doctors that had been distributed before the race, *Clover* was soon talking to a doctor at Beth Israel Deaconess Medical Center in Boston. The treatment he prescribed included placing tea bags in Frazer's mouth to soak up fluids and coagulate the blood. After discussion with the race's crisis management coordinator in Newport about a possible evacuation, Frazer decided to stay with the boat. For three days he made do with a Gatorade diet and declined to take painkillers out of fear they would make him seasick. After Immigration and Customs gave *Clover* special express clearance, Frazer was raced to King Edward VII Hospital.

## Doublehanding It

The two-person crews in the Doublehanded Division survived the hard 2002 race well. The winners were two sailors in their late fifties, Richard du Moulin and Peter Rugg, in du Moulin's 37-footer *Lora Ann*.

# HOW TO WIN A BERMUDA RACE

## Richard du Moulin
(winner Doublehanded Division, *Lora Ann, 2002, 2004*)

*Especially in a smaller boat, you've got to go into it in a way that will optimize the current. You have to throw away the "sail the favored tack" way of thinking. You've got to be willing to make radical deviations of course so you can sail from doughnut to doughnut, from cold eddy to cold eddy. If another boat seems to be doing better than she should, she must be in better current. In 2002 we looked around and found ourselves in weak current, and so we very painfully squared the spinnaker pole and ran off for an hour. If we hadn't, we would have missed 15 hours of four-knot favorable current.*

Introduced in 1994, doublehanded racing is safer than singlehanded because someone is always on deck. It harkens back to a simpler time of small crews, before many boats were packed with large sailors in large numbers who spend much of a Bermuda Race perched on the windward rail as live ballast.

"On any fully crewed boat there is a lot of excess rail-meat time," said Rugg. "I love the fact that doublehanding is non-stop adrenalin. Everything can be done singlehanded with an autopilot and with planning, and takes just a shade more time than a full crew. I get about one hour's sleep every six hours or so, and I split the rest of the time about evenly on deck sailing and below doing chores." Two years later du Moulin and Chris Reyling edged out Hewitt Gaynor and Jay Raymond's *Mireille* by a little over three minutes on corrected time.

## 2004: The Core Constituency

With all its miseries, at least the 2002 race was straightforward. Not so the 2004 race, with its mess of flaky winds and tricky currents. "It was an intensely tactical race," said Gibbs Hill Light Trophy winner Roger Sturgeon. "It is all about good preparation, clever sailing, sharp use of the wind, and sharp use of the Gulf Stream." In the midst of the tactical decisions, most of the larger boats had to make a difficult nighttime jibe in 30 knots of wind in the middle of the Stream in order to catch the best of a favorable meander—and not everybody got through the jibe without damage. The pattern among winners since 1990 had been one of veteran skippers, usually in older boats. This year the winners were very new boats with rookie skippers. Roger Sturgeon was sailing his first-ever Bermuda Race in *Rosebud*, a Transpac 52, pushed hard by three sister

The three MaxZ 86 Class boats with canting keels or water ballast reach away from the startling line in 2004. *Pyewacket* and *Windquest* bracket the eventual winner, *Morning Glory*, which reached Bermuda in slightly over two days. Because this was a Demonstration Division, it was not an official record.

"The Bermuda Race is first and foremost a yacht race and not a navigational exercise."

—Peter Bowker

Joe Dockery's *Carrera* (left), George David's *Idler*, and Eric Swenson's *Toscana* before things got nasty in 2002. "The night in the long meander was some of the most brutal sailing I've done," said *Idler's* Tony Bessinger. "Full main, number 4 jib, 16 to 18 knots over the bottom. Bill Newkirk, trimming main, disappeared every few minutes under a wall of water."

As the classes get away from Newport, the boats look for clear air and begin to act on their pre-race strategy—whether holding high or driving off. If lucky, a crew finds a sistership to match up against. (Opposite) All hands ride the rail throughout the first afternoon, and then as the evening chill begins to set in, half of them go below to eat, the watches are set, and the seagoing routine begins.

ships. The winner of the St. David's Light Trophy, Dominick Porco, in the Swan 45 *Alliance*, was in only his third Bermuda Race and his first as owner.

Up front were three 86-footers sailing in a special Demonstration Division and not eligible for regular prizes. Much larger and faster than the usual maxis, they had radical stability systems not allowed the other boats—in one case water ballast, in the others keels that were canted to windward by hydraulic systems to provide tremendous leverage against immense sails. Despite generally mild weather, the cant-keeler *Morning Glory*, owned by Hasso Plattner, almost broke the two-day mark, beating Roy Disney's new cant-keeler *Pyewacket* to the finish in an elapsed time of 48 hours, 31 minutes. While this astonishing time was recognized by the World Speed Sailing Council as a new record for the Newport-Bermuda run, it was not an official Bermuda Race record.

This was not the first time a special division had been established to provide diversity and stimulate publicity. In the late 1920s, one class was established for Harry Pidgeon and other long-distance cruisers in small boats, and another was set up for very large schooners. More recently, about a dozen mostly professional crews had been competing in the IMS Racing Division. Though small, the Racing Division was important enough to be granted its own Lighthouse Trophy as of 2002.

These decisions evolved from ongoing debate about the Bermuda Race's central identity in a time of increasing diversity in sailboat racing. John Winder, the race chairman for 2002 and 2004, was one of those who believed that the race would stand or fall on the degree to which it satisfied new constituencies (doublehanders, professional sailors in cutting-edge boats, and so on) while continuing to emphasize and satisfy what he called "the core constituency"—the race's historic majority of amateur sailors in normal dual-purpose, cruising-racing boats. Kaighn Smith, a CCA commodore and the winner of the 1994 race, spoke for them when he said that the purpose of the race was "to allow cruising boats to race to Bermuda as racing boats."

Other long-distance races had neglected their traditional core constituencies by emphasizing one subgroup or another, usually the fastest boats, and had proceeded to see entries drop. This in fact had occurred in the Bermuda's Race's early history, when after the initial amateur, small-boat race, Thomas Fleming Day had been persuaded to allow in very large, professionally crewed boats and then watched the race dissolve after five runnings.

"We have held on to being a wholesome, offshore-oriented fleet," Winder said. By that he also meant an amateur fleet. Of the 338 entries in 2002 and 2004, only 22 sailed in the Racing Division for boats with professional crews, while 232 were in the Cruiser/Racer Division, where limits on professional sailors were so strict there was talk of naming it the "Corinthian Division." "We have gone further than most event

With their crews in safety harnesses and inflatable life jackets, *Titan XI* duels *Blue Yankee*, winner of the 2002 Gibbs Hill Lighthouse Trophy.

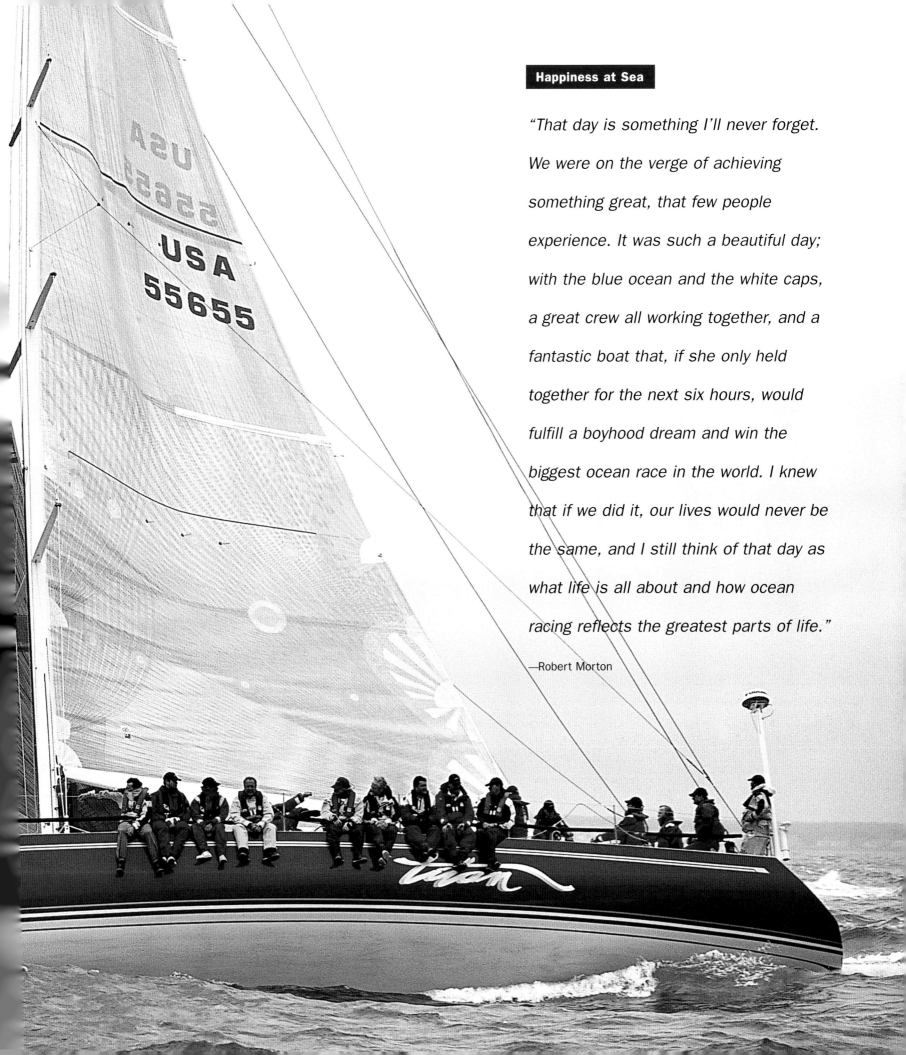

## Happiness at Sea

*"That day is something I'll never forget. We were on the verge of achieving something great, that few people experience. It was such a beautiful day; with the blue ocean and the white caps, a great crew all working together, and a fantastic boat that, if she only held together for the next six hours, would fulfill a boyhood dream and win the biggest ocean race in the world. I knew that if we did it, our lives would never be the same, and I still think of that day as what life is all about and how ocean racing reflects the greatest parts of life."*

—Robert Morton

In the excitement of the early hours, pumping adrenalin can make everybody a little too eager. Here the crew of *Actaea* seems to be scrambling to change jibs.

organizers in marking the delineation between the two, amateurs and professionals," Winder said. Besides encouraging cruising sailors to participate, the system was meant also to block trophy-hunters from leaping into a vulnerable division in which they have an advantage due either to unusually high speed or to an unusually low rating. "The goal," Winder explained, "is to keep the fox out of the henhouse and the hens out of the fox's den." The lesson learned from 2004, Winder said, was this: "Once again, the protection of a particular constituency has allowed for a rekindling of a fleet."

The Demonstration Division boats did not complain. "The race organization was flawless, as in 2002, and it was fun participating in the

East Coast version of the Transpac," Robbie Haines, *Pyewacket*'s sailing master, said. "Both the Transpac and the Bermuda Race are so historic that we liked to be in them both." (The first race to Hawaii started 16 days after the first Bermuda Race in 1906.)

Some critics wondered how something that used to be so simple had become so multifaceted. Yet the race organizers believed that they had to keep trying new things. "Having the involvement of Grand Prix racing boats is integral to the race," Bill Barton, Winder's successor as race chairman, said early in 2006. One motivation, he said, was to keep the sailing industry involved in the race so it would press race organizers to stay in touch with current developments. Barton pointed out that the race was created by one leading sailing magazine's publisher, Thomas Fleming Day, and revived by another, Herbert L. Stone.

At the time he made these observations, Barton and his committee were preparing to include two major rules in the race, the Offshore Racing Rule (ORR), a development of the intensely scientific IMS via Americap) and a simpler rule called the IRC, whose ratings were set in part by an anonymous committee. Barton knew that there was an inherent tension, but he believed the tension was creative:

*The challenge is to keep the core group of amateurs as the main focus while listening to what is happening at the leading edge of the sport. It is*

*clear that without the Bermuda Race and its leadership and role in race development, the landscape of racing for 100 years would have been very different. That landscape will always be changing. For example, the race has been a testing ground for rating rules and a proving ground for safety over the past century.*

*The bottom line is that both the Royal Bermuda Yacht Club and the Cruising Club of America contribute to making the Newport-Bermuda a world-class ocean race that the amateur sailor wants to return to time and again, with the opportunity to set sail, traverse the Stream, engage the competition, and cross the line at St. David's. Then you know you have competed at the top of your sport.*

# *Emily* and Edwin Gaynor

**E**dwin Gaynor and his sloop *Emily* exemplify what John Winder called the core constituency and the ways in which it has changed over the past quarter century.

After seven berths to Bermuda in other sailors' boats, and much cruising in his 28-foot ketch, in 1976 Gaynor, a manufacturer of lighting fixtures, built an aluminum Aage Nielsen-designed 44-foot sloop, *Emily*—home port Southport, Connecticut—for cruising and some racing.

*I thought I'd like to race down, and Betty, my wife, was all for it. She's sailed back with me 14 times. The crew was a bunch of very, very good friends from around here, and we had a lot of lovely meals out there,*

*with a candle on the cabin table, and wine. We didn't sail on a fine edge, like now, when everything you do has to be perfect. That gradually changed when some of the older fellows dropped out and new blood came in. We stepped it up a bit when my son, Hewitt, came aboard with his friends. They were tough guys, and Hewitt has great sea sense. In 1988, he made a decision a couple of days out and we won our class and were third overall. Since then Hewitt's*

*bought a J-120,* Mireille, *and races double-handed. He's doing his thing well, and Emily's still out there doing pretty well, too.*

What is probably the first family team in Bermuda Race history did much better than pretty well. In the 2004 Bermuda Race, *Emily* came within six minutes of winning a Lighthouse Trophy when she finished second in the Cruiser/Racer Division, and *Mireille* was runner-up in the Doublehanded Division by half that margin.

**"Doing pretty well,"** *Emily* **foots her way toward Bermuda. As of 2004 (when she finished second overall), she had sailed 14 Bermuda Races, tying the record for a single boat set by the Gibbons-Neff family's** *Prim.*

## A Bit of an Intrusion

Over the years, the notion has gotten about that the Bermuda Race never changes. Some people liked to believe that on the third Friday of June in every even-numbered year, the same 2,000 men and women gather at Newport for a few parties, crowd into 175 boats, and proceed at greatest possible speed across the Gulf Stream to Bermuda, where the festivities resume. The fact is that the race was constantly being refreshed. One-fourth of the skippers in 2002 were sailing their first Bermuda Race (while just one-tenth had sailed more than ten races), and the two winners in 2004 were both rookie skippers.

One of the many novice crewmembers in 2004 was Sir John Vereker, Governor and Commander in Chief of Bermuda, on appointment by the Queen to a position that dates back to 1609. Because every Bermuda Race ends in Bermuda— and because he so well articulates the race's historic appeal—it is right to end this book about Bermuda racers with him.

An engaging 60-year-old Englishman with long experience in banking and international development, Sir John had been raised around small boats on an estuary in Cornwall. After taking his post in 2002, His Excellency—or "H. E." as Bermudians respectfully referred to him— expressed interest in sailing the race. Word was passed around by the Royal Bermuda Yacht Club's flag officers (including Jane Correia, the first woman commodore at either the club or the Cruising Club of America). Such proposals are usually answered by a friendly suggestion to sail a delivery first. But Sir John wanted to *race*. The only other time a governor of Bermuda had taken part in the Ocean Race, it was 1960

Jane Correia, Commodore of the Royal Bermuda Yacht Club from 2004-06, was a long-time race volunteer and the first woman flag officer of either of the sponsoring clubs.

and the boat he sailed in was dismasted. The possibility that H. E. was a Jonah did not occur to Colin Couper, a Bermudian and the owner of the Swan 46 *Babe*. After gaining the approval of his afterguard, he asked Sir John to join his crew.

Any official anxiety concerning the governor's safety was eased by Couper's credentials. He was an orthopedic surgeon who had first crossed the Gulf Stream at age 16, survived a hurricane with Warren Brown in *Force 7*, and raced so often to his home island that, when asked about the details, in the manner of many Bermuda Race veterans he threw up his hands and declared, "They *all* run together in my mind."

Like most members of the race's core constituency, Couper was a seaman first, then a racer. "My philosophy is, number one, be safe; number two, have fun; then number three, try to win," he said. "I love the camaraderie in the cockpit. Most of my crew are my close personal friends, and if anyone has a serious crack in his personality, it was discovered long ago. We have shared some wonderful experiences. One dawn, when we were getting our first glimpse of the loom of Gibbs Hill Light, we were suddenly surrounded by 200 dolphins. I remember that one of them was leaping unusually high. I'm an atheist, but I admit those dolphins tested me."

Couper's romance ended at the shoreline, however. Asked if it is true that a Bermuda landfall can be made with the assistance of sweet-smelling oleander, he snapped, "*absolute garbage!*"

As the junior member of *Babe*'s crew, Sir John Vereker fit in nicely during the four-and-a-half-day race. "He got along beautifully with everybody, and he related especially well with the young guys," Couper said later. Sir John's memory of his first berth to Bermuda was just as pleasant. He had the qualities of a natural-born ocean racer. "I quickly discovered I was not claustrophobic, not agoraphobic, and not seasick, once I took my pills." He also was resilient, remaining unfazed when the alternator failed and *Babe* finished with jury-rigged navigation and compass lights. Add to those aptitudes the ability to keep competition in perspective; he showed no distress that *Babe* finished in the middle of her class.

He also had something that we have seen on every page of this book, which is the instinctive, deep, and abiding love of the sea and boats that has carried five generations of sailors through gales and calms to St. David's Head. Thomas Fleming Day was thinking of such an individual when he said, on the eve of the first Bermuda Race, "Sailors wanted to get a smell of the sea and forget for the time being that there is such a thing as God's green earth in the universe."

John Vereker said it in his own way: "It's hard not to understand the bond with the sea when you go out on it in a small boat. It made me feel *very English* to sail the race. I loved the vastness. It was just wonderful to be out there for so long under the stars in the Milky Way."

He paused. "When we neared the finish, and the other masthead lights appeared, I actually felt it was a bit of an intrusion."

Sir John Vereker (right) and Jesse DeCouto on *Babe* at the end of the 2004 race.

# Appendix 1: Commodores and Race Chairmen, 1906-2006

**Royal Bermuda Yacht Club Commodores, 1906-Present**

1906, The Honorable Ambrose Gosling

1907-11, Dr. Dudley C. Trott

1912-18, E. W. Gosling

1919, His Excellency Sir James Willcox

1920, Dr. Dudley C. Trott

1921-22, R. Darrell

1923-24, E. H. Trimingham

1925-26, E. C. Gosling

1927, Dr. E. E. Walker

1928-29, K. F. Trimingham

1930-31, Dr. C. B. Wainwright

1932-33, A. T. Gosling

1934-35, H. D. Butterfield Jr.

1936-37, N. B. Dill

1938-39, J. E. Pearman

1940-41, W. D. Wadson

1942-43, B. W. Walker

1944, E. V. Frith and B. T. Gosling

1945, B. T. Gosling

1946-47, Owen P. Darrell

1948-49, Cdr. G. Ridgway, R.N.

1950-51, C. Vail Zuill

1952-53, de Forest Trimingham

1954-55, J. H. Masters

1956-57, H. M. Cooper

1958-59, W. T. Wilson

1960-61, K. Fenton Trimingham Jr.

1962-63, E. M. Cooper

1964-65, E. L. Gibbons

1966-67, L. Vorley

1968-69, S. C. A. Greet

1970-71, H. C. E. Masters

1972-73, E. K. Cooper

1974-75, W. N. Conyers

1976-77, N. B. Dill Jr

1978-79, G. W. Young

1980-81, P. N. Cooper

1982-83, C. N. A. Butterfield Jr.

1984-85, Reid T. Young

1986-87, Douglas F. Fetigan

1988-89, Richard W. Kempe

1990-91, B. W. Walker

1992-93, E. John Thompson

1994-95, Brian W. Billings

1996-97, Thomas E. C. Miller

1998-99, Bruce D. Lines

2000-01, P. Somers Cooper

2002-03, P. Leslie Crane

2004-05, Jane Correia

2006-07, Andrew Cox

**Cruising Club of America Commodores**

1922, William Washburn Nutting
1923, Herbert L. Stone
1924, Martin S. Kattenhorn
1925, Robert N. Bavier
1926, Stuyvesant Wainwright
1927, Martin S. Kattenhorn
1928, George P. P. Bonnell
1929, Edward Crabbe
1930, Daniel Bacon
1931-32, Alexander W. Moffat
1933-34, Hobart Ford
1935-36, George E. Roosevelt
1937, George A. Cutter
1938, George N. Wallace
1939-40, John B. Lord
1941-42, Alfred B. Stanford
1943-44, Hobart Ford
1945-46, Ernest Ratsey
1947-48, Thorvald S. Ross
1949-50, Roderick Stephens Jr.
1951, George H. Richard
1952-53, G. W. Blunt White
1954, Harrison G. Reynolds
1955-56, Harvey Conover
1957, Ralph E. Case
1958-59, Henry B. duPont
1960-61, Prescott B. Huntington
1962-63, Robert M. Love
1964-65, Robert L. Hall
1966-67, Fred Adams

1968-69, Clayton Ewing
1970-71, Alan C. Bemis
1972-73, James Michael
1974-75, Richard S. Nye
1976-77, Stanley Livingston Jr.
1978-79, Peter H. Comstock
1980-81, Richard C. McCurdy
1982-83, Charles L. Ill
1984-85, William B. White
1986-87, James A. McCurdy
1988-89, Walter N. Rothschild Jr.
1990-91, Avery Seaman
1992-93, John L. Merrill Jr.
1994-95, Dr. Kaighn Smith
1996-97, Robert E. Drew
1998-99, James C. Pitney
2000-01, James Harvie
2002-03, William E. Whitney
2004-05, Truman S. Casner
2006-07, Edward S. Rowland

**Bermuda Race Chairmen**

1906-07, Thomas Fleming Day
1908, Henry A. Morss
1909-10, Thomas Fleming Day
1923-26, Herbert L. Stone
1928-30, Edwin H. Tucker
1932, Everett Morss Jr.
1934-38, Herbert L. Stone
1946, Harvey Conover
1948-50, G. W. Blunt White
1952, Ernest Ratsey
1954, Walter H. Wheeler Jr.
1956, Henry B. duPont
1958, Daniel D. Strohmeier
1960, Fred Adams
1962, Pierre S. du Pont III
1964, Thomas J. Watson Jr.
1966, Peter H. Comstock
1968, Sydney H. Rogers
1970, Walter T. Flower
1972, Richard B. Nye
1974, Harman Hawkins
1976, Vincent J. Monte-Sano
1978, Jack M. Brown
1980, Vincent J. Monte-Sano
1982, James A. McCurdy
1984, James B. Grant
1986, Avery Seaman
1988, Robert W. Hubner
1990-92 B. Devereux Barker III
1994, Daniel P. Dyer III
1996, Thomas Hazlehurst
1998, Nicholas Schaus
2000, Ronald C. Trossbach
2002-04, John S. Winder
2006, William R. Barton

# Appendix 2: Bermuda Race Facts and Trivia

## Basic Facts

The Bermuda Race is the oldest ocean race for amateur sailors in normal boats, the oldest regularly scheduled ocean race, and the first ocean race sailed on time allowance.

Organizers—The race was founded by Thomas Fleming Day and *The Rudder* magazine in 1906. After a period of inactivity from 1911 to 1922, it was revived in 1923 by Herbert L. Stone and *Yachting* magazine. Since 1926 it has been run by the Cruising Club of America and the Royal Bermuda Yacht Club (which has managed the finish since 1906).

Start locations and course length—Brooklyn, NY, 668 nautical miles (1906-07, 1908-10); Marblehead, MA, 675 miles (1908); New London, CT, 660 miles (1923-30, 1934); Montauk, NY, 628 miles (1932); Newport, RI, 635 miles (1936-2004).

The Bermuda Race is called "the thrash to the Onion Patch" because most races include some close-hauled sailing in rough water (what sailors call "a hard thrash"); and until the twentieth century Bermuda was an agricultural island where large onions thrived (Bermudians sometimes refer to themselves as "Onions").

Total races—44.

Total entries—4,205 boats with approximately 42,000 sailors.

Total miles sailed (approx.)—2,600,000.

Largest fleet—182 (2002).

Smallest fleet—two (1910).

Tragedies—Lives lost: one, in a fire on the schooner *Adriana*, 1932 (another ten sailors were saved from *Adriana* by a competitor, *Jolie Brise*). Boats lost: two (*Adriana*, 1932, and *Elda*, 1956, when she ran up on Bermuda's reef).

First Bermuda Race—May 1906, Brooklyn to Bermuda. One division, three starters between 28 and 40 feet in length. Winner (Sir Thomas Lipton Trophy), *Tamerlane*, 38-foot yawl owned by Franklin Maier and skippered by the race's founder, Thomas Fleming Day.

Most recent Bermuda Race—June 2004, Newport to Bermuda. Thirteen divisions, 156 starters between 36 and 86 feet in length. Winner, Cruiser/Racer Division (St. David's Lighthouse trophy), *Alliance*, 45-foot sloop, Dominick Porco. Winner, Racing Division (Gibbs Hill Lighthouse trophy), *Rosebud*, 42-foot sloop, Roger Sturgeon.

Bermuda Race progeny—Fastnet Race, Port Huron-Mackinac Race, and the Off Soundings Club (among others).

Rating rules used—1906-26, time allowances based on boats' overall length; 1928-32, modified Royal Ocean Racing Club Rule; 1934-68, Cruising Club of America Rule; 1970-78, 1982-88, International Offshore Rule (IOR); 1976-2004, Measurement Handicap System (MHS), renamed International Measurement System (IMS); 1998-2004, some classes under Americap Rule.

First controversy—(tie) 1906, the race itself and first woman crew.

Most frequent controversies—rating rules, professional sailors, mandatory equipment.

## Race Results

Most overall victories, skipper—three (tie), John Alden in three *Malabar*s (1923, 1926, 1932), and Carleton Mitchell in *Finisterre* (1956, 1958, 1960); two (tie), Robert N. Bavier Sr., *Memory* (1924) and *Edlu* (1934), and Richard S. and Richard B. Nye in two *Carina*s (1952, 1970).

Most overall victories, boat: three, *Finisterre* (1956, 1958, 1960); two, *Baruna* (1938, 1948).

Most first-to-finishes, skipper—four, George Coumantaros in two *Boomerang*s (1984, 1990, 1992, 1996).

Most first-to-finishes, boat—three (tie), *Baruna*, (1936, 1946, 1948); *Bolero* (1950, 1954, 1956); first maxi *Boomerang* (1984, 1990, 1992).

Most wins by a designer—Olin Stephens, 14 (1934-94).

Winning skippers who also won America's Cups—two, Harold S. Vanderbilt, 1910 (1930, 1934, and 1937 America's Cups), and Ted Hood, 1968 (1974 America's Cup).

Fastest race—*Pyewacket*, 53:39:22 (ave. 11.8 knots), 2002.

Slowest race– *Venturer*, 121:13:12 (ave. 5.2 knots), 1960.

## Participation

Most races by a sailor—30, Jim Mertz (every race except two, 1936-2004).

Most races by a boat—14 (tie), *Prim*, Gibbons-Neff family (1954-82), and *Emily*, Edwin Gaynor (1978-2004).

First woman sailor—Thora Lund Robinson, *Gauntlet*, 1906.

First woman skipper—Queene Hooper Foster, *Saphaedra*, 1986.

Oldest winning skipper—DeCoursey Fales, *Nina*, 1962 (74 years old).

Youngest winning skipper—Kyle Weaver, *Constellation*, 1992 (22 years old).

Largest boat—*Amorita*, 100 feet, 1909.

Smallest boat—*Gauntlet*, 28 feet, 1906.

First boat built for the race—*Zena*, 1907.

First entry with Marconi rig—*Zena*, 1907.

First race-winner with Marconi rig—*Memory*, 1924.

Last race-winner with gaff rig—*Malabar X*, 1934.

First Bermuda entry—(tie) *Isolt* and *Zena*, 1907.

First freshwater entry—*Priscilla,* Rochester, NY, 1907.

First freshwater winner—*Scaramouche*, Chuck Kirsch, Sturgis, MI, 1974.

First West Coast entry—*Santana*, W. A. W. Stewart, Los Angeles, 1938.

First Canadian entry—*Gauntlet*, A. E. Dingle, 1923.

First South American entry—*Fjord*, Argentina, 1954.

First Old World entry—*Jolie Brise*, U.K., 1926.

First Australian entry—*Apollo*, 1970.

First non-U.S. Winner—*Noryema*, U.K., 1972.

First service academy entry—*Vamarie*, USNA, 1938.

Best service academy finish—*Constellation*, USNA, overall winner 1992.

# Appendix 3: Bermuda Race Winners: 1906-2004

**OVERALL AND CLASS WINNERS, FIRST TO FINISH, AND ONION PATCH TROPHY WINNERS**

### 1906, Start, Brooklyn, NY, 668 miles, 3 starters

Best time, *Tamerlane*, Frank Maier, 126 hrs: 09 min.:00 sec., ave. speed 5.3 knots

Winner, *Tamerlane*

### 1907, Start, Brooklyn, 12 starters

Best time *Dervish*, Henry A. Morss, 89:00:00, 7.5 knots

Large class, *Dervish*

Small class, *Lila*, Richard D. Floyd

### 1908, Start, Marblehead, MA, 675 miles, 6 starters

Best time, *Venona*, E. Jared Bliss, 100:19:30, 6.7 knots

Large class, *Dervish*, Henry A. Morss

Small class, *Venona*

### 1909, Start, Brooklyn, 5 starters

Best time, *Amorita*, W. L. Baum, 78:19:00, 8.5 knots

Winner, *Margaret*, George S. Runk

### 1910, Start, Brooklyn, 2 starters

Best time, *Vagrant*, Harold S. Vanderbilt, 90:42:00, 7.4 knots

Winner, *Vagrant*

**1923-1934, START AT NEW LONDON, CT, 660 MILES (EXCEPT 1932, MONTAUK)**

### 1923, 22 starters

Best time, *Memory*, Robert N. Bavier, 112:18:45, 5.9 knots

Winner, *Malabar IV*, John G. Alden

### 1924, 14 starters

Best time, *Memory*, Robert N. Bavier, 102:31:21, 6.4 knots

Winner, *Memory*

Class A, *Memory*

Class B, *Hutoka*, G. B. Drake

Class C, *Lloyd W. Berry*, Bayview Yacht Club

### 1926, 16 starters

Best time *Dragoon*, Robert N. Bavier, 118:06:45, 5.6 knots

Winner, *Malabar VII*, John G. Alden

Class A, *Malabar VII*

Class B, *Black Goose*, W. F. Downs

### 1928, 25 starters

Best time *Rugosa II*, Russell Grinnell, 103:13:48, 6.4 knots

Winner, *Rugosa II*

Class A, *Rugosa II*

Class B, *Malay*, Raymond W. Ferris

Special Class, *Flying Cloud III*, Lawrence Grinnell, Jr.

Class under 35 feet, *Islander*, Harry Pidgeon

### 1930, 42 starters

Best time, *Yankee Girl II*, G. W. Warren, 98:29:39, 6.7 knots

Winner, *Malay*, Raymond W. Ferris

Class A, *Malabar X*, John G. Alden

Class B, *Malay*

### 1932, Start, Montauk, NY, 628 miles, 27 starters

Best time, *Highland Light*, Frank C. Paine, 71:35:43, 8.8 knots (new record)

Winner, *Malabar X*, R. I. Gale, John G. Alden

Class A, *Malabar X*

Class B, *Dorade*, Roderick S. Stephens Jr.

### 1934, Start, New London, 29 starters

Best time *Vamarie*, V. W. Makaroff, 75:33:32, 8.7 knots

Winner, *Edlu*, Rudolph J. Schaefer

Class A, *Edlu*

Class B, *Baccarat*, R. A. Alger Jr.

## 1936-PRESENT, START AT NEWPORT, RI, 635 MILES

### 1936, 44 starters
Best time, *Vamarie*, V. W. Makaroff. 114:50:30, 5.5 knots
Winner, *Kirawan*, Robert P. Baruch
Class A, *Stormy Weather*, Philip LeBoutillier
Class B, *Kirawan*
Special Class, over 73 feet, no finishers

### 1938, 38 starters
Best time, *Baruna*, Henry C. Taylor, 91:05:42, 7.0 knots
Winner, *Baruna*
Class A, *Baruna*
Class B, *Blitzen*, R. J. Reynolds

### 1940-1944  RACES CANCELLED DURING WORLD WAR II

### 1946, 31 starters
Best time, *Baruna*, Henry C. Taylor, 119:03:05, 5.3 knots
Winner, *Gesture*, A. Howard Fuller
Class A, *Gesture*
Class B, *Suluan*, R. F. deCoppet

### 1948, 36 starters
Best time, *Baruna*, Henry C. Taylor, 87:09:45, 7.3 knots
Winner, *Baruna*
Class A, *Baruna*
Class B, *Malabar XIII*, Morgan Butler

### 1950, 59 starters
Best time, *Bolero*, John Nicholas Brown, 75:32:09, 8.4 knots
Winner, *Argyll*, William T. Moore
Class A, *Argyll*
Class B, *Merry Maiden*, H. Irving Pratt
Class C, *Loki*, Gifford B. Pinchot

### 1952, 58 starters
Best time, *Royono*, U.S. Naval Academy, 97:16:28, 6.5 knots
Winner, *Carina*, Richard S. Nye
Class A, *Royono*
Class B, *Mustang*, Roderick Stephens Jr.
Class C, *Carina*

### 1954, 77 starters
Best time, *Bolero*, John Nicholas Brown, 108:55:04, 5.8 knots
Winner, *Malay*, Daniel D. Strohmeier
Class A, *Bolero*
Class B, *Circe*, Carl Hovgard
Class C, *Fjord*, R. G. A. Decker (Argentina)
Class D, *Malay*

### 1956, 89 starters
Best time, *Bolero*, Sven Salen (Sweden), 70:11:37, 9.0 knots (new record)
Winner, *Finisterre*, Carleton Mitchell
Class A, *Niña*, DeCoursey Fales
Class B, *Carina*, Richard S. Nye
Class C, *Figaro III*, William T. Snaith
Class D, *Finisterre*

### 1958, 111 starters
Best time, *Good News*, John H. Hedden, 102:23:48, 6.2 knots
Winner, *Finisterre*, Carleton Mitchell
Class A, *Legend*, Wells Morss
Class B, *Touche II*, John T. Potter
Class C, *Glory*, Phillip F. Miller
Class D, *Finisterre*

### 1960, 131 starters
Best time, *Venturer*, H. G. Haskell Jr., 121:13:12, 5.2 knots
Winner, *Finisterre*, Carleton Mitchell
Class A, *Dyna*, Clayton Ewing
Class B, *Palawan*, Thomas J. Watson Jr.
Class C, *Cyane*, Henry B. duPont
Class D, *Katama*, Fred Adams
Class E, *Finisterre*

### 1962, 131 starters
Best time, *Northern Light*, A. Lee Loomis, 80:46:32, 7.9 knots
Winner, *Niña*, DeCoursey Fales
Class A, *Niña*
Class B, *Gaylark*, Charles W. Ufford
Class C, *Lady Linden*, A. M. R. Hughes
Class D, *Swamp Yankee*, Van. Allen Clark Jr.
Class E, *Burgoo*, J. A. Mulcahey

**1964, 143 starters**

Best time, *Stormvogel*, Cornelius Bruynzeel (Netherlands),
    92:10:15, 6.9 knots

Winner, *Burgoo*, Milton Ernstof

Class A, *Ondine*, S. A. Long

Class B, *Carillon*, Wells Morss

Class C, *Tomadrus*, T. Miller

Class D, *Nike*, Charles F. Strohmeier

Class E, *Burgoo*

Onion Patch Trophy Series, United States


**1966, 167 starters**

Best time, *Kialoa II*, John B. Kilroy, 105:02:41, 6.0 knots

Winner, *Thunderbird*, T. Vincent Learson

Class A, *Fortuna*, Argentine Naval Academy (Argentina)

Class B, *Carina*, Richard S. Nye

Class C, *Inverness*, Robert W. McCullough

Class D, *Thunderbird*

Class E, *Tioga*, Bradley P. Noyes

Class F, *Nike*, Curt Steinweg (Argentina)

Onion Patch Trophy Series, England


**1968, 152 starters**

Best time, *Ondine*, S. A. Long, 83:12:35, 7.6 knots

Winner, *Robin*, Ted Hood

Class A, *Good News*, Jakob Isbrandtsen

Class B, *Rage*, Homer Denius

Class C, *Robin*

Class D, *Thunderbird*, T. Vincent Learson

Class E, *Windquest*, Justin Wasley

Class F, *Westray*, Glenn MacNary

Onion Patch Trophy Series, United States


**1970, 679 miles, around Argus Bank Tower, 152 starters**

Best time, *Windward Passage*, 87:03:47, 7.8 knots

Winner, *Carina*, Richard S. Nye

Class A, *Running Tide*, Jakob Isbrandtsen

Class B, *Equation*, John T. Potter

Class C, *Carina*

Class D, *Harpoon*, Mark Ewing

Class E, *Soogie Moogie*, James H. Castle

Class F, *Pageant*, John H. Page

Onion Patch Trophy Series, United States


**1972, Usual Newport course, 178 starters**

Best time, *Robon*, Robert H. Grant, 80:15:15 ,7.9 knots

Winner, *Noryema IV*, Ron W. Amey (U.K.)

Class A, *Robon*

Class B, *Charisma*, Jesse Philips

Class C, *Noryema IV*

Class D, *Dove*, Stewart Greene

Class E, *Maverick*, Rodney Hill (U.K.)

Class F, *Aesop*, Alexander R. Fowler

Onion Patch Trophy Series, United States


**1974, 166 starters**

Best time, *Ondine*, S. A. Long, 67:52:22, 9.4 knots (new record)

Winner, *Scaramouche*, Charles E. Kirsch

Class A, *Dora IV*, Lynn Williams

Class B, *Scaramouche*

Class C, *Recluta III*, C. A. Corna (Argentina)

Class D, *Diane*, James Mattingly

Class E, *Cayenne*, Donald Tate

Class F, *Hot Canary*, Stanley Rubenzahl

Onion Patch Trophy Series, United States


**1976, 150 starters**

Best time, *Tempest*, Eric Ridder, 88:16:20, 7.2 knots

Winner, *Running Tide*, A. G. VanMetre/A. G. VanMetre Jr.

Class A, *Running Tide*

Class B, *Bumblebee 3*, J. Kahlbetzer (Australia)

Class C, *Arieto*, A. Schofield

Class D, *Pride*, Richard Jayson

Class E, *Circe*, E. Greene

Class F, *Abino Robin*, Ted Hood

Onion Patch Trophy Series, United States

**1978, 161 starters: IOR 89, MHS 72**

Best time, *Circus Maximus*, John Raby and Don Ridder,
    105:05:46, 6.0 knots

IOR Winner, *Acadia*, Burt H. Keenan

MHS Winner, *Babe*, Arnold C. Gay

Class A, IOR, *Tempest*, Eric Ridder;

Class B, IOR, *Acadia*

Class B, MHS, *Solution*, Thor Ramsing

Class C, IOR, *Marionette*, C. A. F. Dunning (U.K.)

Class C, MHS, *Snow White*, W. B. White

Class D, IOR, *Wildflower*, R. B. Scarborough

Class D, MHS, *Blaze*, Edward du Moulin/Harold Oldak

Class E, IOR, *Mareva II*, H. S. L. Murfey Jr.

Class E, MHS, *Alaris*, T. K. Iliff

Class F, IOR, *Krshna*, R. Pellicano

Class F, MHS, *Babe*

Onion Patch Trophy Series, United States


**1980, 160 starters, MHS only**

Best time, *Bumblebee 4*, J. D. Kahlbetzer (Australia), 70:07:45, 9.1 knots

Winner, *Holger Danske*, Richard Wilson

Class A, *Tenacious*, James R. Mattingly

Class B, *Merrythought*, Jack King

Class C, *Acadia*, Burt H. Keenan

Class D, *Hilaria*, C. F. Chapin/G. H. Schryver

Class E, *Katrinka*, Winder family

Class F, *Holger Danske*

Onion Patch Trophy Series, U. S. Northeast Team


**1982, 178 starters: IOR 76, MHS 102**

Best time, *Nirvana*, Marvin Green, 62:29:16, 10.2 (new record)

MHS winner, *Brigadoon III*, Robert W. Morton

IOR winner, *Carina*, Richard B. Nye

Class A, IOR, *Retaliation*, F. P. Heinemann

Class B, MHS, *Brigadoon III*

Class C, IOR, *Carina*

Class D, MHS, *Spindrift*, R. Munro

Class E, IOR, *Conamor*, S. A. Lieber

Class F, MHS, *Elixir*, David C. Noyes

Onion Patch Trophy Series, Canada


**1984, 115 starters: IMS 49, IOR 66**

Best time, *Boomerang*, George Coumantaros, 82:11:50, 7.7 knots

IMS Winner, *Pamir*, Francis H. Curren Jr.

IOR Winner, *Merrythought*, Jack King

Class A, IOR, *Retaliation*, F. P. Heinemann

Class B, IMS, *Pamir*

Class C, IOR, *Merrythought*

Class D, IMS, *Full Cry*, Robert Crompton

Class E, IOR, *Road Warrior*, John Kolius

Class F, IMS, *Wave Train*, Albert Saunders

Onion Patch Trophy Series, United States


**1986, 125 starters: IMS 82, IOR 35, Maxi 8**

Best time, *Condor*, Robert A. Bell, 90:46:47, 7.0 knots

IMS Winner, *Puritan*, Donald P. Robinson

IOR Winner, *Silver Star*, D. H. Clarke

Class A, IOR, *Springbok*, D. A. Rosow

Class B, IMS, *Stainless*, B. S. Hall

Class C, IOR, *Abracadabra*, Mark C. Ploch

Class D, IMS, *Froya*, Oivind Lorentzen Jr.

Class E, IOR, *Silver Star*

Class F, IMS, *Puritan*

Class M, Maxis, *Condor*

Onion Patch Trophy Series, U.S. Blue Team


**1988, 120 starters: IMS 78, IOR 42**

Best time, *Congere*, Beven Koeppel, 87:24:08, 7.3 knots

IMS Winner, *Cannonball*, Charles A. Robertson

IOR Winner, *Congere*

Class A, IMS, *Cannonball*

Class B, IOR, *Springbok*, David Rosow

Class C, IMS, *Brigadoon III*, James Bishop

Class D, IMS, *Scaramouche of Warwick*, E. Paul du Pont

Class E, IMS, *Emily*, Edwin Gaynor

Class F, IMS, *Anthem*, Peter Geis

Class M, IOR Maxis, *Congere*

Onion Patch Trophy Series, United States

**1990, 145 starters, IMS only**

Best time, *Boomerang*, George Coumantaros, 87:20:01, 7.3 knots

Winner, *Denali*, Lawrence S. Huntington

Cruising Winner, *Pirate*, Juan Corradi

Class A, *Arcadia*, Robert Stone

Class B, *Collaboration*, Oliver Grin

Class C, *Etoile*, Eugene Sydnor

Class D, *Leda*, William Apthorp

Class E, *Denali*

Class F, Cruising, *Chasseur*, Frank Snyder

Class G, Cruising, *Pirate*

Onion Patch Trophy Series, United States


**1992, 117 starters: 90 racing, 27 cruising**

Best time, *Boomerang*, George Coumantaros, 72:19:29, 8.8 knots

Winner, *Constellation*, U. S. Naval Academy

Cruising Winner, *Freestyle*, Paul Fireman

Class A, *Bully*, Richard Heffering

Class B, *Equinox*, Marty Siagowitz

Class C, *Constellation*

Class D, *Cepheus*, Sheppard Poor

Class E, *Mutiny*, Gibbs Kane

Class F, Cruising, *Monterey*, Leslie Crane (Bermuda)

Class G, Cruising, *Freestyle*

Onion Patch Trophy Series, Bermuda


**1994, 149 starters: 2 Grande Voile, 110 Lighthouse, 20 Cruising, 17 Doublehanded**

Best time, *Windquest*, Rich DeVos/Doug DeVos, 72:15:09, 8.8 knots

Winner, *Gaylark*, Kaighn Smith

Class 1, Grande Voile, *Essence*, J. Scoroposki

Class 2, Grand-Prix, *Conspiracy*, Donald Elliman

Class 3, Cruiser/Racer, *Wonder*, Steven Van Dyke

Class 4, Cruiser/Racer, *Challenge IV*, G. Willis

Class 5, Cruiser/Racer, *Toscana*, Skipper Helme

Class 6, Cruiser/Racer, *Loose Cannon*, J. Dunne

Class 7, Cruiser/Racer, *Froya*, Robert Gunther

Class 8, Cruiser/Racer, *Gaylark*

Class 9, Cruising, *Gamelan*, A. M. Winchester

Class 10, Doublehanded, *Halcyon*, D. A. Antoniadis

Class 11, Doublehanded non-spinnaker, *Morgan's Cloud*, J. H. Harries

Onion Patch Trophy Series, New York Yacht Club


**1996 145 Starters: 98 Cruiser/Racer, 6 Racing A, 6 Racing B, 19 Cruising, 14 Doublehanded, 2 Club Certificate**

Best time, *Boomerang*, George Coumantaros, 57:31:50, 11 knots (new record)

Winner, *Boomerang*

Class 1, Racing, *Sagamore*, James Dolan

Class 2, Cruiser/Racer, *Boomerang*

Class 3, Cruiser/Racer, *Defiance*, K. Morrell

Class 4, Cruiser/Racer, *Gold Digger*, James D. Bishop

Class 5, Cruiser/Racer, *Mensae*, E. C. Kristiansen

Class 6, Cruiser/Racer, *As Larks Harmoniously*, C. Knowlton

Class 7, Cruiser/Racer, *Temptress*, Richard Shulman/Kirk Cooper

Class 8, Cruiser/Racer, *Restless*, E. E. Crawford

Class 9, Cruising, *Nirvana*, R. Beck

Class 10, Doublehanded, *Next Boat*, M. Ellman

Class 11, Doublehanded non-spinnaker, *Morgan's Cloud*, J. H. Harries

Class 12, Club Certificate, *Simpatico*, W. F. Riley

Onion Patch Trophy Series, United States


**1998 162 Starters: 10 IMS Racing, 117 IMS Cruiser/Racer, 26 Americap Cruising, 9 Americap Doublehanded**

Best time, *Alexia*, Alberto Roemmers, 90:56:16, 7.0 knots

Winner, *Kodiak*, E. Llwyd Ecclestone

Class 1, Cruiser/Racer, *Emily*, Edwin Gaynor

Class 2, Cruiser/Racer, *Froya*, Robert Gunther

Class 3, Cruiser/Racer, *Jacqueline*, R. Forman

Class 4, Cruiser/Racer, *Hound*, Frank Eberhart

Class 5, Cruiser/Racer, *Temptress*, Richard Shulman/Kirk Cooper

Class 6, J-44, *Stampede*, J. Sundstrom

Class 7, Cruiser/Racer, *Kodiak*

Class 8, Cruiser/Racer, *Encore*, James Dolan

Class 9, Racing, *Snow Leopard*, Lawrence Huntington

Class 10, Racing, *Blue Yankee*, Robert C. Towse

Class 11, Cruising, *Simpatico*, W. Riley

Class 12, Cruising, *Starr Trail*, Robert Mulderig (Bermuda)

Class 13, Doublehanded, *Macintosh*, D. Steigenga

Onion Patch Trophy Series, United States

**2000 175 Starters: 11 IMS Racing, 126 IMS Cruiser/Racer, 25 Americap Cruising, 13 Americap Doublehanded**

Best time, *Sagamore*, James Dolan, 80:42:39, 7.7 knots

Winner, *Restless*, E. E. Crawford

Class 1, Cruiser/Racer, *Restless*

Class 2, Cruiser/Racer, *Sapphire Seas*, Avery

Class 3, Cruiser/Racer, *Carina*, Rives Potts Jr.

Class 4, Cruiser/Racer, *Winden*, Schwartz

Class 5, J-44, *Stampede*, Sundstrom

Class 6, Cruiser/Racer, *Temptress*, Richard Shulman

Class 7, Cruiser/Racer, *Appreciation*, Siegal

Class 8, Racing, *Idler*, David

Class 9, Grand-Prix Racing, *Heatwave*, Giordano

Class 10, Classic Cruising, *Borderlaw*, Sherwin

Class 11, Cruising non-spinnaker, *Spirit*, Imbriale

Class 12, Doublehanded, *Next Boat*, M. Ellman

Class 13, Doublehanded non-spinnaker, *Emerald Trader*, Murphy

Onion Patch Trophy Series, Cruising Club of America


**2002 182 Starters: 11 IMS Racing, 127 IMS Cruiser/Racer, 28 Americap Cruising, 10 Americap Doublehanded**

Best time, *Pyewacket*, Roy Disney, 53:29:22, 11.8 knots (new record)

Cruiser/Racer Winner, *Zaraffa*, Huntington Sheldon

Racing Winner, *Blue Yankee*, Robert Towse

Class 1, Cruiser/Racer, *Sinn Fein*, Peter Rebovich

Class 2, Cruiser/Racer, *Ariel*, Jim Thompson

Class 3, Cruiser/Racer, *Carina*, Rives Potts Jr.

Class 4 Cruiser/Racer, *Galadriel*, John Santa

Class 5, J-44, *Mabuhay II*, Edwardo Salvati

Class 6, Cruiser/Racer, *Hound*, Frank Eberhart

Class 7, Cruiser/Racer, *Neva*, Robert Watson

Class 8, Cruiser/Racer, *Zaraffa*

Class 9, Racing, *Blue Yankee*

Class 10, Cruising, *Palawan*, Joseph Hoopes

Class 11, Cruising, *Restive*, George Denny III

Class 12, Doublehanded, *Lora Ann*, Richard T. du Moulin

Onion Patch Trophy Series, Storm Trysail White Team


**2004 156 Starters: 11 IMS Racing, 105 IMS Cruiser/Racer, 3 MaxZ86 Demonstration Division, 27 Americap Cruising, 10 Americap Doublehanded**

Best time, *Carrera*, J. T. Dockery, 68:15:54, 9.4 knots

Best time, Demonstration Division, *Morning Glory*, Hasso Plattner (Germany), 48:38:31

Cruiser/Racer Winner, *Alliance*, Dominick Porco

Racing Winner, *Rosebud*, Roger Sturgeon

Class 1, Cruiser/Racer, *Sinn Fein*, Peter Rebovich

Class 2, Cruiser/Racer, *Lively*, Andrew Hurst

Class 3, Cruiser/Racer, *Cygnette*, W. J. Mayer

Class 4, Cruiser/Racer, *Orion*, Pat Patterson Jr.

Class 5, J-44, *Mabuhay II*, Edwardo Salvati

Class 6, Cruiser/Racer, *Alliance*, Dominick Porco

Class 7, Cruiser/Racer, *Ace*, F. W. Stelle

Class 8, Cruiser/Racer, *Zaraffa*, Huntington Sheldon

Class 9, Racing, *Rosebud*

Class 10, Demonstration Division, *Morning Glory*

Class 11, Cruising, *Starlight*, A. C. Bulger

Class 12, Cruising, *J'Erin*, James J. Flaherty

Class 13, Doublehanded, *Lora Ann*, Richard du Moulin

Onion Patch Trophy Series, Storm Trysail Club Blue Team

# Appendix 4: Bermuda Race Fleet Results: 2000, 2002, 2004

## 2000 Newport Bermuda Race

### CLASS AND DIVISION RESULTS

#### IMS RACING DIVISION—GRAND PRIX

CLASS 9

| Cls Pos | Div Pos | Yacht Name | Captain | Affiliation | Elapsed H M S | Corrected H M S |
|---|---|---|---|---|---|---|
| 1 | 1 | HEATWAVE | Giordano | Edgartown | 86 15 14 | 70-04-32 |
| 2 | 2 | RIMA | Kabbani | New York | 82 14 08 | 74-13-03 |
| 3 | 3 | LOCO | Braidwood | CYC – AUS | 85 21 42 | 74-31-25 |
| 4 | 4 | SAGAMORE | Dolan | New York | 80 42 39 | 80-34-15 |
| 5 | 5 | SAYONARA | Ellison | St. Francis | 80 55 50 | 80-55-51 |

#### IMS RACING DIVISION

CLASS 8

| Cls Pos | Div Pos | Yacht Name | Captain | Affiliation | Elapsed H M S | Corrected H M S |
|---|---|---|---|---|---|---|
| 1 | 111 | IDLER | David | New York | 86 14 04 | 71-00-43 |
| 2 | 114 | SALINE SOLUTION | Mahoney | Richmond | 87 39 42 | 71-10-51 |
| 3 | 124 | BLUE YANKEE | Towse | Storm Try | 81 43 44 | 75-29-38 |
| 4 | 126 | SNOW LION | Huntington | CCA | 92 12 58 | 76-00-32 |
| 5 | 129 | CHESSIE RACING | Collins | New York | 86 13 10 | 77-04-26 |
| 6 | 132 | BOOMERANG | Coumantaros | CCA | 81 53 59 | 81-53-57 |

#### IMS CRUISER/RACER DIVISION

CLASS 1

| Cls Pos | Div Pos | Yacht Name | Captain | Affiliation | Elapsed H M S | Corrected H M S |
|---|---|---|---|---|---|---|
| 1 | 1 | RESTLESS | Crawford | Tred Avon | 93 15 39 | 52-47-54 |
| 2 | 2 | BANGALORE | Tefft | RHADC | 94 15 15 | 56-23-48 |
| 3 | 3 | GAYLARK | Watson | Corinthian | 92 54 41 | 58-03-44 |
| 4 | 4 | NICOLE | duPont | Tred Avon | 93 14 18 | 58-09-28 |
| 5 | 5 | PHANTOM | Comerford | Annapolis | 93 06 05 | 58-15-30 |
| 6 | 6 | ANTHEM | Geis | Annapolis | 93 02 56 | 58-26-31 |
| 7 | 7 | ACTAEA | Cone | Corin-Phil | 96 15 33 | 58-28-25 |
| 8 | 8 | SINN FEIN | Rebovich | Raritan | 93 42 21 | 58-30-46 |
| 9 | 9 | LIGHT FANTASTIC | Shemitz | Milford | 92 42 09 | 58-40-24 |
| 10 | 10 | EMILY | Gaynor | CCA | 93 48 28 | 58-56-12 |
| 11 | 11 | TAZZARIN | Barton | Manchester | 93 04 02 | 59-00-38 |
| 12 | 12 | REMORA VIII | Hopkins | Barrington | 94 09 20 | 59-10-11 |
| 13 | 13 | DARK HORSE | Naroski | Palmers Cv | 92 29 24 | 60-02-37 |
| 14 | 15 | ANTARES | Donahue | Edgartown | 94 04 57 | 60-11-20 |
| 15 | 17 | EXUBERANT | Hammar | Portsmouth | 96 12 32 | 61-09-27 |
| 16 | 43 | MONTEREY | Crane | R Bermuda | 94 13 38 | 63-08-45 |
| 17 | 44 | CATHERINE ELIZA | Mauritz | NYAC | 96 17 15 | 63-10-16 |

## CLASS 2

| Cls Pos | Div Pos | Yacht Name | Captain | Affiliation | Elapsed H M S | Corrected H M S |
|---|---|---|---|---|---|---|
| 1 | 14 | SAPPHIRE SEAS | Avery | Newport | 92 43 02 | 60-07-31 |
| 2 | 16 | ZEPHYR | Waddington | Windjammer | 92 21 11 | 60-36-22 |
| 3 | 18 | DAWN TREADER | Cohen | Fishing Ba | 93 34 38 | 61-12-56 |
| 4 | 20 | SWIFT | Panayiotou | NASS | 91 45 04 | 61-18-42 |
| 5 | 21 | CARPE DIEM | Fracchia | Setauket | 92 33 28 | 61-30-14 |
| 6 | 22 | LINDY | Dickerson | Niantic Ba | 92 42 04 | 61-43-37 |
| 7 | 25 | EDDYSTONE LIGHT | Hall | USCGA | 94 14 10 | 61-47-56 |
| 8 | 27 | THE UGLY DUCKLING | Kardash | New York | 92 51 52 | 61-53-12 |
| 9 | 31 | CILISTA | Eberle | Manchester | 94 06 29 | 62-17-00 |
| 10 | 33 | SAFARI | Schutt | Chesapeake | 93 00 44 | 62-19-28 |
| 11 | 34 | ARIEL | Thompson | Tred Avon | 92 42 05 | 62-21-16 |
| 12 | 35 | LIVELY | Cerrito | NASS | 93 17 26 | 62-30-21 |
| 13 | 36 | MISTY | Allardyce | Watch Hill | 92 38 32 | 62-35-26 |
| 14 | 39 | SAZERAC | Ettie | New York | 92 48 30 | 62-42-52 |
| 15 | 41 | FLIRT | Crowley | NASS | 93 57 13 | 63-02-16 |
| 16 | 47 | VIGILANT | Demeyer | NASS | 94 53 43 | 63-40-12 |
| 17 | 53 | SIMBA | Knapp | Saugatuck | 94 39 01 | 64-11-46 |
| 18 | 60 | IMPALA | Sanford | Nantucket | 94 47 14 | 64-36-02 |
| 19 | 63 | JUBILANT | Lundell | Huntington | 95 35 10 | 64-47-53 |

## CLASS 3

| Cls Pos | Div Pos | Yacht Name | Captain | Affiliation | Elapsed H M S | Corrected H M S |
|---|---|---|---|---|---|---|
| 1 | 19 | CARINA | Potts | CCA | 90 02 26 | 61-15-11 |
| 2 | 24 | REGATTA | Koste | Tred Avon | 92 05 52 | 61-47-49 |
| 3 | 28 | XENOPHON | Rabuffo | Baldwin | 91 35 35 | 61-59-22 |
| 4 | 29 | BLACKWATCH | Harrington | New York | 91 12 25 | 61-59-40 |
| 5 | 30 | BREAKAWAY | Tarbell | Kittery Pt | 92 06 16 | 62-11-30 |
| 6 | 32 | INCESSANT | Paul Kapla | Annapolis | 92 13 46 | 62-18-39 |
| 7 | 37 | JACQUELINE IV | Forman | New York | 93 19 41 | 62-37-31 |
| 8 | 40 | CYGNETTE | Mayer | New York | 92 00 12 | 62-48-43 |
| 9 | 45 | JOSS | Ferretti | Indian Hbr | 93 00 38 | 63-26-45 |
| 10 | 46 | BANDANA | Benson | TAYC | 92 15 48 | 63-36-19 |
| 11 | 48 | RAINMAKER | McFaul | Port Wash | 93 08 47 | 63-41-10 |
| 12 | 49 | CYBELE | Burnes | CCA | 93 50 11 | 63-45-49 |
| 13 | 51 | UPBEAT | Smith | Edgartown | 92 28 10 | 63-58-09 |
| 14 | 52 | CLOVER | Finnegan | New York | 91 45 14 | 63-59-28 |
| 15 | 54 | MORGAN OF MARIE | Golder | Raritan | 93 12 58 | 64-14-23 |
| 16 | 55 | DOLPHIN | Morgan | NY/GIYS | 92 46 15 | 64-20-43 |
| 17 | 56 | FINESSE | Merrill | CCA | 93 30 13 | 64-24-38 |
| 18 | 58 | ALIBI | Breck | Riverside | 93 16 54 | 64-28-29 |
| 19 | 64 | PANTHER | Rogers | Annapolis | 94 02 09 | 64-53-19 |
| 20 | 98 | APACHE | Kelly | Ctrboard | 99 19 04 | 68-43-22 |
| DNC | DNC | GREEN DRAGON | Carr | Essex | | |

## CLASS 4

| Cls Pos | Div Pos | Yacht Name | Captain | Affiliation | Elapsed H M S | Corrected H M S |
|---|---|---|---|---|---|---|
| 1 | 23 | WENDEN | Schwartz | Riverside | 88 57 17 | 61-46-02 |
| 2 | 26 | CRESCENDO | Jacobson | Indian Riv | 89 27 38 | 61-50-19 |
| 3 | 38 | LOCOMOTION | Barnard | RNSYS | 91 21 37 | 62-37-36 |
| 4 | 42 | MUTINY | Kane | American | 90 00 38 | 63-03-40 |
| 5 | 50 | PALANTIR | Kendrick | Lloyd Hbr | 91 48 31 | 63-54-55 |
| 6 | 57 | SOMERSET | Alder | Riverside | 90 43 28 | 64-27-40 |
| 7 | 59 | CHASSEUR | Snyder | New York | 92 10 19 | 64-34-52 |
| 8 | 61 | BABE | Couper | R Bermuda | 91 39 48 | 64-39-26 |
| 9 | 62 | RAMPAGE | Borden | USCGA | 92 44 51 | 64-47-45 |
| 10 | 65 | ORION | Patterson | Hampton | 90 56 05 | 64-58-04 |

| | 11 | 66 | MIDNIGHT SUN | Eisenberg | New York | 91 49 04 | 64-59-02 |
|---|---|---|---|---|---|---|---|
| | 12 | 67 | LYRA | Gregory | CCA | 91 34 27 | 65-01-18 |
| | 13 | 68 | WHISPER | Brotman | | 91 24 59 | 65-13-26 |
| | 14 | 69 | BYE BYE BLUES | Monro | Stamford | 90 29 00 | 65-28-25 |
| | 15 | 70 | SWEPT AWAY | Mandell | Huntington | 89 10 02 | 65-39-24 |
| | 16 | 74 | JAM SESSION | Weiner | New York | 91 31 30 | 66-12-23 |
| | 17 | 77 | HOUND | Eberhart | New York | 92 03 47 | 66-24-34 |
| | 18 | 81 | MANTRA | Devereaux | Manchester | 92 45 31 | 66-38-38 |
| | 19 | 92 | SCREAMIN' MIMI | Gillette | Lauderdale | 93 22 26 | 67-35-15 |
| | 20 | 104 | PETITES CAYES | Spurling | GIYS | 94 25 46 | 69-38-05 |

## CLASS 5 (J-44)

| Cls Pos | Div Pos | Yacht Name | Captain | Affiliation | Elapsed H M S | Corrected H M S |
|---|---|---|---|---|---|---|
| 1 | 71 | STAMPEDE | Sundstrom | American | 88 51 08 | 65-55-29 |
| 2 | 73 | GOLD DIGGER | Bishop | American | 88 57 32 | 66-10-21 |
| 3 | 75 | CHALLENGE IV | Willis | Storm Try | 89 49 48 | 66-18-06 |
| 4 | 78 | MABUHAY II | Salvati | New York | 89 32 57 | 66-31-12 |
| 5 | 79 | DIOGENES 2 | Clark | American | 89 48 45 | 66-32-20 |
| 6 | 80 | RESOLUTE | Scribner | Lloyd Hbr | 89 23 47 | 66-35-10 |
| 7 | 82 | RUNAWAY | Glenn | Sewanhaka | 89 48 37 | 66-38-49 |
| 8 | 84 | VAMP | Sitar | American | 89 47 27 | 66-51-31 |
| 9 | 86 | ANTWERP EXPRESS | Kalish | SRNA | 91 05 40 | 66-59-16 |
| 10 | 90 | CELEBRATION | Stuart | New York | 91 36 50 | 67-25-01 |

## CLASS 6

| Cls Pos | Div Pos | Yacht Name | Captain | Affiliation | Elapsed H M S | Corrected H M S |
|---|---|---|---|---|---|---|
| 1 | 72 | TEMPTRESS | Shulman | New York | 88 32 24 | 65-59-26 |
| 2 | 76 | WAHOO | Fretz | Chester RI | 87 11 44 | 66-18-08 |
| 3 | 83 | SIRENA | Loeb | New York | 87 54 28 | 66-50-49 |
| 4 | 85 | ANDIAMO | Rush | Shelter Is | 88 35 19 | 66-54-39 |
| 5 | 87 | WHITE JACKET | Hurlock | New York | 90 57 49 | 67-06-23 |
| 6 | 88 | WINDSONG | Reynolds | New York | 90 56 27 | 67-15-33 |
| 7 | 89 | WAR BABY | Brown | R Bermuda | 88 31 54 | 67-23-41 |
| 8 | 91 | DIAMOND | Evans | New York | 91 35 56 | 67-28-41 |
| 9 | 93 | NOW | Davies | Columbia | 91 13 03 | 67-49-37 |
| 10 | 94 | FAUST | Kieffer | | 92 07 18 | 67-54-24 |
| 11 | 95 | SUNDAY DRIVER | Carballal | Lloyd Hbr | 91 20 02 | 68-12-11 |
| 12 | 97 | GRYPHON | Harris | Manchester | 92 30 19 | 68-35-51 |
| 13 | 99 | MORNING GLORY | Olsson | Larchmont | 89 59 06 | 68-47-11 |
| 14 | 101 | CARIBE | Swingle | GIYS | 91 17 28 | 68-52-53 |
| 15 | 102 | BONAVENTURE V | Tsamasfyro | R Hellenic | 91 41 41 | 69-20-27 |
| 16 | 103 | SYROCCO | Fortenbaug | Indian Hbr | 93 33 17 | 69-28-27 |
| 17 | 105 | HINANO | Rego/ Bill | RHADC | 91 16 28 | 69-54-08 |
| 18 | 106 | EQUINOX | Rhea | | 91 16 03 | 70-03-10 |
| 19 | 109 | TOSCANA | Swenson | Indian Hbr | 93 09 39 | 70-34-24 |
| 20 | 110 | SCEPTRE'D ISLE | Weismann | New York | 91 54 15 | 70-52-22 |
| 21 | 116 | QUADRILLE | Terajewicz | Bristol | 94 43 08 | 71-13-31 |
| 22 | 117 | ALEXIS | D'Alessand | Boston | 95 29 25 | 71-15-22 |
| 23 | 123 | WINDWALKER | Cullen | Corinthian | 97 32 56 | 74-12-07 |

## CLASS 7

| Cls Pos | Div Pos | Yacht Name | Captain | Affiliation | Elapsed H M S | Corrected H M S |
|---|---|---|---|---|---|---|
| 1 | 96 | APPRECIATION | Siegal | New York | 84 53 05 | 68-31-17 |
| 2 | 100 | BRIGHT STAR | Breeden | New York | 87 18 06 | 68-52-13 |
| 3 | 107 | LOLITA | Savage | Indian Hbr | 86 59 33 | 70-23-04 |
| 4 | 108 | MENSAE | Kristianse | Lloyd Hbr | 88 17 01 | 70-29-39 |
| 5 | 112 | JULIANNA | Gould | USS | 89 09 51 | 71-06-11 |
| 6 | 113 | WONDER | Van Dyck | New York | 88 26 49 | 71-07-34 |

| | 7 | 115 | ARCADIA | Stone | New York | 85 06 56 | 71-13-00 |
|---|---|---|---|---|---|---|---|
| | 8 | 118 | NEVA | Watson | New York | 88 45 13 | 71-49-04 |
| | 9 | 119 | HARRIER | Munger | Riverside | 89 40 51 | 71-49-51 |
| | 10 | 120 | KODIAK | Ecclestone | CCA | 87 10 05 | 71-55-07 |
| | 11 | 121 | EXCALIBUR | Apold | RNSYS | 89 14 15 | 71-57-24 |
| | 12 | 122 | BOMBARDINO | Sykes | American | 88 17 59 | 72-13-19 |
| | 13 | 125 | ENCORE | Langan | CCA | 84 58 12 | 75-48-22 |
| | 14 | 127 | JAVELIN | Bulman | STC | 86 50 17 | 76-21-53 |
| | 15 | 128 | MISCHIEVOUS | Fitzgibbon | Indian Hbr | 86 42 12 | 76-55-34 |
| | 16 | 130 | TRADER | Detwiler | New York | 83 01 10 | 78-20-06 |
| | 17 | 131 | ZARAFFA | Sheldon | New York | 82 30 37 | 79-04-10 |

## AMERICAP CRUISING DIVISION

CLASS 10 (Classic)

| Cls Pos | Div Pos | Yacht Name | Captain | Affiliation | Elapsed H M S | Corrected H M S |
|---|---|---|---|---|---|---|
| 1 | 1 | BORDERLAW | Sherwin | R Bermuda | 92 47 05 | 69-04-17 |
| 2 | 2 | LIVELY LADY II | Hubbard | New York | 96 53 25 | 71-40-42 |
| 3 | 3 | FUERA | Nicholas | American | 94 23 32 | 72-16-00 |
| 4 | 4 | KIRAWAN | Horowitz | California | 93 47 45 | 75-38-28 |

CLASS 11 (Non Spinnaker)

| Cls Pos | Div Pos | Yacht Name | Captain | Affiliation | Elapsed H M S | Corrected H M S |
|---|---|---|---|---|---|---|
| 1 | 1 | SPIRIT | Imbriale | Jamestown | 92 48 41 | 68-13-41 |
| 2 | 2 | SIMPATICO | Riley | Stage Hbr | 92 29 39 | 70-34-20 |
| 3 | 3 | DAWN TREADER | Deichmann | Shenecosse | 96 21 03 | 71-43-49 |
| 4 | 4 | TIANNA | Drum | Newport | 94 09 14 | 71-53-23 |
| 5 | 5 | BERMUDA OYSTER | Hubbard | R Bermuda | 92 58 49 | 72-24-12 |
| 6 | 6 | PARADISO | Zenone | | 91 17 06 | 72-30-46 |
| 7 | 7 | DIVA | Fischer | New York | 92 25 31 | 72-41-13 |
| 8 | 8 | SYMPHONY | Mertz | American | 90 33 54 | 72-56-30 |
| 9 | 9 | CONSTANCY | Miltimore | Pequot/NY | 97 03 29 | 73-39-21 |
| 10 | 10 | VIVALDI | Fiori | Burr Bros | 91 14 22 | 75-22-23 |
| 11 | 11 | SEAQUILL | Brown | CCA | 92 24 10 | 77-21-28 |
| 12 | 12 | DRAGONSBANE | van Heynin | Ida Lewis | 95 52 15 | 77-49-50 |
| 13 | 13 | ACADIA | Keenan | Storm Try | 93 31 54 | 78-09-44 |
| 14 | 14 | ARION | Johnson | Belhaven | 92 44 55 | 78-58-35 |
| 15 | 15 | TIGER TOO | Ritter | New York | 95 19 29 | 79-33-57 |
| 16 | 16 | AVALANCHE | Whipple | New York | 96 25 10 | 79-44-42 |
| 17 | 17 | MOONSHINE | Duerden | New York | 89 39 47 | 81-03-50 |
| 18 | 18 | ESCAPADE | Seynhaeve | Annapolis | 93 16 55 | 81-09-29 |
| 19 | 19 | MAGIC FLUTE | Zwig | Island | 92 32 39 | 81-59-18 |
| 20 | 20 | PAMIR | Curren | Conanicut | 92 57 43 | 81-59-59 |
| 21 | 21 | ESSENCE | Scoroposki | Sewanhaka | 100 10 25 | 96-05-45 |

## AMERICAP DOUBLEHANDED CRUISING DIVISION

CLASS 12 (DH Spinnaker)

| Cls Pos | Div Pos | Yacht Name | Captain | Affiliation | Elapsed H M S | Corrected H M S |
|---|---|---|---|---|---|---|
| 1 | 1 | NEXT BOAT | Ellman | Beach Pt. | 92 00 43 | 64-05-51 |
| 2 | 2 | MARIAH | Thurston | Barrington | 91 38 02 | 66-35-10 |
| 3 | 3 | SEAQUESTER | Shepard | Corinthian | 94 21 04 | 67-05-54 |
| 4 | 4 | VICTORIA | Reppert | New Bed | 94 10 25 | 68-22-02 |
| 5 | 5 | FIRST LIGHT | Kipp | CCA | 91 53 19 | 69-43-00 |

| Cls Pos | Div Pos | Yacht Name | Captain | Affiliation | Elapsed H M S | Corrected H M S |
|---|---|---|---|---|---|---|
| 6 | 6 | FREEBIRD | Asche | New York | 92 29 40 | 73-04-37 |
| 7 | 7 | HALCYON | Antoniadis | N Bedford | 91 22 48 | 73-35-33 |
| 8 | 8 | MACINTOSH | Steigenga | Cath Bluff | 89 59 54 | 74-12-54 |
| 9 | 9 | ANTARES | Sharpe | Annapolis | 91 26 22 | 81-01-24 |
| 10 | 10 | PEGASUS | Biagioli | Boston | 88 49 10 | 81-05-41 |
| 11 | 11 | SHERE KHAN | Johnson | New York | 91 39 05 | 82-12-17 |

CLASS 12 (DH Non Spinnaker)

| Cls Pos | Div Pos | Yacht Name | Captain | Affiliation | Elapsed H M S | Corrected H M S |
|---|---|---|---|---|---|---|
| 1 | 1 | EMERALD TRADER | Murphy | US Sailing | 95 20 48 | 75-37-58 |
| 2 | 2 | STRELLA ENCORE | Mangin | New York | 92 18 07 | 80-49-48 |

## MAXI FLEET SCORING

| | |
|---|---|
| 1 | SAYONARA |
| 2 | SAGAMORE |
| 3 | BOOMERANG |

## 2002 Newport Bermuda Race

## CLASS AND DIVISION RESULTS

### IMS RACING DIVISION

CLASS 9

| Cls Pos | Div Pos | Yacht Name | Captain | Affiliation | Elapsed H M S | Corrected H M S |
|---|---|---|---|---|---|---|
| 1 | 1 | BLUE YANKEE | RC Towse | Stamford YC | 58 29 24 | 51 59 23 |
| 2 | 2 | BOOMERANG | GS Coumantaros | CCA | 54 02 44 | 52 57 37 |
| 3 | 3 | PYEWACKET | RE Disney | Los Angeles | 53 39 22 | 53 14 42 |
| 4 | 4 | CARRERA | J Dockery | Stamford YC | 62 13 44 | 53 15 21 |
| 5 | 5 | TITAN XI | T Hill | | 59 37 34 | 53 49 57 |
| 6 | 6 | PTARMIGAN | LF Dickie | Riverside | 72 53 37 | 54 29 28 |
| 7 | 7 | IDLER | G David | STC | 70 35 50 | 54 50 31 |
| 8 | 8 | BRIGHT STAR | RC Breeden | NYYC / STC | 58 50 53 | 56 18 59 |
| 9 | 9 | MORNING GLORY | H Plattner | RBYC | 58 17 52 | 58 17 54 |
| 10 | 10 | R WAVE 3 | IH Futterman | Knickerboc | 84 06 10 | 61 55 48 |
| 11 | 11 | DOGSLED | TF Barnard | RNSYS | 96 50 48 | 69 06 33 |

### IMS CRUISER/RACER DIVISION

CLASS 1

| Cls Pos | Div Pos | Yacht Name | Captain | Affiliation | Elapsed H M S | Corrected H M S |
|---|---|---|---|---|---|---|
| 1 | 5 | SINN FEIN | PS Rebovich Sr. | Raritan YC | 94 36 37 | 62 21 14 |
| 2 | 8 | EMILY | ES Gaynor | CCA | 93 41 42 | 62 38 50 |
| 3 | 10 | RESTLESS | EE Crawford | Tred Avon | 102 20 42 | 62 58 15 |
| 4 | 24 | BANGALORE | CB Tefft | RHADC | 100 26 16 | 64 27 48 |
| 5 | 33 | BORDERLAW | SJ Sherwin Dr | RBYC | 98 49 47 | 65 06 12 |
| 6 | 51 | DAISY II | WN Hubbard | NYYC | 95 19 09 | 65 52 41 |
| 7 | 58 | ILLWIND | CL Ill | CCA | 95 37 47 | 66 15 30 |
| 8 | 73 | CROSSBOW | RF Halvorsen | NYYC | 100 03 52 | 67 44 25 |
| 9 | 81 | DEVOCEAN | M Melvin | Liberty YC | 94 08 16 | 67 54 20 |
| 10 | 85 | LIGHT FANTASTIC | SR Shemitz | STC | 100 57 55 | 68 16 17 |

| 11 | 89 | TWISTER | JE Ellsworth | Stamford L | 99 38 27 | 68 35 25 |
| 12 | 96 | INVICTUS | D Franzel | Boston SC | 99 49 57 | 69 01 35 |
| 13 | 105 | FOXFIRE | Came / Brechter | Shelter Is | 100 54 18 | 69 43 08 |
| 14 | 106 | SOLUTION | CS Bacon, Jr. | NYYC | 105 07 13 | 70 11 52 |
| 15 | 107 | ANNY | LJ Vultee | Housatonic | 104 39 25 | 70 14 53 |
| 16 | 109 | WARRIOR I | TE Burrows | | 102 00 46 | 70 20 01 |
| 17 | 119 | SPIRIT | R Imbriale | Jamestown | 109 08 20 | 72 35 03 |
| 18 | 122 | ACTAEA | MM Cone | Corinthian | 109 37 05 | 73 51 05 |
| 19 | 125 | SONG OF JOY | CA Lytton | Yankee Point | 114 18 48 | 76 16 16 |

## CLASS 2

| Cls Pos | Div Pos | Yacht Name | Captain | Affiliation | Elapsed H M S | Corrected H M S |
|---|---|---|---|---|---|---|
| 1 | 11 | ARIEL | JP Thompson | Tred Avon | 88 42 47 | 63 20 50 |
| 2 | 12 | AURA | WJ Kardash | CCA / NYYC | 90 14 17 | 63 21 44 |
| 3 | 13 | JACQUELINE IV | RS Forman | NYYC | 90 16 56 | 63 22 57 |
| 4 | 15 | FLIRT | BE Ray, Ens | NASS | 90 01 35 | 63 30 44 |
| 5 | 16 | CYBELE | RM Burnes, Jr. | CCA | 89 04 32 | 63 35 14 |
| 6 | 19 | SWIFT | GP Roland, Ens | NASS | 90 41 30 | 63 58 24 |
| 7 | 26 | VIGILANT | JL Chen, Ens | NASS | 91 34 45 | 64 37 57 |
| 8 | 61 | CHOUCAS | F Cosandey | Stuyvesant | 94 24 06 | 66 21 58 |
| 9 | 64 | LINDY | DG Dickerson | Niantic Ba | 94 26 20 | 66 25 35 |
| 10 | 69 | XENOPHON | J Rabuffo | Baldwin YC | 93 18 58 | 66 56 53 |
| 11 | 92 | DAWN TREADER | LG Cohen | STC | 98 13 56 | 68 46 30 |
| 12 | 97 | LIVELY | MC Smith, Ens | NASS | 97 28 05 | 69 08 30 |
| 13 | 98 | MISTY | FA Allardyce | Watch Hill | 96 53 33 | 69 11 32 |
| 14 | 103 | SISTER ROSE | JJ Milyasevich | Lakewood YC | 96 48 05 | 69 33 07 |
| 15 | 110 | ANTARES | RM Donahue | Edgartown | 97 31 58 | 70 22 40 |
| 16 | 114 | GAMELAN | AM Winchester | American YC | 99 07 36 | 70 47 23 |
| | | SIMBA | SJ Knapp | Saugatuck | DNF | |

## CLASS 3

| Cls Pos | Div Pos | Yacht Name | Captain | Affiliation | Elapsed H M S | Corrected H M S |
|---|---|---|---|---|---|---|
| 1 | 6 | CARINA | AR Potts, Jr. | CCA | 87 14 15 | 62 29 36 |
| 2 | 22 | DOLPHIN | HS Morgan | CCA | 87 55 28 | 64 17 24 |
| 3 | 25 | MOON RACER | KR Comerford | Annapolis | 88 59 07 | 64 31 37 |
| 4 | 31 | TEMAGAMI | LA English | Royal Cana | 90 46 05 | 64 57 35 |
| 5 | 32 | INCESSANT | P Kaplan | Annapolis | 91 11 33 | 65 05 18 |
| 6 | 40 | FINESSE | NPS Merrill | CCA | 89 55 26 | 65 18 34 |
| 7 | 41 | RAGTIME | RS Johnstone | NYYC | 89 09 09 | 65 19 28 |
| 8 | 44 | CYGNETTE | WJ Mayer | NYYC / IHY | 90 49 29 | 65 31 54 |
| 9 | 70 | ALTHEA | W Ewing III | Noroton YC | 91 50 51 | 67 05 00 |
| 10 | 74 | SCOUT | KA Maloney | Beverly YC | 93 07 40 | 67 49 03 |
| 10 | 74 | CYGNET | WR Sylvanovich | NYYC | 92 56 08 | 67 49 03 |
| 12 | 80 | XTREME | JM Naroski | Palmers Co | 93 46 27 | 67 53 03 |
| 13 | 87 | MYSTERY | RA Jones | Cooper River | 93 25 54 | 68 28 31 |
| 14 | 101 | REGATTA | CG Koste | Tred Avon | 96 56 19 | 69 22 35 |
| 15 | 116 | UPBEAT | OC Smith | CCA | 96 56 42 | 70 53 09 |
| 16 | 118 | MORGAN OF MARIE | C Golder | RHKYC / RY | 99 02 00 | 72 11 00 |
| | | BLACK WATCH | TJ Harrington | NYYC | DNF | |
| | | DIRIGO | EM Johnson | Eastport YC | DNF | |
| | | TRUE NORTH | RG Cragg | RNSYS | DNC | |

## CLASS 4

| Cls Pos | Div Pos | Yacht Name | Captain | Affiliation | Elapsed H M S | Corrected H M S |
|---|---|---|---|---|---|---|
| 1 | 21 | GALADRIEL | JS Santa | Black Rock | 86 36 00 | 64 12 32 |
| 2 | 29 | ORION | DH Patterson,Jr | STC | 86 43 21 | 64 46 17 |
| 3 | 30 | BABE | CE Couper MD | RBYC | 88 03 28 | 64 52 33 |
| 4 | 42 | BANDANA | CF Benson | Tred Avon | 90 01 43 | 65 26 40 |

| Cls Pos | Div Pos | Yacht Name | Captain | Affiliation | Elapsed H M S | Corrected H M S |
|---|---|---|---|---|---|---|
| 5 | 52 | MUTINY | TG Kane, Jr. | American YC | 89 13 40 | 65 59 55 |
| 6 | 77 | DOVE | JE Bornhofft | Annisquam | 88 18 06 | 67 51 43 |
| 7 | 83 | CLOVER | NF Finnegan | NYYC | 92 14 50 | 68 03 03 |
| 8 | 100 | PALANTIR | RD Kendrick | Lloyd Harb | 94 11 42 | 69 18 17 |
| 9 | 112 | LE CYGNE | DC Chapman | South Rive | 94 23 06 | 70 34 10 |
| 10 | 113 | RAMPAGE | Lt. M Nasitka | CGA SC | 95 32 49 | 70 36 29 |
| 11 | 124 | STAGGER LEE | MD Hochberg | | 100 51 59 | 74 46 19 |
| 12 | 127 | MANTRA | WA Devereaux | Manchester | 104 37 16 | 79 37 06 |
| | | TALISMAN | RL Herndon | Breakwater | DNF | |
| | | SOMERSET | WW Alder | Riverside | DNF | |

## CLASS 5 (J-44)

| Cls Pos | Div Pos | Yacht Name | Captain | Affiliation | Elapsed H M S | Corrected H M S |
|---|---|---|---|---|---|---|
| 1 | 36 | MABUHAY II | EA Salvati, MD | LYC / NYYC | 83 23 45 | 65 11 33 |
| 2 | 43 | STAMPEDE | JL Sundstrom | American YC | 83 50 44 | 65 30 05 |
| 3 | 48 | GOLD DIGGER | JD Bishop | American YC | 83 59 57 | 65 38 43 |
| 4 | 49 | RUNAWAY | LR Glenn | Seawanhaka | 84 06 12 | 65 45 49 |
| 5 | 53 | BROWN EYED GIRL | SH Dinhofer | NYYC | 84 32 10 | 66 00 45 |
| 6 | 57 | CHARLIE V | NH Schulman | NYYC / Sea | 84 55 10 | 66 13 50 |
| 7 | 62 | CHALLENGE IV | JW Willis | STC / Lloy | 85 18 26 | 66 22 18 |
| 8 | 63 | VAMP | LJ Sitar | American YC | 84 45 29 | 66 22 58 |
| 9 | 67 | DIOGENES II | MD Clarke | American YC | 85 29 14 | 66 36 03 |
| 10 | 99 | MONHEGAN | PB Hilgendorff | CCA | 88 54 00 | 69 16 55 |
| 11 | 108 | RESOLUTE | RK Scribner | Charleston | 89 31 24 | 70 15 40 |
| 12 | 117 | PASSION | A Perni | Manhasset | 91 12 21 | 70 54 01 |
| 13 | 120 | TRILOGY | D Carlson | | 93 52 57 | 73 16 11 |

## CLASS 6

| Cls Pos | Div Pos | Yacht Name | Captain | Affiliation | Elapsed H M S | Corrected H M S |
|---|---|---|---|---|---|---|
| 1 | 14 | HOUND | F Eberhart | CCA | 84 22 49 | 63 26 29 |
| 2 | 17 | TEMPTRESS | RS Shulman | NYYC | 81 43 49 | 63 39 37 |
| 3 | 28 | ELAN | A Blair | Essex YC | 84 00 45 | 64 41 35 |
| 4 | 35 | SWEPT AWAY | RM Mandell | | 83 59 58 | 65 07 52 |
| 5 | 47 | TOSCANA | EP Swenson | IHYC | 83 08 03 | 65 37 51 |
| 6 | 50 | WANDERER | WS Cushman | NYYC | 84 38 09 | 65 52 25 |
| 7 | 56 | CARPE DIEM | MJ Fracchia | NYYC | 84 48 42 | 66 13 35 |
| 8 | 71 | BROADSWORD | JG Brim | NYYC | 84 43 57 | 67 27 45 |
| 9 | 84 | ALEXIS | AC Dalessandro | Boston YC | 86 30 32 | 68 04 05 |
| 10 | 90 | CARIBE | RS Swingle | | 86 01 01 | 68 45 22 |
| 11 | 93 | NOW | AL Davies MD | Columbia SC | 88 24 46 | 68 50 27 |
| 12 | 94 | ESCAPADE | D Seynhaeve | American YC | 90 15 53 | 68 55 15 |
| 13 | 104 | WINDWALKER | CW Cullen | Corinthian | 87 13 44 | 69 40 28 |
| 14 | 111 | WHISPER | S Brotman | | 93 25 10 | 70 26 22 |
| 15 | 115 | KINSHIP | JT Selldorff | New Bedford | 88 08 40 | 70 52 36 |
| 16 | 121 | CHIEFTAIN | RM Chuda, MD | NYAC YC | 96 03 56 | 73 19 12 |
| | | SEVERIN | EJ Tobin | American YC | DNF | |

## CLASS 7

| Cls Pos | Div Pos | Yacht Name | Captain | Affiliation | Elapsed H M S | Corrected H M S |
|---|---|---|---|---|---|---|
| 1 | 18 | NEVA | RC Watson | STC | 74 59 09 | 63 54 19 |
| 2 | 23 | RUSH | TL Stark | NYYC | 79 04 59 | 64 19 58 |
| 3 | 34 | SCEPTRE'D ISLE | D Weismann | NYYC | 79 50 33 | 65 06 17 |
| 4 | 37 | NOVA | SC Barker | | 76 45 54 | 65 16 23 |
| 5 | 38 | MOONDANCE | D Opatrny | NYYC / Riv | 80 24 58 | 65 17 16 |
| 6 | 39 | HARRIER | SR Munger | Riverside | 77 53 45 | 65 18 12 |
| 7 | 46 | NATALIE J | PD Oniel, III DDS | Bayview YC | 79 43 30 | 65 34 23 |
| 8 | 55 | JULIANNA | AL Gould, Jr. | US Sailing | 78 11 57 | 66 09 45 |
| 9 | 59 | GOOMBAY SMASH | WA Douglass III | NYYC | 81 32 04 | 66 17 22 |

| | | | | | Elapsed | Corrected |
|---|---|---|---|---|---|---|
| 10 | 65 | AGINCOURT | PG Lowell | NYYC | 84 13 26 | 66 31 09 |
| 11 | 66 | NOONMARK VI | CSR Walker | Royal Yach | 78 07 28 | 66 32 23 |
| 12 | 72 | MENSAE | EC Kristiansen | Lloyd Harb | 80 14 48 | 67 35 13 |
| 13 | 76 | EXCALIBUR | W Apold | RNSYS | 79 59 52 | 67 50 08 |
| 14 | 78 | CAPELLA VIII | JG Stanley | CCA / NYYC | 80 17 37 | 67 52 46 |
| 15 | 86 | CWENE II | R Dominique | USMMA | 85 20 22 | 68 17 31 |
| 16 | 88 | TANGO | TC Smith, Jr. | Eastern YC | 83 39 40 | 68 30 11 |
| 17 | 91 | SIRENA | SM Loeb | NYYC | 85 49 01 | 68 46 06 |
| 18 | 123 | SEA HAWK | SA Friedel | 20 Hundred | 90 58 50 | 74 42 57 |
| 19 | 126 | HINANO | RD Spurling | | 94 17 38 | 76 21 39 |

## CLASS 8

| Cls Pos | Div Pos | Yacht Name | Captain | Affiliation | Elapsed H M S | Corrected H M S |
|---|---|---|---|---|---|---|
| 1 | 1 | ZARAFFA | H Sheldon, MD | | 58 53 25 | 58 25 15 |
| 2 | 2 | ENCORE | JL Dolan | NYYC | 65 04 28 | 60 34 42 |
| 3 | 3 | SPANK ME BT | RW Limoggio | Port Wash | 61 49 29 | 61 49 28 |
| 4 | 4 | KODIAK | EL Ecclestone | CCA | 71 25 25 | 61 57 48 |
| 5 | 7 | DENALI | WF Mckinley | Bayview YC | 64 51 38 | 62 29 42 |
| 6 | 9 | MISCHIEVOUS | AJ Fitzgibbons,III | NYYC | 67 14 06 | 62 57 34 |
| 7 | 20 | ACE | FW Stelle | Breakwater | 74 58 19 | 64 08 36 |
| 8 | 27 | CHIPPEWA | CG Deutsch | New York | 73 15 30 | 64 38 12 |
| 9 | 45 | ARCADIA | RG Stone, Jr. | NYYC | 74 42 20 | 65 32 00 |
| 10 | 54 | NIRVANA | CF Kiefer III | | 69 49 05 | 66 01 43 |
| 11 | 60 | BRIGADOON VII | RW Morton | NYYC | 75 44 37 | 66 19 26 |
| 12 | 68 | STARR TRAIL | RA Mulderig | RBYC | 74 41 43 | 66 56 43 |
| 13 | 79 | VANISH | RW Monro | IHYC | 77 22 22 | 67 52 59 |
| 14 | 82 | BOMBARDINO | JW Sykes | American YC | 78 54 20 | 67 56 52 |
| 15 | 95 | ENTRADA | JW Thompson | The Royal | 79 15 20 | 68 57 39 |
| 16 | 102 | ANTIPODES | JF Miller | NYYC | 80 40 52 | 69 25 20 |
| | | TRADER | FB Detwiler | Bayview YC | DNF | |

**AMERICAP CRUISING DIVISION**

## CLASS 10

| Cls Pos | Div Pos | Yacht Name | Captain | Affiliation | Elapsed H M S | Corrected H M S |
|---|---|---|---|---|---|---|
| 1 | 1 | PALAWAN | JC Hoopes | CCA | 80 11 58 | 60 23 58 |
| 2 | 2 | SKY | J Reiher | Breakwater | 85 13 50 | 61 00 16 |
| 3 | 3 | MARLOW | JT Middleton | | 91 36 28 | 61 18 25 |
| 4 | 4 | STARLIGHT | AC Bulger | NYYC | 91 18 39 | 61 20 32 |
| 5 | 8 | LADY B | JP Madden | | 88 56 16 | 63 22 46 |
| 6 | 10 | CANVASBACK | LC Howley | Vermillion | 93 02 25 | 63 50 35 |
| 7 | 11 | AMELIA | JE Hughes | Shelter Is | 86 25 30 | 64 01 43 |
| 8 | 12 | SONNY | JS White | Stamford YC | 84 14 52 | 64 17 34 |
| 9 | 13 | PAMIR | FH Curren | Conanicut | 92 08 19 | 64 50 36 |
| 10 | 14 | FOX | EG Verney | Nantucket | 91 44 53 | 65 12 05 |
| 11 | 17 | WAIANIWA | C Bouzaid | New York | 95 31 16 | 65 52 20 |
| 12 | 18 | NIGHT TRAIN | WF Riley | Stage Harb | 98 41 44 | 66 11 20 |
| | | GITANA | LF Rooney, III | | DNC | |
| | | PERSEVERANCE | TI Puett | CCA / NYYC | DNC | |

## CLASS 11

| Cls Pos | Div Pos | Yacht Name | Captain | Affiliation | Elapsed H M S | Corrected H M S |
|---|---|---|---|---|---|---|
| 1 | 5 | RESTIVE | GP Denny, III | Kollegewid | 101 08 23 | 62 16 09 |
| 2 | 6 | J'ERIN | JJ Flaherty | Mattapoise | 105 10 18 | 62 43 34 |
| 3 | 7 | BERMUDA OYSTER | PB Hubbard | RBYC, Rhad | 101 38 03 | 62 52 42 |

| 4 | 9 | INESSA II | K Grubecki | Polish Sai | 98 14 29 | 63 33 39 |
| 5 | 15 | ALLEGRA | JM Mertz | Rye YC | 98 35 14 | 65 13 49 |
| 6 | 16 | SHEARWATER | CM Hall | Norfolk YC | 104 22 38 | 65 14 55 |
| 7 | 19 | DIVA | EG Fischer, MD | NYYC / Ida | 105 05 52 | 66 18 14 |
| 8 | 20 | DAME OF SARK | S Donovan | Edgartown | 113 24 28 | 66 20 50 |
| 9 | 21 | TIGER TOO | TG Ritter | NYYC | 98 57 06 | 66 28 06 |
| 10 | 22 | ASOLARE | W Marsh | Stage Harb | 111 59 19 | 71 26 42 |
| 11 | 23 | GRYF II | K Kaminski | Polish Sai | 115 15 35 | 72 28 35 |
| 12 | 24 | AVATAR | J Kedzierski | Polish Sai | 140 55 00 | 91 35 23 |
| | | FEO | EP Best | Seawanhaka | DNF | |
| | | SEASTAR | CV Wait | New York | DNF | |

## AMERICAP DOUBLEHANDED (SPINNAKER) DIVISION

CLASS 12

| Cls Pos | Div Pos | Yacht Name | Captain | Affiliation | Elapsed H M S | Corrected H M S |
|---|---|---|---|---|---|---|
| 1 | 1 | LORA ANN | RT Du Moulin | Larchmont | 90 49 51 | 54 02 28 |
| 2 | 2 | MIREILLE | EH Gaynor | Pequot YC | 87 39 23 | 55 24 14 |
| 3 | 3 | PIPE DREAM IX | S Piper III | Biscayne Bay | 80 22 24 | 56 17 45 |
| 4 | 4 | GRYPHON | JS Harris | CCA / Manc | 86 50 27 | 56 20 02 |
| 5 | 5 | SHERE KHAN | BR Johnson | NYYC / CCA | 87 55 00 | 57 40 13 |
| 6 | 6 | KILLUA | JG Binch | CCA / NYYC | 108 48 55 | 60 38 25 |
| 7 | 7 | ANTARES | DE Sharpe | Annapolis | 92 47 10 | 61 23 30 |
| 8 | 8 | MOJO | RS Bockman MD | NYYC | 86 07 53 | 64 38 35 |
| 9 | 9 | MOMENTUM | R Womsley | | 100 55 46 | 65 09 25 |
| | | KIVA | M Stevens | Portsmouth | DNF | |

## 2004 Newport Bermuda Race

## CLASS AND DIVISION RESULTS

### IMS RACING DIVISION

CLASS 9

| Cls Pos | Div Pos | Yacht Name | Captain | Affiliation | Elapsed H M S | Corrected H M S |
|---|---|---|---|---|---|---|
| 1 | 1 | ROSEBUD | Roger Sturgeon | Hyannis | 68 24 43 | 59 44 12 |
| 2 | 2 | BRIGHT STAR | RC Breeden | NYYC | 70 23 46 | 61 39 04 |
| 3 | 3 | LIGHTWAVE | Carsten Petersen | NYYC | 72 45 33 | 62 59 04 |
| 4 | 4 | SJAMBOK | MJ Brennan | NASS | 72 01 00 | 63 54 22 |
| 5 | 5 | SNOW LION | LS Huntington | CCA | 84 18 54 | 65 30 47 |
| 6 | 6 | HARRIER | SR Munger | Riverside | 77 29 21 | 66 21 45 |
| 7 | 7 | TITAN 12 | Tom Hill | NYYC | 67 56 03 | 67 14 48 |
| 8 | 8 | CARRERA | JT Dockery | NYYC, CCA | 67 15 54 | 67 15 51 |
| 9 | 9 | AERA | N Lykiardopulo | RYS | 77 30 24 | 67 31 16 |
| 10 | 10 | BLUE YANKEE | Robert C. Towse | STC | 76 40 12 | 68 13 28 |
| 11 | 11 | RIMA | John G. Brim | NYYC | 82 51 45 | 70 54 02 |

### IMS CRUISER/RACER DIVISION

CLASS 1

| Cls Pos | Div Pos | Yacht Name | Captain | Affiliation | Elapsed H M S | Corrected H M S |
|---|---|---|---|---|---|---|
| 1 | 18 | SINN FEIN | PS Rebovich | Raritan | 116 32 52 | 76 52 39 |
| 2 | 20 | EMILY | Edwin S. Gaynor | CCA | 116 17 19 | 77 58 21 |
| 3 | 22 | NICOLE | TC DuPont | CCA | 120 23 08 | 79 21 45 |
| 4 | 32 | LIVELY LADY II | WN Hubbard, III | NYYC | 124 14 53 | 81 05 36 |
| 5 | 33 | BANGALORE | Carvel B. Tefft | RHADC | 125 14 22 | 81 07 32 |
| 6 | 35 | ACTAEA | Michael M. Cone | CYC of Phila | 121 43 19 | 81 17 57 |
| 7 | 38 | LIGHT FANTASTIC | Sylvan R. Shemitz | | 120 20 49 | 81 32 08 |
| 8 | 45 | REMORA VIII | RA Hopkins | Barrington | 123 32 20 | 82 32 39 |
| 9 | 51 | AURORA | Andrew Kallfelz | JYC | 120 05 45 | 83 06 16 |
| 10 | 54 | CROSSBOW | Roy F. Halvorsen | NYYC | 121 05 20 | 83 20 05 |
| 11 | 65 | PIRATE | Juan E. Corradi | NYYC | 127 00 46 | 84 42 40 |
| 12 | 69 | SONG OF JOY | Charles A. Lytton | YPYC | 129 17 58 | 84 51 04 |
| 13 | 75 | CHOUCAS | F Cosandey | Stuyvesant | 120 57 12 | 85 34 37 |

CLASS 2

| Cls Pos | Div Pos | Yacht Name | Captain | Affiliation | Elapsed H M S | Corrected H M S |
|---|---|---|---|---|---|---|
| 1 | 21 | LIVELY | Andrew Hurst | NASS | 111 24 50 | 79 05 34 |
| 2 | 25 | JACQUELINE IV | RS Forman, Jr. | NYYC | 112 34 19 | 79 53 59 |
| 3 | 27 | AURA | William Kardash | CCA, NYYC | 112 17 43 | 80 08 33 |
| 4 | 29 | DREAMCATCHER | Stephen Kylander | DCYC | 113 57 36 | 80 49 46 |
| 5 | 31 | SO FAR | L Hillman | Northshore | 113 12 46 | 81 03 33 |
| 6 | 39 | MISTY | Fred A. Allardyce | Watch Hill | 114 43 07 | 81 39 26 |
| 7 | 44 | ANTARES | R Donahue and J McGrath | Edgartown | 115 30 02 | 82 26 46 |
| 8 | 52 | REGATTA | CG Koste | Tred Avon | 116 01 26 | 83 18 23 |
| 9 | 53 | FLIRT | ZC Conatser | NASS | 117 20 36 | 83 18 51 |
| 10 | 59 | MORGAN OF MARIETTA | Colin G. Golder | Raritan | 116 12 05 | 83 57 24 |
| 11 | 63 | KYRIE | John DiMatteo | Centerport | 118 34 56 | 84 17 02 |
| 12 | 67 | MOONDANCE | Cliff Crowley | Black Rock | 119 35 10 | 84 50 32 |
| 13 | 89 | VELADARE | John Myles | PYC | 123 58 25 | 88 47 20 |
| 14 | 95 | COURAGE | ES Madara, III | AYC | 129 11 48 | 93 24 26 |

## CLASS 3

| Cls Pos | Div Pos | Yacht Name | Captain | Affiliation | Elapsed H M S | Corrected H M S |
|---|---|---|---|---|---|---|
| 1 | 23 | CYGNETTE | WJ Mayer | NYYC, IHYC | 110 04 22 | 79 42 51 |
| 2 | 26 | CRESCENDO | James Wilmot | Indian Hbr | 108 01 28 | 79 55 58 |
| 3 | 28 | GALADRIEL | John Santa | Black Rock | 108 57 43 | 80 46 50 |
| 4 | 37 | CARINA | Rives Potts | CCA | 111 51 02 | 81 25 08 |
| 5 | 41 | XENOPHON | Jeff Rabuffo | Baldwin | 112 23 18 | 81 58 55 |
| 6 | 42 | BANDANA | CF Benson | Tred Avon | 112 31 21 | 82 07 46 |
| 7 | 48 | AMIGO VI | BP Coyne | BYC | 114 43 35 | 82 53 31 |
| 8 | 50 | BABE | Colin E. Couper | RBYC | 113 40 54 | 83 03 14 |
| 9 | 56 | FREE FALL | Wiliam McFaul | Port Wash | 112 29 11 | 83 46 53 |
| 10 | 60 | HOUND | Frank Eberhart | NYYC, CCA | 110 03 50 | 84 00 17 |
| 11 | 71 | ALTHEA | Wm. Ewing, III | Noroton | 115 49 46 | 84 56 55 |
| 12 | 77 | GOOGOLPLEX | MJ McNamara | STC | 115 44 56 | 85 46 06 |
| 13 | 78 | DOLPHIN | Henry S. Morgan | CCA | 117 51 42 | 85 46 17 |
| 14 | 93 | WHISPER | Sheldon Brotman | SCYCC | 120 23 54 | 91 45 40 |
| 15 | 94 | MANTRA | WA Devereaux | CCA, MYC | 122 48 57 | 92 42 19 |
| | | DREAM CATCHER TOO | Greg F. Snowball | RYCV, PWY | DNF | |
| | | FINESSE | NPS Merrill | CCA | DNF | |
| | | RUSE | William Marsh | Wychmere | DNF | |

## CLASS 4

| Cls Pos | Div Pos | Yacht Name | Captain | Affiliation | Elapsed H M S | Corrected H M S |
|---|---|---|---|---|---|---|
| 1 | 10 | ORION | Pat Patterson, Jr. | STC | 98 54 40 | 74 13 19 |
| 2 | 34 | RESOLUTE | TD Arndt | LYC, STC | 109 04 53 | 81 17 13 |
| 3 | 46 | WINDBORN | Richard W. Born | RBYC | 107 59 21 | 82 33 49 |
| 4 | 47 | FIREFLY | P Wilmerding | NYYC, KYC | 104 22 22 | 82 47 24 |
| 5 | 55 | ALIBI | GL Grant, Jr. | CPYC, ROR | 110 42 36 | 83 41 38 |
| 6 | 61 | LADY B | John P Madden | RBYA | 108 03 42 | 84 02 47 |
| 7 | 64 | BLUE MINGO | Edward J. Tobin | AYC | 109 33 31 | 84 24 37 |
| 8 | 66 | JUGGERNAUT | RC Musetti | AYC | 111 29 11 | 84 42 44 |
| 9 | 72 | ALEXIS | AC D'Alessandro | BYC | 107 30 46 | 85 00 24 |
| 10 | 74 | DOGSLED | Todd F. Barnard | RNSYS | 110 40 13 | 85 32 32 |
| 11 | 79 | TABASCO | John C. Levinson | Pequot | 110 57 30 | 85 53 03 |
| 12 | 80 | UPGRADE | Bill Read | PCYC, CCA | 111 35 39 | 86 01 17 |
| 13 | 81 | STAR | EG Verney | Nantucket | 111 18 03 | 86 11 25 |
| 14 | 86 | WANDERER | Bill Cushman | NYYC | 112 59 39 | 87 29 04 |
| | | GARBO | Gerald W. Sears | NYYC | DNF | |

## CLASS 5 (J-44)

| Cls Pos | Div Pos | Yacht Name | Captain | Affiliation | Elapsed H M S | Corrected H M S |
|---|---|---|---|---|---|---|
| 1 | 36 | MABUHAY II | EA Salvati, MD | LYC, NYYC | 104 27 13 | 81 23 05 |
| 2 | 57 | CHARLIE V | NH Schulman, MD | Sea Cliff | 107 56 05 | 83 49 33 |
| 3 | 58 | RUNAWAY | LR Glenn | CCA | 107 55 51 | 83 52 37 |
| 4 | 70 | BROWN-EYED GIRL | SH Dinhofer | Indian Hbr | 108 55 23 | 84 53 36 |
| 5 | 73 | GOLD DIGGER | James D. Bishop | AYC | 110 02 11 | 85 27 20 |
| 6 | 82 | TRILOGY | Douglas Carlson | WYC | 111 16 50 | 86 16 49 |
| 7 | 83 | SAGITTA | Jon Somes | Bayview | 111 04 25 | 86 42 11 |
| 8 | 96 | MONHEGAN | M van Breems | Sound Sail | 122 15 22 | 94 31 58 |

## CLASS 6

| Cls Pos | Div Pos | Yacht Name | Captain | Affiliation | Elapsed H M S | Corrected H M S |
|---|---|---|---|---|---|---|
| 1 | 1 | ALLIANCE | Dominick Porco | AYC | 84 18 40 | 69 50 35 |
| 2 | 5 | BETTER THAN | Andrzej Rojek | NYYC | 87 23 15 | 72 25 41 |
| 3 | 9 | PLENTY | Alex Roepers | Stonington | 89 00 11 | 74 04 36 |
| 4 | 13 | DEVOCEAN | S De Voe, III | NYYC | 91 15 52 | 76 06 56 |
| 5 | 15 | TEMPTRESS | RS Shulman | STC | 95 38 03 | 76 42 33 |

| 6 | 43 | SPITFIRE | Brian Fantel | USMMA | 97 49 39 | 82 26 05 |
| 7 | 49 | CYBELE | RM Burnes, Jr. | CCA | 104 07 05 | 83 02 42 |
| 8 | 68 | AFFINITY | AJ Santry, III | NYYC | 106 49 21 | 84 50 49 |
| 9 | 76 | RAIDER | David Ross | Rhode River | 102 15 20 | 85 39 08 |
| 10 | 84 | TRINITY | DD Pinciaro | PYC | 107 37 44 | 86 57 06 |
| 11 | 87 | TANGO | David Millet | CCA | 106 43 07 | 87 37 35 |
| 12 | 91 | PENINGO | Alexander Vietor | CCA | 109 21 45 | 89 20 09 |
| 13 | 97 | JACKAROO | John N. Vultee | HBC | 117 21 59 | 95 36 07 |
| 14 | 98 | MADRIGAL | WL Kimbell, Jr | Corinthian | 119 35 05 | 96 20 03 |
| | | VIXEN | D Weismann | NYYC | DNF | |

## CLASS 7

| Cls Pos | Div Pos | Yacht Name | Captain | Affiliation | Elapsed H M S | Corrected H M S |
|---|---|---|---|---|---|---|
| 1 | 2 | ACE | FW Stelle | Breakwater | 84 31 45 | 71 37 14 |
| 2 | 4 | ANTIPODES | James F. Miller | NYYC | 83 52 33 | 72 24 33 |
| 3 | 6 | BOMBARDINO | James W. Sykes | AYC, NYYC | 85 08 12 | 72 51 03 |
| 4 | 11 | STARR TRAIL | RA Mulderig | RBYC | 85 14 35 | 74 49 06 |
| 5 | 14 | ARCADIA | RG Stone, Jr. | NYYC | 87 49 07 | 76 26 57 |
| 6 | 17 | CABARET | Robert Limoggio | PWYC | 90 44 11 | 76 50 18 |
| 7 | 24 | SPIRIT OF MINERVA | Adrian Faiers | RORC | 90 52 20 | 79 50 54 |
| 8 | 30 | KODIAK | RA Greene | NYYC | 93 47 27 | 80 58 43 |
| 9 | 62 | EXCALIBUR | William Apold | RNSYS | 99 41 19 | 84 08 45 |
| 10 | 85 | MENSAE | EC Kristiansen | LHYC | 104 09 56 | 86 59 03 |
| 11 | 88 | FIRST LIGHT | Andre A. Laus | NYYC | 111 20 13 | 88 34 32 |
| 12 | 90 | MONTEREY | P. Leslie Crane | RBYC | 110 39 33 | 88 58 29 |
| | | JULIANNA | AL Gould, Jr. | US Sailing | DNF | |
| | | WINDWALKER | Craig W. Cullen | CCA | DNF | |

## CLASS 8

| Cls Pos | Div Pos | Yacht Name | Captain | Affiliation | Elapsed H M S | Corrected H M S |
|---|---|---|---|---|---|---|
| 1 | 3 | ZARAFFA | Skip Sheldon | CCA | 72 23 42 | 72 23 43 |
| 2 | 7 | DONNYBROOK | James Muldoon | Annapolis YC | 72 24 55 | 72 51 22 |
| 3 | 8 | PTARMIGAN | LF Dickie | Riverside | 82 57 03 | 73 37 30 |
| 4 | 12 | SERENGETI | Charles Weiss | Seawanhka | 83 13 22 | 75 27 54 |
| 5 | 16 | FALCON | M. Mincus and S. Barker | NYYC | 85 01 15 | 76 43 17 |
| 6 | 19 | MISCHIEVOUS | AJ Fitzgibbons, III | NYYC | 82 39 17 | 77 44 41 |
| 7 | 40 | NIRVANA | Charles F. Kiefer, III | | 87 37 01 | 81 51 48 |
| 8 | 92 | KETURAH | EL Ecclestone, Jr. | CCA | 93 41 05 | 90 49 02 |

**IMS MAXZ DIVISION**

## CLASS 10

| Cls Pos | Div Pos | Yacht Name | Captain | Affiliation | Elapsed H M S | Corrected H M S |
|---|---|---|---|---|---|---|
| 1 | 1 | MORNING GLORY | Hasso Plattner | KYC | 48 28 31 | 48 28 31 |
| 2 | 2 | WINDQUEST | Dick DeVos and Doug DeVos | MBYC | 55 35 08 | 50 51 23 |
| 3 | 3 | PYEWACKET | Roy E. Disney | LAYC | 53 55 23 | 53 44 02 |

## CLASS 11

| Cls Pos | Div Pos | Yacht Name | Captain | Affiliation | Elapsed H M S | Corrected H M S |
|---|---|---|---|---|---|---|
| 1 | 9 | STARLIGHT | AC Bulger | NYYC | 113 50 56 | 67 40 43 |
| 2 | 12 | CYGNET | WR Sylvanovich | NYYC | 116 58 52 | 69 22 16 |
| 3 | 13 | RUTAINE | DP McLoughlin | Newport | 118 28 31 | 69 36 49 |
| 4 | 16 | CRACKERJACK | Alan H. Krulisch | Petit Manan | 122 35 53 | 71 14 26 |
| 5 | 17 | TIGER TOO | Toby G. Ritter | NYYC | 120 38 22 | 71 16 26 |
| 6 | 19 | VALOUR | Harold R. Denton | Miles River | 119 01 03 | 72 21 31 |
| 7 | 20 | REMEDIOS | Frans J. Kok | GIYS | 116 10 44 | 72 45 35 |
| 8 | 21 | CANVASBACK | Lee Howley | Vermillion | 118 06 16 | 72 55 02 |
| 9 | 23 | NOVA | Mark DiStefano | NYYC | 110 37 06 | 76 33 00 |
| 10 | 24 | FLYING GOOSE | DC van Starrenburg | NYYC | 112 22 31 | 76 44 50 |
| | | PAMIR | Francis H. Curren | NYYC | DNF | |
| | | AMELIA 3 | JE Hughes, Jr. | CCA | DNF | |
| | | MARLOW | Michael Paolucci | | DNF | |

## CLASS 12

| Cls Pos | Div Pos | Yacht Name | Captain | Affiliation | Elapsed H M S | Corrected H M S |
|---|---|---|---|---|---|---|
| 1 | 1 | J'ERIN | James J. Flaherty | Mattapoisset | 123 06 46 | 64 27 41 |
| 2 | 2 | DAME OF SARK | SP Donovan, Jr. | Edgartown | 128 16 20 | 65 12 46 |
| 3 | 3 | PANACHE | Mark W. Shakley | NYYC | 119 31 28 | 65 38 23 |
| 4 | 4 | RESTIVE | George P. Denny | Kollegewid | 121 32 38 | 65 48 10 |
| 5 | 5 | SPIRIT | Krzysztof Bogdan | South Bay | 124 53 42 | 65 53 40 |
| 6 | 6 | REVEILLE | Jim Hammitt | New Bedford | 119 28 02 | 66 44 01 |
| 7 | 7 | DIVA | EG Fischer, MD | CCA | 119 13 49 | 66 56 39 |
| 8 | 8 | PREVAIL | Mark B. Shaw | NYYC | 116 39 44 | 67 08 39 |
| 9 | 10 | AVATAR | Janusz Kedzierski | PSYC | 127 42 12 | 68 15 39 |
| 10 | 11 | ALLEGRA | James M. Mertz | CCA, RBYC | 117 45 12 | 69 21 00 |
| 11 | 14 | DRAGONSBANE | RK van Heyningen | Ida Lewis | 123 01 09 | 69 46 08 |
| 12 | 15 | INESSA II | K Grubecki | PYA Poland | 122 07 06 | 69 52 45 |
| 13 | 18 | NOSTOS | LD Weisman | BYC | 126 21 18 | 71 34 14 |
| 14 | 22 | COUNTERPOINT | D Kazanowski | OCC | 127 34 58 | 72 57 35 |

## CLASS 13

| Cls Pos | Div Pos | Yacht Name | Captain | Affiliation | Elapsed H M S | Corrected H M S |
|---|---|---|---|---|---|---|
| 1 | 1 | LORA ANN | R duMoulin | STC, LYC | 112 59 37 | 69 00 28 |
| 2 | 2 | MIREILLE | E. Hewitt Gaynor | CCA | 107 03 14 | 69 03 39 |
| 3 | 3 | KIVA | Mark Stevens | PYC | 110 37 53 | 69 53 40 |
| 4 | 4 | WILDHORSE | RL Meisner | Watch Hill | 124 56 29 | 70 24 07 |
| 5 | 5 | LINDY | DG Dickerson | Niantic Bay | 120 37 40 | 74 26 42 |
| 6 | 6 | VALKYRIE | Bjorn Johnson | CCA, NYYC | 114 09 38 | 74 42 53 |
| 7 | 7 | TIANNA | Robert Drum | NPYC | 128 59 20 | 75 10 13 |
| 8 | 8 | FREEBIRD | Philip M. Asche | NYYC | 122 26 29 | 75 17 02 |
| 9 | 9 | ANTARES | David E. Sharpe | Annapolis YC | 119 31 30 | 79 12 24 |
| | | SISTER ROSE | Joe Milyasevich | LYC | DNC | |
| | | KILLUA | James G Binch | Edgartown | DNF | |

# Acknowledgments, Selected Sources, Notes

My thanks go first to the Cruising Club of America for making this book possible. Commodores Truman Casner and Ned Rowland, and Sheila McCurdy and Bill Barton, have understood my purpose from the beginning.

At the Royal Bermuda Yacht Club, Commodores Jane Correia and Andy Cox, with Kirk Cooper, Peter Cooper, Hilary Roberts, and others, arranged for interviews with Bermudians who make the race succeed, and for photocopies of minutes of club meetings and articles in the island's major newspaper, *The Royal Gazette*. Kirk and Helen Cooper were gracious hosts and (through their stories and library) fonts of information about the race, Bermuda, and those fascinating characters, Bermudians.

At Mystic Seaport, my appreciation goes first to Andy German for his commitment and multitude of contributions to this book—our fourth in four years, each a prize to be proud of. I thank Mary Anne Stets for pushing the book along, and Amy German, Dennis Murphy, and Claire White-Peterson for their assistance with the many illustrations. At the G. W. Blunt White Library and the New York Yacht Club library, Paul O'Pecko (and his staff) and Teresa Bogar provided all any writer can ask for: materials, time, working space, calm, and order. To Clare Cunningham goes my gratitude for another beautiful design.

Sheila McCurdy, David Brown, Frank Bohlen, Dallas Murphy, and Kirk Cooper read all or portions of the manuscript and saved me from many errors, though (of course) any that remain are mine.

I am indebted to the great many people who provided Bermuda Race facts, stories, anecdotes, or photographs. Because only so much space is available, not all their contributions have made their way into these pages. If any one lesson comes out of this effort, it is the limitless power of an ocean racing sailor to find humor in miserable situations.

I thank: Harry Anderson, Paul Antrobus, Arthur Bugs Baer, Bill Barton, John Baxter, Tony Bessinger, Jim Bishop, Frank Bohlen, Buddy Bombard, Peter Bowker, Pat Britton, Nancy Broeckl, Clive Brown, Nick Brown, Warren Brown, Peter Bruce, John Burnham, Karin J. Olsen Campia, Jenifer Clark, Kirk Cooper, Peter Cooper, Jane Correia, Andy Cox, Bob Coulson, Colin Couper, Rad Daly, Bob Darbee, Nicholas B. Dill, Mindy Gunther Drew, Edward du Moulin, Richard du Moulin, Dan Dyer, George Eddy, Kirk Elliott, Daniel Forster, Queene Foster, Edwin Gaynor, Mitch Gibbons-Neff, Larry Glenn, Dick Goennel, Bob Gunther Jr., Bob Gunther Sr., and Guy Gurney;

Also Robbie Haines, Edward Harris, George Hinman, Ellen Jane Hollis, Stan Honey, Robert W. Hubner, Larry Huntington, Matthew Huntington, Tim James, Gary Jobson, Stan Keck, Walter Keenan, Mayotta Southworth Kendrick, Bruce Kirby, Karl Kirkman, Jane Lawrence, Stanley Livingston Jr., Doug Logan, Al Loomis, Harvey Loomis, Worth Loomis, Sheila McCurdy, Patricia Makin, Jacques Megroz, Jack Merrill, Jim Mertz, Peter Millard, Carleton Mitchell, Henry Morgan, Bob Morton, Robert Mulderig, Dallas Murphy, Dan Nerney, Jeff Neuberth, Nick Nicholson, Richard B. Nye, Sean O'Connell, Norman Olsen, and Scott Osler;

Not to mention Ron Packer, Eugene Rayner, Peter Rugg, Ross Sherbrook, Kaighn Smith, Owen Smith, Geoffrey Spranger, T. J. M. Steele, Olin Stephens, Rod Stephens, Kenneth Stone, Randy Tankoos, Steve Thing, Toby Tobin, Shorty Trimingham, Eldon Trimingham, David Vietor, Sir John Vereker, John Wadson, Jeremy Gordon Walker, Jordy Walker, Onne van der Wal, Eric Wallischeck, Morton Weintraub, Kim Whitney, Richard Wilson, Talbot Wilson, John Winder, and Tom Young.

Portions of the text were previously published in *Cruising World*, *Practical Sailor*, *Sail*, and *Sailing World* magazines.

—*John Rousmaniere*

## Selected Sources

Bruce, Erroll. *When the Crew Matter Most: An Ocean Racing Story*. New York: D. Van Nostrand, 1961. The great English sailor's story of nearly winning the 1960 race is the best book about a Bermuda Race. See also Bruce's *Deep Sea Sailing* about an earlier race.

Carrick, Robert W., and Richard Henderson. *John G. Alden and His Yacht Designs*. Camden, ME: International Marine, 1984. The great designer (and three-time race winner) and his schooners, which helped stimulate the race's revival and dominated the race in the 1920s and early thirties.

Cruising Club of America Archives, G. W. Blunt White Library, Mystic Seaport. The voluminous records and correspondence of Bermuda Race committees, recently archived by Douglas Stein.

Loomis, Alfred F. *Ocean Racing*. New York: Morrow, 1936 (2nd ed., 1946). The definitive history of the sport into its second generation, with rosters of boats and sailors who raced at sea through 1935 (first edition only).

McNitt, R. W. *Sailing at the U.S. Naval Academy: An Illustrated History*. Annapolis: Naval Institute Press, 1996. A history of the academy's sailing program.

Morris, Everett B., and Robert Coulson, eds. *Racing at Sea*. Princeton: Van Nostrand, 1959). Essays by noted sailors, including Chick Larkin and Dan Strohmeier.

Parkinson, John, Jr. *Nowhere is Too Far: The Annals of the Cruising Club of America*. New York: CCA, 1960. The history of the CCA.

Robinson, William W. *A Berth to Bermuda*. Princeton: Van Nostrand, 1961. A photo essay on the difficult 1960 race. So good that I have intentionally borrowed its title.

Rousmaniere, John. *In a Class by Herself: The Yawl Bolero and the Passion for Craftsmanship*. Mystic, CT: Mystic Seaport, 2006. The story of the three-time elapsed-time winner *Bolero*.

———. *The Golden Pastime*. New York: W. W. Norton, 1987. A history of yachting with a chapter on early ocean racing.

———, ed. *Desirable and Undesirable Characteristics of Offshore Yachts*. New York: W. W. Norton, 1987. A survey of yacht design and construction with chapters by Olin and Rod Stephens, Jim McCurdy, Bill Lapworth, Tom Young, and other members of the CCA's Technical Committee.

Stephens, Olin J., II. *All This and Sailing, Too*. Mystic, CT: Mystic Seaport, 1999. The yacht designer's autobiography. Much on ocean racing, rating rules, and the Bermuda Race.

———. *Lines: A Half-Century of Yacht Designs by Sparkman & Stephens, 1930-1980*. Jaffrey, NH: Godine, 2003. The boats profiled include *Finisterre*, *Running Tide*, and *Bolero*.

Trimingham, R. W. *Under the Calabash Tree: 150 Years of the Royal Bermuda Yacht Club*. Hamilton: The Bermudian, 1996. A lively history of one of the world's oldest and most important yacht clubs, with several chapters on the Ocean Race.

## Race reports

Reports of races are based on material in one or more of the following: CCA Archives (1906-2004 races); *The Rudder* (1906-10); *The Royal Gazette*, Hamilton (1906-23); Loomis, *Ocean Racing* (1906-34); *Yachting* (1910-80); Trimingham, *Under the Calabash Tree* (1906-94); Parkinson, *Nowhere is Too Far* (1923-58); *The Bermudian* (1923-60); *Sail* (1972-present); *Sailing World* and predecessors (1972-present); *Cruising World* (1996); *Grand Prix Sailor* (1998); *2004 Bermuda Race Magazine* (2002); *Ocean Navigator* (2002); *Practical Sailor* (2004); and CCA yearbooks (various years).

## Notes:

### CHAPTER 1: TOM DAY INVENTS A SPORT, 1906-1910

Ocean racing history: Loomis, *Ocean Racing*; D. H. Clarke, *The Singlehanders* (New York: David McKay, 1976).

Race rules: 1906 Bermuda Race conditions (copy provided by Captain Eric Wallischeck of the U.S. Merchant Marine Academy).

"If one wishes": E. F. Knight, *The Falcon on the Baltic*, chapter 1.

Larry Huntington: *Yachting*, February 1947.

**Thomas Fleming Day:** Charles G. Davis, "Tom Day As I Knew Him," *The Rudder*, November 1927; Winfield M. Thompson, "He Could Read the Stars," *Yachting*, December 1927.

"To Captain Day": CCA Archives, 1922 Bermuda Race files.

"Day himself": L. Francis Herreshoff, *An Introduction to Yachting* (New York: Sheridan House, 1963), 145.

"Sailors wanted," "in the world of": *Brooklyn Daily Eagle*, May 26, 1906.

"My dear boy": *Royal Gazette* supplement, June 15, 1907.

"Some thought": Wetherill, "Ocean Racing in Small Yachts"; Edwin J. Schoettle, ed., *Sailing Craft* (New York: Macmillan, 1928), 137.

"The bow waves": *The Rudder*, July 1906.

RBYC support: minutes of club meetings in the spring of 1906, copies in author's possession.

"By 6 a.m.": *Royal Gazette*, June 26, 1906.

"I shall be": *Royal Gazette* Supplement, June 8, 1907.

"We had made": Carrick and Henderson, *John G. Alden*, 18.


## Chapter 2: The Schooner Era, 1923-1932

"An instinctive": Herbert L. Stone, "Racing to Bermuda: Past and Present," *The Bermudian*, June 1936, 8.

Subchasers: John Rousmaniere, "The Romance of the Subchasers," *Naval History*, summer 1992.

"We did it": Rousmaniere, *Golden Pastime*, 181.

"We popularize": Parkinson, *Nowhere*, 17.

Herbert L. Stone: obituary, *New York Times*, September 29, 1955.

"I hope": *Yachting*, July 1923.

"The next time": Loomis, *Ocean Racing*, 86.


Fastnet race: Ian Dear, *Fastnet: The Story of a Great Ocean Race* (London: Batsford, 1981).

"The gaff-headed": Loomis, *Ocean Racing*, 90.

"That beat confirmed": Stephens, *All This*, 54.

"Bermuda Fever": *Yachting*, July 1930.

*Jolie Brise*: E. G. Martin, *Deep Water Cruising* (New York: Yachting, 1928); Robin Bryer, *Jolie Brise: A Tall Ship's Tale* (London: Secker & Warburg, 1982).

**Adriana fire**: C. Sherman Hoyt, *Sherman Hoyt's Memoirs* (New York: Van Nostrand, 1950); James H. Ottley to Everett Morss Jr., June 29, 1932, CCA Archives, Bermuda Race box 1, folder 4; Edward Southworth, "The 1932 Bermuda Race," typescript provided by Mayotta Southworth Kendrick.


## Chapter 3: Wet Fannies and Rod Stephens, 1934-1938

"Another of": *Yachting*, August 1934.

"Extremely fast": Loomis, *Ocean Racing*, 108.

"Lucky was": Albert Pratt, "*Grenadier* Sails the Bermuda Race," *The Sportsman*, August 1934.

"We broke": K. B. Hudson, "The Bermuda Ocean Yacht Race, 1934," *The Bermudian*, August 1934.

"*Baccarat*'s skipper": *Yachting*, August 1934.

Lorna Whittlesey Hibberd, oral history, 1987, G. W. Blunt White Library, Mystic Seaport.

Rating rules: Olin Stephens, "Trends in Yacht Design," in Rousmaniere, ed., *Desirable and Undesirable*, chapter 1.

"Ye gods": *Yachting*, August 1936.

*Kirawan*: John Rousmaniere, "*Kirawan* Redux: The 1936 Bermuda Race Winner Returns," *WoodenBoat*, January-February 2001.

"Fannies wet": Loomis, *Ocean Racing*, 103.

"The phosphorus": Edward Southworth, "The 1932 Bermuda Race."

Inspections: Everett Morss Jr., report on 1932 race, CCA Archives, Bermuda Race box 1, folder 4.

*Vamarie*: R. W. McNitt, "To Bermuda with *Vamarie*," *United States Naval Institute Proceedings*, December 1938.

"Like human": McNitt, *Sailing at the U.S. Naval Academy*, 63.

"I decided": C. Sherman Hoyt, "Ocean Racing as I Have Found It," *The Bermudian*, June 1936.

"The committee": Stone report on 1936 race, CCA Archives, Bermuda Race box 1, folder 6.

"A man who": *Yachting*, August 1934.


**Rod Stephens.** Roderick S. Stephens Jr., oral history, 1991, G.W. Blunt White Library, Mystic Seaport; Stephens to Robert W. Hubner, October 8, 1987 (copy in author's possession); Rousmaniere, *In a Class by Herself*, 77-82; Francis S. Kinney *"You are First": The Story of Olin and Rod Stephens of Sparkman & Stephens, Inc.* (New York: Dodd Mead, 1978).

"It was": Stephens, oral history.

"Rod feels": Carleton Mitchell, "Notes on Conversation with Rod Stephens, December 22, 1953," Carleton Mitchell Papers, G.W. Blunt White Library, Mystic Seaport, box 1, folder 5.

Professionalism debate: Parkinson, *Nowhere*, 136-41; Edward R. Greeff, oral history, 1987, G. W. Blunt White Library, Mystic Seaport.

"I'll defend": *Yachting*, March 1937.

**CHAPTER 4: THE LURE OF BERMUDA, 1946–1950**

"It wasn't": *Yachting*, August 1946.

Illingworth and contemporary British boats: John Illingworth, *Further Offshore* (London: Adlard Coles, 1969).

"Keeping *Argyll*": Carleton Mitchell, *Yachtsman's Camera* (New York: D. Van Nostrand, 1950), 145.

"We got 90 miles": Carrick and Henderson, *John G. Alden*, 28.

Alfred F. Loomis, *Bermuda Race Post-Mortem of the Race of 1948* (New York: *Yachting*, 1950).

*Bolero* and *Baruna*: Rousmaniere, *In a Class by Herself*, 96-98.

*Vega*: "Last to Bermuda in '38," Charles W. Crouse, typescript, CCA Archives, Bermuda Race box 1, folder 7.

**Bermuda.** "You may be": *Royal Gazette*, June 26, 1906.

"Do you like": *Yachting*, June 1938.

Bermuda history: John J. Jackson, *Bermuda* (London: David & Charles, 1988); Hudson Strode, *The Story of Bermuda* (New York: Harrison Smith, 1932); William Zuill, *Bermuda Journey: A Leisurely Guide* (Hamilton: Bermuda Book Store, 1946).

Bermuda sailing: Trimingham *Under the Calabash Tree*; J. C. Abbell, *Sailing in Bermuda: Sail Racing in the Nineteenth Century* (Hamilton: Royal Hamilton Amateur Dinghy Club, 1982); Eldon H. Trimingham, "The Development of the Bermuda Rig," *Bermuda Journal of Archeology and Maritime History* 2 (1990); Michael Jarvis, "The Fastest Vessels in the World: The Origin and Evolution of the Bermuda Sloop, 1620-1800," *Bermuda Journal of Archeology and Maritime History* 7 (1995).

"It is Bermuda": Stone, "Racing to Bermuda: Past and Present."

"Everybody in": Trimingham, *Under the Calabash Tree*, 10.

St. David's Island: Strode, *The Story of Bermuda*, 115; E. A, McCallam, *Life in Old St. David's Bermuda*. 2nd ed. (Hamilton: Bermuda Historical Society, 1986).

"A conjurer," "American yachtsmen": Guy S. Ridgway, "*Viking* Wins the Prince of Wales Cup," *The Bermudian*, June 1932.

"Then Teddy": Loomis, *Ocean Racing*, 86.

"Nobody even": Parkinson, *Nowhere*, 40-1.

"Gorgeous aquamarine," "We felt": Edward Streeter, "Log of the *Trade Wind*," typescript (copy provided by Harry Anderson).

**CHAPTER 5: *FINISTERRE* COMES THROUGH—AND AGAIN, AND AGAIN, 1952-1960**

"He drove *Royono*": McNitt, *Sailing at the U.S. Naval Academy*, 84-5.

*Samuel Pepys*: Erroll Bruce, *Deep Sea Sailing* (New York: D. Van Nostrand, 1954). *Malay*: Daniel Strohmeier, "The Crew," *Racing at Sea*;

Waldo Howland, *A Life in Boats: The Concordia Years* (Mystic, CT: Mystic Seaport, 1988); Elizabeth Meyer, ed., *Concordia Yawls, 1938-1978* (1979).

"A weird": *New York Times*, June 20, 1956.

"Reckless person": Minutes of meeting held aboard USS *Rhodes*, June 23, 1956, CCA Archives, Collection 13 (1950-58), 1956 Bermuda Race folder.

**Carleton Mitchell**: Carleton Mitchell, oral history, 1987, G.W. Blunt White Library, Mystic Seaport; John Rousmaniere, "The Sailing Lives of Carleton Mitchell," *Sail*, March 2006; Amy D. German, "A Sense of Participation," *The Log of Mystic Seaport*, Spring 2000; Tony Bessinger, "Past the End of the Land," *Sailing World*, May 2001.

"To desire nothing": Mitchell, *The Wind's Call* (New York: Scribner's 1971), 11.

"A small centerboard": Mitchell, "Report on a Boat: *Finisterre*," *Yachting*, August 1955. "On *Finisterre*": Mitchell, "Fabulous *Finisterre* Again," *Sports Illustrated*. June 30, 1958.

"For one thing": Ezra Bowen, "Ocean Racing," *Sports Illustrated*, June 18, 1956.

"My theory": Mitchell oral history.

"I realize": Mitchell to Ernest Ratsey, December 26, 1953, Carleton Mitchell Papers, Mystic Seaport, box 1, folder 5.

"Her skipper": Olin Stephens, *Lines*, 70.

"Good admiralship," "these conditions": H. K. Rigg, "The Secret Life of *Finisterre*," *The Skipper*, September 1958.

"It has been": Mitchell to Rod Stephens, July 27, 1956, CCA Archives, Bermuda Race box 4, folder 18.

"I know no one": Loomis to Mitchell, November 14, 1957, Carleton Mitchell Papers, Mystic Seaport, box 6, folder 5.

Radar: L. A. Adair and John Nicholas Brown, "Radar Signaling," *Yachting*, April 1953.

"Sooner or later": Talcott M. Banks Jr. to Ham de Fontaine, December 15, 1954, CCA Archives, Bermuda Race box 4, folder 6.

**1960 storm:** "Which gear": *Yachting* questionnaire, CCA Archives, Bermuda Race box 5, folder 13.

"Racing a yacht": Bruce, *Deep Sea Sailing*, 18.

"It is," "to put on," "what about," "to be a better man": Bruce, *When the Crew*, 76, 77, 99, 105. My sources include Harry Anderson, Bob Coulson, Larry Glenn, Jacques Megroz, Jack Merrill, Henry Morgan, David Noyes, Norman Olsen, Theodore A. Jones, *The Dog Watch* (New York: W. W. Norton, 1981), and David R. Owen, "Some Unusual Aspects of the 1960 Newport-Bermuda Race," typescript, CCA Archives, Bermuda Race box 5, folder 13.

*Figaro*: William Snaith, *On the Wind's Way* (New York: Putnam's, 1973).

"Here we are": Mitchell, *Passage East*, 171.


## Chapter 6: Controversy and Big Winds, 1962–1972

"God, no": *Yachting*, August 1966.

"An ocean race": Norris Hoyt, *Addicted to Sail* (New York: W. W. Norton, 1987).

"*Finisterre*'s record": Stephens, *All This*, 143.

*Niña's Sea Routine*, Fales correspondence: New York Yacht Club Archives.

"The world's": Morris to Thomas J. Watson Jr., June 11, 1963, CCA Archives, Bermuda Race box 12, folder 15.

"You realize": Peter Comstock to E. Newbold Smith, March 5, 1965, CCA Archives, Bermuda Race box 19, folder 1.

"Because the": Ernstof to Watson, February 20, 1964, CCA Archives, Bermuda Race box 18, folder 7.

"When someone": Geoffrey Spranger, "*Burgoo*'s Bermuda, from Start to Finish," *The Rudder*, September 1964.

"Imperturbably cheerful": *Yachting*, August 1966.


*Alfred F. Loomis*: John Rousmaniere, "The Man Who was Spun Yarn," *Nautical Quarterly* 8 (1979).

Bermuda Race song lyrics from Worth and Harvey Loomis.

"A particularly": Frederick Sanders, "A Meteorologist Looks at the 1970 Bermuda Race," *Cruising Club News*, May 1972.

Damage reports: Report of the CCA Design and Construction Committee, November 6, 1970, in bound CCA minutes, 1969-71.

"I've been": *New York Times*, June 28, 1970.

1972 race: John Rousmaniere, "Rough Ride to Bermuda," *Yacht Racing*, September 1972, and the *Bermuda Sun Newport-Bermuda Pictorial*, June 1972.


## Chapter 7: Taking Risks, 1974–1988

German Frers: Barry Pickthall, *German Frers* (Walberton, U.K.: South Atlantic, 2003).

"It would be": Justin E. Kerwin and John N. Newman, "A Summary of the H. Irving Pratt Ocean Race Handicapping Project," Society of Naval Architects and Marine Engineers, *The Fourth Chesapeake Sailing Yacht Symposium, Annapolis, Maryland* (1979).

*Navigation:* "Personally": Fred Adams to Pierre S. du Pont III, November 20, 1963, CCA Archives, Bermuda Race box 6, folder 3.

"The rumors": Loomis, *Ocean Racing*, 101.

Fly turd: Poultney Bigelow, "Under Storm Sails to Bermuda," *The Independent*, November 26, 1903.

"Crawling from": Edward Streeter, "Log of the *Trade Wind*."

"They are," "These are": Charles Larkin II, "Navigation," *Racing at Sea*, 63.

"All the self-doubts": Nick Nicholson, "Navigation, Then and Now," *Practical Sailor*, June, 2004.

"We were," "We took": *Yachting*, August 1954.


*Holger Danske*:  Richard Wilson, "The Dane Awakens," *Cruising Club News*, January 1981.

*Denali* evacuation: John Rousmaniere, "A Matter of Evacuation," *Sailing World*, October 1988.

Crew list: Tony Gibbs, "Racing to Bermuda," *The New Yorker*, July 18, 1983. Seasickness: John Parkinson Jr. *Yarns for Davy Jones* (1966), 28-29.

1988 race: Douglas Logan, "Stalking the Elusive Onion," *Sailing World*, September 1988.


## Chapter 8: Sporting Character, 1990–2004

*The Gulf Stream:* "It is the Stream," "I can conclude": Loomis, "How About Those 'Meanders,'" *Yachting*, June 1952.

"The Gulf Stream": Bigelow, "Under Storm Sails to Bermuda."

"One of the," "On a calm": Bruce, *Deep Sea Sailing*, 76-7.

"Reduced to": Gibbs, "Racing to Bermuda"; Columbus O'D. Iselin, "The Gulf Stream System," *Oceanus*. June 1960; "Rules of Thumb for Crossing the Gulf Stream," *Oceanus*, June 1964; W. Frank Bohlen, "Gulf Stream Currents," June 9, 2004.

Loomis interview: *Yachting*, June 1938.

"That was": John Rousmaniere, "Crew Overboard Safety," *Practical Sailor*, August 1, 2005.

"It was": Talbot Wilson, "2004 Newport-Bermuda Race," *CCA Yearbook*, 2005, 362.

# Illustration Credits

1: © Jane Crosen

2: Carleton Mitchell photo, © Mystic Seaport, 1996.31.2589

3: © Onne van der Wal

6: © Mystic Seaport, Rosenfeld Collection 1984.187.

7: © Daniel Forster

8-9: © Onne van der Wal

10: Mystic Seaport 1996.96.669

11: Courtesy Eldon H. Trimingham II

12: (top) © Mystic Seaport, Rosenfeld Collection 1984.187.B12;
(bottom) Mystic Seaport 1955.965

13: The Mariners' Museum, Newport News, VA

14: *The Rudder*, August 1906

15: *The Rudder*, 1905

16: *The Rudder*, August 1906

17: *The Rudder*, August 1906

19: *The Rudder*, August 1906

20: Courtesy Eldon H. Trimingham II

21: *The Rudder*, August 1906

22: (all) Cruising Club of America Archives, G. W. Blunt White Library,
Mystic Seaport

23: © Mystic Seaport, Rosenfeld Collection 1984.187.671

24: © Mystic Seaport, Rosenfeld Collection 1984.187.9918F

25: © Mystic Seaport, Rosenfeld Collection 1984.187.28742F

26: © Mystic Seaport, Rosenfeld Collection 1984.187.68257F

28: © Mystic Seaport, Rosenfeld Collection 1984.187.9931F

29: © Mystic Seaport, Rosenfeld Collection 1984.187.18615F

30: © Mystic Seaport, Rosenfeld Collection 1984.187.9892F

31: © Mystic Seaport, Rosenfeld Collection 1984.187.12309F

32: © Mystic Seaport, Rosenfeld Collection 1984.187.18616F

33: © Mystic Seaport, Rosenfeld Collection 1984.187.18642F

34-35: © Mystic Seaport, Rosenfeld Collection 1984.187.28755F

36: © Mystic Seaport, Rosenfeld Collection 1984.187.61205F

37: © Mystic Seaport, Rosenfeld Collection 1984.187.61163F

38: © Mystic Seaport, Rosenfeld Collection 1984.187.61197F

39: © Mystic Seaport, Rosenfeld Collection 1984.187.61146F

40: © Mystic Seaport, Rosenfeld Collection 1984.187.61165F

42: © Mystic Seaport, Rosenfeld Collection 1984.187.26983F

43: Norris Hoyt photo, Mystic Seaport

44: © Mystic Seaport, Rosenfeld Collection 1984.187.68356F

45: © Mystic Seaport, Rosenfeld Collection 1984.187.18695F

46: © Mystic Seaport, Rosenfeld Collection 1984.187.40334F

47: © Mystic Seaport, Rosenfeld Collection 1984.187.75526F

48-49: © Mystic Seaport, Rosenfeld Collection 1984.187.75513F

50: © Mystic Seaport, Rosenfeld Collection 1984.187.91476F

51: *Yachting*, August 1936

53: (left) © Mystic Seaport, Rosenfeld Collection 1984.187.9928F;
(right) © Mystic Seaport, Rosenfeld Collection 1984.187.113917F

54-55: © Mystic Seaport, Rosenfeld Collection 1984.187.87716F

56: © Mystic Seaport, Rosenfeld Collection 1984.187.11386F

57: © Mystic Seaport, Rosenfeld Collection 1984.187.113965F

58: © Mystic Seaport, Rosenfeld Collection 1984.187.113956F

60: © Dan Nerney

61: © Mystic Seaport, Rosenfeld Collection 1984.187.113856F

62: © Mystic Seaport, Rosenfeld Collection 1984.187.114014F

63: © Mystic Seaport, Rosenfeld Collection 1984.187.113849F

64: Carleton Mitchell photo, © Mystic Seaport 1996.31.4967

65: © Mystic Seaport, Rosenfeld Collection 1984.187.126951F

66-67: © Mystic Seaport, Rosenfeld Collection 1984.187.126947F

68: © Mystic Seaport, Rosenfeld Collection 1984.187.598T

69: Norris Hoyt photo, Mystic Seaport

70: © Mystic Seaport, Rosenfeld Collection 1984.187.126992F

71: Carleton Mitchell photo, © Mystic Seaport 1996.31.2655

72: Courtesy Eldon H. Trimingham II

73: © Mystic Seaport, Rosenfeld Collection 1984.187.67374F

74: (left) Bermuda News Bureau photo, courtesy Royal Bermuda Yacht
Club; (right) © Mystic Seaport, Rosenfeld Collection
1984.187.141780F

75: © Mystic Seaport, Rosenfeld Collection 1984.187.114068F

76: © Mystic Seaport, Rosenfeld Collection 1984.187.91593F

77: © Mystic Seaport, Rosenfeld Collection 1984.187.79691F

78: Cruising Club of America Archives, G. W. Blunt White Library,
Mystic Seaport

79: Bermuda News Bureau photo, courtesy *Sailing World*

80: (both) © R. Steven Thing

81: © Barry Pickthall/PPL

82: © R. Steven Thing

83: © Mystic Seaport, Rosenfeld Collection 1984.187.67314F

84: © Mystic Seaport, Rosenfeld Collection 1984.187.141751F

86: © Mystic Seaport, Rosenfeld Collection 1984.187.1063T

87: © Mystic Seaport, Rosenfeld Collection ANN.1984.187.6862

88: © Mystic Seaport, Rosenfeld Collection 1984.187.133164F

89: © Mystic Seaport, Rosenfeld Collection ANN.1984.187.6861

90: © Mystic Seaport, Rosenfeld Collection ANN.1984.187.6863

91: Bermuda News Bureau photo, courtesy Richard Goennel

92: © Mystic Seaport, Rosenfeld Collection 1984.187.159765F

93: © Mystic Seaport, Rosenfeld Collection 1984.187.159762F

94: (top) © Mystic Seaport, Rosenfeld Collection 1984.187.160036F; (bottom) Carleton Mitchell photo, © Mystic Seaport 1996.31.5361

95: © Mystic Seaport, Rosenfeld Collection 1984.187.151355F

96: Norris Hoyt photo, Mystic Seaport

97: Norris Hoyt photo, Mystic Seaport 1889.85.11B

98: © Mystic Seaport, Rosenfeld Collection 1984.187.166240F

99: © Mystic Seaport, Rosenfeld Collection 1984.187.166637F

100: © Mystic Seaport, Rosenfeld Collection 1984.187.166357F

101: Norris Hoyt photo, Mystic Seaport 1989.85.123

102: Bermuda News Bureau photo, courtesy *Sailing World*

103: © John Rousmaniere

104: © Mystic Seaport, Rosenfeld Collection 1984.187.172320F

105: © Mystic Seaport, Rosenfeld Collection 1984.187.172339F

106: © Mystic Seaport, Rosenfeld Collection 1984.187.172272F

107: Bermuda News Bureau photo, courtesy *Sailing World*

108: (both) Bermuda News Bureau photo, courtesy *Sailing World*

110–11: © Dan Nerney

112: Howay Caufman photo, *Sports Illustrated*

113: (top) courtesy Sally Loomis Campbell; (bottom) courtesy Cruising Club of America

116: (top) ©2005, Sparkman & Stephens, Inc.; (bottom) © McCurdy & Rhodes, Inc.

117: © Dan Nerney

118: © Dan Nerney

120: (both) Bermuda News Bureau photo, courtesy *Sailing World*

121: Norris Hoyt photo, Mystic Seaport 1989.85.80B

122: © Karin J. Olsen Campia

123: © R. Steven Thing

124: Bermuda News Bureau photo, courtesy *Sailing World*

125: (both) Bermuda News Bureau photo, courtesy *Sailing World*

126: © Karin J. Olsen Campia

127: (both) Bermuda News photo, courtesy *Sailing World*

128: © Dan Nerney

130: (top) Carleton Mitchell photo, © Mystic Seaport, 1996.31.2589; (bottom) © Mystic Seaport, 1996.31.2631

131: Norris Hoyt photo, Mystic Seaport

132: (both) © John Rousmaniere

133: Norris Hoyt photo, Mystic Seaport 1989.85.122

135: (top) courtesy Tim James; (bottom) © Mystic Seaport, Rosenfeld Collection 1984.187.126966F

136: Edwin Hills photo, courtesy Barb Hills

138: © Dan Nerney

139: © Dan Nerney

140: © Mystic Seaport, Rosenfeld Collection 1984.187.133214F

141: Courtesy *Sailing World*

142: Courtesy Frank Bohlen

143: © Douglas Logan

144: © John Rousmaniere

145: © Tom Leutweiler

146: © Daniel Forster/DCNAC (Daimler-Chrysler North Atlantic Challenge)

147: © Onne van der Wal

148: © Sheila McCurdy

149: (top) Norris Hoyt photo, Mystic Seaport 1989.85.80B; (bottom) courtesy Jenifer Clark

150-51: © John Rousmaniere

152: Courtesy Jenifer Clark

153: Bermuda News Bureau photo, courtesy *Sailing World*

154: Bermuda News Bureau photo, courtesy *Sailing World*

156: Courtesy R. Steven Thing

157: (top) Bermuda News Bureau photo, courtesy *Sailing World*; (bottom) © Barry Pickthall/PPL

159: (above left) © Sheila McCurdy; (above right and bottom) © John Rousmaniere

160: (left) Clive Brown photo, courtesy Burt and Walter Keenan; (right) © Barry Pickthall/PPL

161: © R. Steven Thing

163: © Onne van der Wal

164-65: © Onne van der Wal

166: © Onne van der Wal

167: © Onne van der Wal

168-69: © Barry Pickthall/PPL

170: © Onne van der Wal

171: © Barry Pickthall/PPL

173: Courtesy Colin Couper

# Index